DUMBARTON OAKS STUDIES

ᴇᴄ XIII ᴊᴏ

LEONTIUS OF BYZANTIUM

AN ORIGENIST CHRISTOLOGY

LEONTIUS OF BYZANTIUM

AN ORIGENIST CHRISTOLOGY

by

DAVID BEECHER EVANS

Dumbarton Oaks
Center for Byzantine Studies
Trustees for Harvard University
Washington, District of Columbia
1970

Distributed by
J.J. Augustin, Publisher
Locust Valley, New York

LIBRARY OF CONGRESS CATALOG CARD NUMBER 62–17509
PRINTED IN GERMANY AT J.J. AUGUSTIN, GLÜCKSTADT

Acknowledgements

This study is a slightly expanded version of a doctoral dissertation of the same title submitted in 1966 to Harvard Divinity
School, and consequently is in debt to a particularly large number
of my teachers and friends. At Harvard, Professor Zeph Stewart of
Harvard University patiently endured my initiation into Greek
palaeography and *Editionstechnik*. Libraries in Berlin, the Escurial,
Genoa, Oxford, Paris, Rome, and Venice all promptly and courte-
ously provided microfilms or photostats of the manuscripts; and
Helen Joan Evans assisted me in collating them. The Dumbarton
Oaks Center for Byzantine Studies in Washington, D. C., afforded
me two full years of uninterrupted study in surroundings only more
stimulating than pleasant. My debt to its faculty and staff is in-
calculable, but I record with particular thanks the diligence and
concern of the Reverend Professor John Meyendorff, who read the
drafts, and the patient encouragement of the Director of Studies,
Professor Ernst Kitzinger. At Princeton Theological Seminary
Alice McElhinny typed the manuscript. Later, while at Dumbarton
Oaks in 1967, Antoine Guillaumont read and commented the piece.
In bringing the manuscript to print, Mrs. Fanny Bonajuto of
Dumbarton Oaks has served as editor; for her carefulness with the
text and her patience with the author in the face of countless de-
lays and annoyances, I thank her most sincerely. Russell Becker,
John Hatherley, and James McPherson, all students at Princeton
Theological Seminary, helped read the galleys. Above all, however,
I am indebted to my advisor in the dissertation, the Very Reverend
Professor Georges Florovsky, then of Harvard Divinity School
and now of Princeton University. I do not presume to call myself
his disciple; but my fondest hope for this work is that it may not
be found unworthy of the time and counsel with which he has
assisted me.

Princeton, New Jersey   David B. Evans
April 1969

CONTENTS

List of Abbreviations

This list includes all abbreviations used in the text, whether of *termini technici* (e.g., *ep* = *epistula*), names of persons (e.g., BasMag = Basil the Great), or works cited (e.g., Aristotle, *Cat* = Aristotle, *Categoriae*). Abbreviations regularly appearing only after other abbreviations are not listed separately. (E.g., EvagPont, *KephGn* is considered a single abbreviation and listed under E; the title *KephGn* is not listed under K.)

Abbreviations are listed alphabetically by their first letters, whether or not that letter is one ordinarily considered significant: e.g., GDMansi, *SacConcColl* is listed under G, not under M.

ACO = *Acta conciliorum oecumenicorum*, ed. Eduard Schwartz, 4 tomes in 13 volumes (Berlin, Berlin-Leipzig, Strasbourg, 1914–1940 [incomplete])

AGuillaumont, *KephGn* = Antoine Guillaumont, *Les "Kephalaia gnostica" d'Evagre le Pontique et l'histoire de l'Origénisme chez les Grecs et chez les Syriens*, Patristica sorbonensia, 5 (Paris, 1962)

AJFestugière, *Moines d'Orient* = André-Jean Festugière (ed. and trans.), *Les moines d'Orient*, 4 vols. (Paris 1961–1965 [incomplete])

AMai, *SpicRom* = Angelo Mai (ed.), *Spicilegium romanum*, 10 vols. (Rome, 1839–1844), X, 2 (1844)

Aristotle, *Cat* = Aristotle, *Categoriae*, in *Aristotelis Categoriae et liber de interpretatione*, ed. L. Minio-Paluello, Oxford Classical Texts (Oxford, 1956)

BasMag = Basil of Caesarea in Cappadocia (Basil the Great)

CMoeller, "Chalcédonisme et néo-chalcédonisme," *KonzChalk*, I = Charles Moeller, "Le chalcédonisme et le néo-chalcédonisme en Orient de 451 à la fin du VIe siècle," in *Das Konzil von Chalkedon: Geschichte und Gegenwart*, eds. Aloys Grillmeier and Heinrich Bacht, 3 vols., revised (Würzburg, 1959), I, 637–720

CorpJurCiv = *Corpus juris civilis*, eds. Paul Krüger *et al.*, 3 vols. (Berlin, 1928–1929)

CyrScyth = Cyril of Scythopolis. The works of Cyril of Scythopolis are cited from ESchwartz, *KyrSkyth*. The abbreviations of their titles are:

> *VCyriaci* = *Vita Cyriaci* = *Leben des Kyriakos*, in ESchwartz, *KyrSkyth*, 222–235
> *VEuthymii* = *Vita Euthymii* = *Leben des Euthymios*, in ESchwartz, *KyrSkyth*, 6–85
> *VSabae* = *Vita Sabae* = *Leben des Sabas*, in ESchwartz, *KyrSkyth*, 85–200
> and so on

ep = *epistula*

ESchwartz, *KyrSkyth* = Eduard Schwartz, *Kyrillos von Skythopolis*, Texte und Untersuchungen zur Geschichte der altchristlichen Literatur, Reihe 4, Band XLIX, Heft 2 (Leipzig, 1939)

EStein, *BasEmp* = Ernest Stein, *Histoire du Bas-Empire*, 2 vols. (Paris, 1949 [vol. II] – 1959 [vol. I])

EvagPont = Evagrius of Pontus. The titles of his works are abbreviated as follows:

> *CapPrac* = *Capita practica*, in PG, 40, 1219–1252
> *KephGn* = Antoine Guillaumont (ed. and trans.), *Les six centuries des "Kephalaia gnostica" d'Evagre le Pontique*. Edition critique de la version syriaque commune et édition d'une nouvelle version syriaque, intégrale, avec une double traduction française = *Patrologia orientalis*, tome XXVIII, fasc. I (Paris, 1958)
> [EvagPont] *sub* BasMag, *ep* 8 = Basil the Great, *epistula* 8, in SBasile, *Lettres*, I (Paris, 1957), 22–37—a letter now positively assigned to Evagrius of Pontus

LIST OF ABBREVIATIONS

FDiekamp, *OrigStreit* = Franz Diekamp, *Die origenistischen Strei-tigkeiten im sechsten Jahrhundert und das fünfte allgemeine Concil* (Münster in Westphalia, 1899)

FLoofs, *LeontByz* = Friedrich Loofs, *Leontius von Byzanz und die gleichnamigen Schriftsteller der griechischen Kirche*, Texte und Untersuchungen zur Geschichte der altchristlichen Literatur, Band III, Heft 1–2 (Leipzig, 1887)

GDMansi, *SacConcColl* = Giovanni Domenico Mansi (ed.), *Sacrorum conciliorum nova et amplissima collectio...*, 31 vols. (Florence and Venice, 1759–1798)

HCanisius, *AntLect* = Henricus Canisius (ed.), *Antiquae lectionis* (*sic*) ..., 6 vols. (Ingolstadt, 1601–1604), IV, 1 (1603)

IHausherr, "NouvFrag," *OrChrPer*, V (1939) = Irénée Hausherr, "Nouveaux fragments grecs d'Evagre le Pontique," *Orientalia Christiana Periodica*, V (1939), 229–233

InnMar, *DeColl* = *Innocentii Maronitae epistula de collatione cum Severianis habita*, in *ACO*, IV, 2 ([Strasbourg], 1914), pp. 167–184

JMuyldermans, *Evagriana* = Joseph Muyldermans, *Evagriana* (Paris, 1931)

JPJunglas, *LeontByz* = Johannes Peter Junglas, *Leontius von Byzanz. Studien zu seinen Schriften, Quellen und Anschauungen*, Forschungen zur christlichen Literatur- und Dogmengeschichte, Band VII, Heft 3 (Paderborn, 1908)

LeontByz = Leontius of Byzantium. The works of Leontius of Byzantium are cited in the page and column numbers of PG, 86. The abbreviations of their titles are:

  AdvFraudes = *Adversus fraudes Apollinaristarum*, in PG, 86, 1947–1976

  CapTrig = *Capita triginta contra Severum*, in PG, 86, 1902–1916

LIST OF ABBREVIATIONS

CNE = *Tres libri contra Nestorianos et Eutychianos*, in PG, 86, 1267–1396

SolArgSev = *Solutio argumentorum a Severo objectorum*, in PG, 86, 1915–1946

LeontJer, *AdvNest* = Leontius of Jerusalem, *Adversus Nestorianos*, in PG, 86, 1399–1768[i]

MRichard, "Léonce et Pamphile," *RevScPhilTheol*, XXVII (1938) = Marcel Richard, "Léonce et Pamphile," *Revue des sciences philosophiques et théologiques*, XXVII (1938), 27–52

— "LéonceJér et LéonceByz," *MélScRel*, I (1944) = Marcel Richard, "Léonce de Jérusalem et Léonce de Byzance," *Mélanges de science religieuse*, I (1944), 35–88

— "Léonce ... origéniste?" *RevEtByz*, V (1947) = Marcel Richard, "Léonce de Byzance était-il origéniste?" *Revue des études byzantines*, V (1947), 31–66

PG = Jacques-Paul Migne (ed.), Patrologiae cursus completus ... series graeca, 161 vols. (Paris, 1857–1868)

prol = *prologus*

SBasile, *Lettres* = Saint Basile, *Lettres*, ed. and trans. Yves Courtonne, Collection Budé, 3 vols. (Paris, 1957–1966)

VGrumel, "LéonceByz," *DTC*, IX = Venance Grumel, "Léonce de Byzance," *Dictionnaire de théologie catholique*, eds. Alfred Vacant *et al.*, 15 vols. (Paris, 1903–1950), IX (1926), cols. 400–426

WFrankenberg, *EuagPont* = Wilhelm Frankenberg (ed.), *Euagrius Ponticus*, Abhandl. d. Königl. Gesellsch. d. Wiss. zu Göttingen, Philol.-hist. Klasse, Neue Folge, Band XIII, 2 (Berlin, 1912)

WRügamer, *LeontByz* = Wilhelm Rügamer, *Leontius von Byzanz. Ein Polemiker aus dem Zeitalter Justinians* (Würzburg, 1894)

Manuscript Designations

The manuscripts and their designations are described on pages 4–7. The designations most frequently used thereafter are:

G = Codex Genuensis bibliothecae missionis urbanae Sancti Caroli graecus 27 (saeculum XI)

M = Codex Venetus Marcianus graecus Z 575 (849) (saeculum XV)

O = Codex Oxoniensis Bodleianus Laudianus graecus 92B (saeculum X)

P = Codex Parisinus bibliothecae nationalis graecus 1335 (saeculum XIV)

T = Versio Turriani

V = Codex Vaticanus graecus 2195 (saeculum X)

LEONTIUS OF BYZANTIUM
AN ORIGENIST CHRISTOLOGY

CHAPTER ONE

INTRODUCTION

I. THE *Corpus Leontianum*

Who was Leontius of Byzantium? What did he write? We spare the reader the arid academic epic of the *corpus Leontianum* and its agonies, but simply say: Leontius of Byzantium is that sixth-century Byzantine theologian who composed three or perhaps four theological treatises; that is, the *Tres libri contra Nestorianos et Eutychianos (CNE)*, the *Solutio argumentorum a Severo objectorum (SolArgSev)*, the *Capita triginta contra Severum (CapTrig)*, and, if the manuscript tradition is to be believed, the *Adversus fraudes Apollinaristarum (AdvFraudes)*.[1]

---

[1] In what follows, the works of Leontius of Byzantium — hereafter abbreviated in bibliographical notices as LeontByz — will be cited from PG, 86, pts. 1–2. PG, 86, is *not* among those volumes re-edited with a slightly different pagination and division of the text by the Librairie Garnier after that firm purchased Migne's rights from his estate (1876) on his death in 1875 — or so L. Marchal, "Migne, Jacques-Paul," *Dictionnaire de théologie catholique*, eds. A. Vacant *et al.*, X (Paris, 1928), 1738. As this book goes to press, two articles have appeared attacking the consensus on the *corpus Leontianum* at a critical point: J. H. I. Watt, "The Authenticity of the Writings Ascribed to Leontius of Byzantium," *Studia Patristica*, VII (Vol. XCII of Texte und Untersuchungen zur Geschichte der altchristlichen Literatur [Berlin, 1966]), 320–336, and Silas Rees, "The Literary Activity of Leontius of Byzantium," *The Journal of Theological Studies*, XIX (1968), 229–242, have insisted on the identity of Leontius of Byzantium (that is, the author of *CNE*, *SolArgSov*, and *CapTrig*) with Leontius of Jerusalem (that is, the author of *Adversus Nestorianos* [PG, 86, 1399–1768[1]] and *Contra Monophysitas* [*ibid.*, 1769–1901]). Neither attack succeeds. Watts' article offers a statistical analysis of three stylistic characteristics of the texts printed in PG, 86. Unfortunately, he neither attempts to ascertain the value of the texts before him nor takes slightest account of the profound dissimilarities of thought in the two groups of writings. Rees offers brief analyses of the chronology and thought of the writings in question, but dismisses all but the first of the arguments of Marcel Richard against the identification without so much as reporting them; see MRichard, "Léonce Jér et LéonceByz," *MélScRel*, I (1944), 35–88. Richard's arguments nonethe-

LEONTIUS OF BYZANTIUM

A. *The Date of Composition*

The date of the *corpus* and the order in which its parts were written? *CapTrig* and *AdvFraudes* cannot be dated at all, but *CNE* was certainly published after the year 528.[2] A *terminus ad quem?* Since Leontius of Byzantium the theologian is surely identical with the Origenist monk of Cyril of Scythopolis' *Vita Sabae*,[3] and the Origenist Leontius died about 543, he must have composed the *corpus* before that year. However, the identification of Leontius the theologian with the Origenist Leontius allows us to attempt an even closer approximation. First, we have good reason to believe that Leontius began his public career with his journey to Constantinople in 531. *CNE*, therefore, was almost certainly written in or after 531; and, we must add, more probably *after* than *in* 531, because Leontius expressly says that *CNE* reduces to writing certain public lectures—which, he says, he had delivered frequent-

---

less seem to me decisive. Further, Rees does not know of the objections to the identification of the two Leontii in Herbert Reindl, *Der Aristotelismus bei Leontios von Byzanz* (unpublished doctoral dissertation; Ludwig-Maximilians-Universität zu München, 1953), and in my own dissertation, *Leontius of Byzantium: an Origenist Christology* (Harvard University, 1966), on which, of course, this book expands; see Chapter Five, pp. 139–143, *infra*. These three works, however, lay a particularly heavy burden of proof on those who maintain the identity of Leontius of Jerusalem with Leontius of Byzantium.

[2] FLoofs, *LeontByz*, 32, notes that *CNE* 3 (PG, 86, 1364D 1–3) speaks of τῇ ...ἐκκλησίᾳ τῆς πάλαι μὲν Ἀντιόχου, νῦν δὲ Θεουπόλεως καλουμένης; and according to Theophanes, *Chronographia* (ed. Carolus de Boor, 2 vols. [Leipzig: Teubner, 1883], I, p. 178, ll. 5–7), Antioch was renamed Theopolis only at the reconstruction of the city after the earthquake of 29 November 528. Now since all three pieces were published together—*CNE prol*, PG, 86, 1269A 14–1272B 17, lists all three—and since besides the whole cannot have been published before each of its parts was written, it follows that *CNE* cannot have been published before 528. Two *caveats* here. To say that the three pieces were published together is not to say that they were written at the same time. Nor is it to say that one or more of them had not been published earlier. The latter question, I note, concerns us only at one point. As we shall notice immediately below, *SolArgSev* is almost certainly a reply to criticism of *CNE* 1. The question then: did Leontius' adversaries find *CNE* 1 in *CNE* or in a separate edition? In the absence of evidence for the latter, I assume the former. For the rest, I apologize to the academic community for so sketchy an analysis of the chronology of Leontius' works and the considerable literature about it; my excuse is that the conclusions of this piece will require a re-examination of that chronology.

[3] For all documentation and discussion of Leontius' life, see Chap. Six.

ly[4]—and so introduces an interval between composition and publication. On the other hand Leontius tells us that *SolArgSev* is a reply to a criticism of what seems to be *CNE* 1[5]; and so the *terminus ad quem* recedes from the date of his death by just so much time as we may suppose necessary for his adversary to reply to *CNE* 1 and for Leontius to draft an apology. A final precision, then. We shall see in the last chapter that Leontius lived in Constantinople for two periods; the first, from the summer of 531 through the Council of 536 to perhaps 537 and his return to Palestine; the second, from about 540 to his death in, as I believe, 543. Now, if we may assume—and the assumption seems safe—that Leontius published *CNE* and *SolArgSev* not in Palestine but in Constantinople, we may ask: in which of these two periods did he publish them? Here we are reduced to speculation, for either period is possible. Nevertheless, it is tempting to suppose that Leontius composed his treatise against Theodore of Mopsuestia, *CNE* 3—or at least published it—in the campaign against Theodore which the Origenists launched in or after 540 as a reprisal for the attacks on Origen begun in Palestine about that time.[6] If so—and we recall that we are speculating—then *CNE* and *SolArgSev* were probably published in Constantinople between 540 and 543; and *a fortiori* the same might be said of *CapTrig*. The date of *AdvFraudes*—if it is by Leontius at all—remains a puzzle.

B. *The History of the Text: the Manuscript Tradition*

Once composed, what was the fate of the *corpus Leontianum*? That is, what is the history of the text? We know first, that Leontius' works were excerpted as early as the seventh century[7] and that these excerpts seem to have formed a tradition of what we may

---

[4] See the opening lines of *CNE prol* (PG, 86, 1268B 2–7).

[5] See the opening lines of *SolArgSev* (PG, 86, 1916C 1–15), with which compare *CNE prol* to *CNE* 1 (*ibid.*, 1269A 15–B 2).

[6] So MRichard, "Léonce ... origéniste?" *RevEtByz*, V (1947), 50–53. However, I cannot agree that it is necessary to date the publication of *CNE* only after the publication of the decree against Origen in 543.

[7] E. g., in the massive florilegium called *Doctrina patrum de incarnatione Verbi*, ed. Franz Diekamp (Münster i. Westphalia, 1907), which contains, among other things, the *CapTrig* entire.

call the *fragmenta Leontii*.[8] Second, we know that Leontius' works
exercised a certain influence upon later generations: e.g., upon Leontius of Jerusalem,[9] Pamphilus,[10] Maximus the Confessor,[11] and John
of Damascus.[12] We note that it may well have been in these two
traditions that Leontius first came to be confused with Leontius of
Jerusalem and Leontius, the author of *De sectis*. However, there is a
third tradition, too, in which Leontius' identity is carefully maintained: the manuscript tradition properly so called. This tradition,
as always, is available to us only after a relatively late date; in the
case of Leontius, only in the tenth century, in VO. Nevertheless—
to say the obvious—we hold it, as always, to be especially important, because it transmits to us the text of Leontius. We therefore
undertake a brief survey of the manuscript tradition.[13]

Of Leontius' works, excluding fragments, we possess seven Greek
manuscripts and a Latin translation by the Spanish Jesuit Francisco
Torres, better known as Turrianus.[14] Among these eight sources,
there are three originals and three copies, including the translation:

[8] The point of departure for any examination of the tradition of the
fragmenta Leontii remains FLoofs, *LeontByz*, 108–120, Loofs' examination of
the *fragmenta Leontii* in PG, 86, 2003C 1–2016D 2.

[9] As we shall see below, Leontius of Jerusalem attacks Leontius of
Byzantium.

[10] On Pamphilus' dependence upon Leontius, see the argument and
bibliography in MRichard, "Léonce et Pamphile," *RevScPhilTheol*, XXVII
(1938), 27–52.

[11] For the influence of Leontius on Maximus, see Hans Urs von Balthasar,
Kosmische Liturgie. Das Weltbild Maximus' des Bekenners, 2d ed. (Einsiedeln,
1961).

[12] The influence of Leontius on John of Damascus has not yet been
studied, to the best of my knowledge, but certain of their texts are
strikingly similar. See, e.g., FLoofs, *LeontByz*, 122–125. However, John may
well inherit his Leontius from Maximus.

[13] My description of Leontius' manuscript tradition rests upon direct
positive photostats or microfilms of all seven of the extant manuscripts, and
complete collations of five texts (except the modern Latin translation T) of
the argument of *CNE* 1, i.e. VOGBS.

[14] My point of departure: Robert Devreesse's list of manuscripts in his
"Le florilège de Léonce de Byzance," *Revue des sciences religieuses*, X
(1930), 548 ff., 551 [–552], note 2. To his list I add M; and report besides that
microfilm of the piece in Codex Escorialensis graecus 458 establishes that
it is not a work of Leontius but the opusculum usually entitled *De duabus
Christi naturis* and assigned to Maximus the Confessor (*Opuscula theologica
et polemica*, PG, 91, 145A 7–149A 19). To be sure, the same piece stands
among Leontius' works in O.

INTRODUCTION

V = Codex Vaticanus graecus 2195 of the tenth century. One of the two complete collections of Leontius' works, it contains, in order: *CNE prol; CNE* 1; *SolArgSev; CapTrig; CNE* 2; *CNE* 3; *AdvFraudes*. For *AdvFraudes*, V is the *codex unicus*. It was from V that Angelo Mai first published the Greek text of all of Leontius' works except *CapTrig*[15] in his *Spicilegium romanum* (*SpicRom*), X, 2 (Rome, 1844), 1–151; and his text is that reproduced in PG, 86.

T = Versio Turriani, the translation of the collection of V into Latin by the Jesuit Torres or Turrianus in the late sixteenth century and published as the *editio princeps* of these works in Henricus Canisius (ed.), *Antiquae lectionis*, etc. (*AntLect*), IV, 1 (Ingolstadt, 1603), pp. xv (unnumbered)–157. Scholars have long wondered from what manuscript Turrianus made his translation. The search was by no means advanced by the comment of Friedrich Loofs that his exemplar could not have been V,[16] for my own close analysis of *CNE* 1 and its florilegium in T—I spare my readers the details[17]— establishes beyond all reasonable doubt that T is indeed a translation of V.

O = Codex Oxoniensis Bodleianus Laudianus graecus 92B of the early tenth century.[18] The second complete collection of Leontius' works, it contains, in order: *CNE prol; CNE* 1; *SolArgSev; CapTrig; CNE* 2; *CNE* 3, the argument; *De duabus Christi naturis*; *CNE* 3, the florilegium.

S = Codex Parisinus bibliothecae nationalis supplementi graeci 163. S is a copy of O, almost certainly made or commissioned by

---

[15] *Editio princeps* of the Greek text of *CapTrig* was Angelo Mai's publication of selections of the *Doctrina patrum de incarnatione verbi* in *Scriptorum veterum nova collectio*, etc., VII, 1 (Rome, 1833), 6–73, including *CapTrig* on pp. 40–45, reproduced in PG, 86, 1902–1916, with Turrianus' Latin.

[16] FLoofs, *LeontByz*, 11–12 and 12, note.

[17] A summary of the evidence:
The Greek words and phrases in the marginalia and notes of T conform closely to V.
A collation of all significant variants in *CNE* 1, the argument, among VOG—see below—to T justifies all but the last degree of certainty that V is the exemplar of T.
The florilegium of *CNE* 1 in T corresponds with that in V in every particular.

[18] For this date, a letter from Miss Ruth Barbour, The Bodleian Library, Oxford, England, 25 April 1962, whom I thank most sincerely both for her judgement and for her permission to publish it.

Johann Ernst Grabe during his stay in England between 1697 and 1711, the year of his death.

G = Codex Genuensis bibliothecae missionis urbanae Sancti Caroli graecus 27[19] of the eleventh century. A miscellany of dogmatic works both trinitarian and Christological, G contains only *CNE prol* and *CNE* 1.

B = Codex Berolinensis Phillippicus 80 (*olim* Phillippicus 1484, Meermannianus 152, Claromontanus 175).[20] B is a theological miscellany copied by Jacques Sirmond (1559–1651), including *CNE prol* and *CNE* 1 copied from G.

Of these six, then, only three, VOG, are not copies or translations of other extant manuscripts. The relations among VOG, however, I have not yet been able to determine, and so I adduce all three in the brief *apparatus* to follow.

There remain only:

P = Codex Parisinus bibliothecae nationalis graecus 1335 of the fourteenth century, containing, of Leontius' works, only *CNE* 3, introduced by as much of *CNE prol* as describes that book. I have not yet examined P carefully.

M = Codex Venetus Marcianus (*i.e.*, Divi Marci Bibliothecae) graecus Z 575 (849), a theological miscellany of the fifteenth century, containing of Leontius' writings precisely the same work included in P *supra*, in precisely the same form: that is, *CNE* 3 only, introduced by as much of *CNE prol* as describes *CNE* 3. I have not yet closely studied M, but a preliminary examination of its contents and readings—in microfilm kindly supplied by the Biblioteca nazionale di San Marco—suggests that the text of Leontius in M is very closely related to the same text in P. I note in passing that, to the best of my knowledge, M has been introduced into the scholarly literature on Leontius only in the past two decades: specifically, in 1952 in Henri de Riedmatten, *Les actes du*

---

[19] However, the library of the Congregazione della Missione urbana di San Carlo was destroyed during World War II, and the manuscript is now in the Biblioteca Franzoniana, Via Giustiniana 11/6, Genoa, Italy. To the librarian of the Biblioteca Franzoniana, the Reverend Piero Martini, I owe my sincerest thanks both for his advice as to the wherebouts of G and for his co-operation in obtaining microfilm of it.

[20] Now in the Deutsche Staatsbibliothek, (Ost-)Berlin W8, Unter den Linden 8, which has kindly furnished photographs.

procès de Paul de Samosate. Étude sur la christologie du IIIe au IVe siècle, Paradosis: Etudes de littérature et de théologie ancienne, 4 [Fribourg, 1952]).

II. THE TREATISE *Contra Nestorianos et Eutychianos*

However, it is not with the whole of the *corpus Leontianum* that we have to do now, but only with such parts of it as expound Leontius' doctrine of the person and nature of Christ, his Christology. Consequently we shall not concern ourselves here with the *AdvFraudes*; for the *AdvFraudes* is, properly speaking, not a theological treatise at all, but an annotated collection of documents proving that certain among them are works not of the Fathers, as their titles represent them, but of Apollinaris and his disciples, in short, *fraudes*. The *CapTrig*, too, will be little heard of; for though it is indeed a theological treatise, it adds little to, but indeed seems to summarize, the arguments of *CNE* and *SolArgSev*. *CNE* and *SolArgSev*: these are our sources here; and still more precisely, of the three treatises compounded into *CNE*, it is above all *CNE* 1 which we must examine. We begin by setting *CNE* 1 in its context, that is, the whole of *CNE*, the *Tres libri contra Nestorianos et Eutychianos*.

A. *The Title of CNE*

The treatise before us is now known as the *Libri tres contra Nestorianos et Eutychianos*, a title lent it in 1603 by Heinrich Canisius (1548–1610) in his *editio princeps* of the Latin translation by Francisco Torres, that is, Turrianus; unless, of course, Canisius inherited it from Turrianus himself.[21] The name stuck. In his new edition of Canisius' collection, begun in 1725, Jacques Basnage (1653–1723) copied Canisius' title[22]; and when in 1844 Angelo Mai sought a Greek title for his *editio princeps* of the Greek text of V,

---

[21] HCanisius, *AntLect*, IV, 1. The title stands on an unnumbered page at the beginning of the volume.
[22] Jacobus Basnage (Jacques Basnage de Beauval) (ed.), *Thesaurus monumentorum ecclesiasticorum et historicorum*, etc., 4 vols. (Amsterdam, 1725), I, 525.

he seems simply to have translated Basnage.[23] Finally, in 1865, both Canisius' Latin and Mai's Greek were canonized by the Patrologia graeca.[24]

The manuscript tradition will have it otherwise, of course. As a piece, CNE has no title at all in the manuscripts, but must make do with the title of its prologue, that is, in the version of O: τοῦ μακαρίου λεοντίου τοῦ ἐρημίτου πρόλογος ἤγουν προθεωρία τῆς ὑποκειμένης συντάξεως.[25] Even Leontius' Byzantine scribes, it seems, have no better name for CNE than "the treatise [immediately] below." Nor is Leontius himself of any help; unless his mention of τὰ πρώην ἡμῖν κατὰ τὸν ἀληθῆ λόγον ἐκ τῶν ἁγίων Πατέρων συνειλεγμένα πρὸς τοὺς ἀπὸ Νεστορίου τε καὶ Εὐτυχοῦς in the opening sentence of AdvArgSev refers to the whole of CNE and not, as the context suggests, only to CNE 1.[26]

However, the lack of a title ought not surprise us. CNE is not a literary unity, but a collection of three very different pieces, linked only by their common Christology and—we must suppose—the theological situation in which their author developed it. A name for CNE was hard to come by; a better name than it finally obtained, almost impossible.

B. *The Prologue to CNE*

We have suggested above that Leontius published CNE in Constantinople in the campaign of the Origenists against Theodore of Mopsuestia, and more exactly sometime between his return to the capital from Palestine about 540 and a time long enough before his death in 543 to allow him to defend CNE 1 against the attacks reported in SolArgSev. We must now ask: what does Leontius him-

---

[23] AMai, *SpicRom*, X, 2, p. 1: λόγοι γ' κατὰ νεστοριανῶν καὶ εὐτυχιανιστῶν.

[24] PG, 86, 1267–1268.

[25] τοῦ μακαρίου *om*. G. τοῦ ἐρημίτου] μονάχου G. πρόλογος ἤγουν προθεωρία] ἐκ τοῦ λόγου ἢ προθεωρίας P. προθεωρία] θεωρία G. That "the treatise [immediately] below" is the whole of CNE, that is, three books and not CNE 1 alone, is plain from the preface itself: it describes the three books to follow in some detail (PG, 86, 1269A 15–1272B 17).

[26] PG, 86, 1916C 1–3.

self say about the circumstances in which he published *CNE*, and what does it contain—remembering always that the date and occasion of its publication need not be identical with the date and occasion (or dates and occasions) of its composition.

1. The Publication of *CNE*

Leontius' answer lies in his brief prologue to *CNE*.[27] Its first paragraph[28] tells us the occasion of his writing: certain "god-loving men"[29] who have heard and applauded "the public lectures which [he has] frequently held" have encouraged him to put into writing for them "some kind of outlines of the *dubitationes* and *solutiones*" which he has so often discussed.[30] Leontius hesitates; he has, he tells us, neither the gift of the pen nor the gift of the Spirit. Not, to be sure, that Leontius is thereby discouraged! "For I am not ashamed that I know myself ⟨ only ⟩ in some slight degree, when those now counted wise are utterly ignorant of themselves."[31] "Their wilful ingratitude towards the ancient labors of the holy Fathers" does indeed give him pause, for if they have not been moved by "writings set forth with so much of God's grace and wisdom, and indeed also with so excellent an understanding of philosophy and the other disciplines, how will this insignificant treatise persuade them ... ?"[32]

This brief passage is of interest on two counts. First, Leontius tells us here that *CNE* is intended to furnish "outlines of the *dubitationes* and *solutiones*" discussed by him in his "public lectures." Where he held those lectures and why, we shall consider in our last chapter. Second, in his cryptic words about "those now counted wise," Leontius grants us a fleeting glimpse—of whom? His adversaries, that is, Nestorians and Eutychians? Other theologians of his

---

[27] *Ibid.*, 1268B 1–1272D 7, copied from Angelo Mai's *editio princeps* of the Greek text in *SpicRom*, X, 2, pp. 1–5.

[28] PG, 86, 1268B 2–1269A 9.

[29] *Ibid.*, 1268B 2: ἄνδρες ... θεοφιλεῖς. FLoofs, *LeontByz*, 22, note: "θεοφιλής ist in Justinians Zeit fast stehendes Epitheton der Bischöfe; vgl. den *Codex Justinianus* und die *Novellen*."

[30] PG, 86, 1268B 2–7.

[31] *Ibid.*, 1268B 10–1269A 1. *N. B.*: 1269A 1 *post* ἑαυτοὺς *add.* ἀγνοούντων· ἔπειτα δὲ καὶ ἡ τούτων πρὸς τοὺς VOG.

[32] *Ibid.*, 1269A 1–9.

9

party, that is, other Chalcedonians? Whoever they may be, οἱ νυνὶ σοφοί in the prologue to *CNE* are certainly one and the same with οἱ νῦν ὄντες σοφοί whom Leontius attacks in the opening lines of *CNE* 1;[33] and so we may safely leave them until we meet them again there. Meantime we note with regret that Leontius' prologue tells us very much less of his intentions in *CNE* than we would like to hear.

2. The Contents of *CNE*

The second part of the prologue[34] describes each of the three books to follow. A mercy, let us confess, not only because Leontius closes his description of each book with its title, otherwise easily garbled, but also because only here do we learn upon sure authority that the three books were published as one.[35]

First Leontius describes *CNE* 1,[36] of which much more soon. Its title in the text: τῆς κατὰ τὴν θεότητα τοῦ Χριστοῦ καὶ ἀνθρωπότητα ἐναντίας δοκήσεως Νεστορίου τε καὶ Εὐτυχοῦς ἔλεγχος καὶ ἀνατροπή, adducing VOG.[37] Turrianus' translation: *contrariae inter se fictionis Nestorii et Eutychis circa divinitatem ac humanitatem Christi confutatio.*[38]

---

[33] *Ibid.*, 1273A 1 ff. and especially A 4.

[34] *Ibid.*, 1269A 14–1272B 17.

[35] The only two complete texts of *CNE* are VO, in which, as the description on page 5 shows, *CNE* is divided by the insertion of *SolArgSev* and *CapTrig* after *CNE* 1, and could not easily be reconstructed on the evidence of the manuscript tradition alone.

[36] Leontius' description in PG, 86, 1269A 15–B 10. For *CNE* 1 itself: 1273A 1–1316B 5, copied from A. Mai's *editio princeps* of the Greek text, V, in *SpicRom*, X, 2, pp. 5–39. Of the florilegium, however, Mai published only twelve of eighty-nine items, and only one of Leontius' scholia (*ibid.*, 33–39); so that the whole florilegium is available only in Turrianus' Latin translation of V in HCanisius, *AntLect*, IV, 1, pp. 19–39. For a description of the florilegium of *all three books* of *CNE* in V, together with Leontius' scholia, see R. Devreesse, *op. cit.*, 545–576.

[37] PG, 86, 1269B 8–10. *Apparatus:* νεστορίου τε καὶ εὐτυχοῦς *om.* O. At the head of *CNE* 1 itself (1273–1274) the title in VO is virtually identical, omitting only τε; but τοῦ αὐτοῦ λεοντίου ἀσχητοῦ ἔλεγχος καὶ ἀνατροπὴ τῆς κατὰ τοῦ χριστοῦ ἐναντίας δοκήσεως νεστορίου καὶ εὐτυχοῦς G. A subscription to *CNE* 1 in V, fol. 50, exactly reproduces the title in V.

[38] HCanisius, *AntLect*, IV, 1, ii (unnumbered). Turrianus' translation of the same title at the head of *CNE* 1 (*ibid.*, 1) is slightly different.

Next, *CNE* 2.[39] Its title in the texts: πρὸς τοὺς ἐξ ἡμῶν προσθεμένους τῇ κατεφθαρμένῃ γνώμῃ τῶν Ἀφθαρτοδοκητῶν διάλογος,
adducing VOG.[40] *CNE* 2 is a long dialogue between an Orthodox
and an Orthodox disciple of the Monophysite bishop Julian of
Halicarnassus, who sometime after 518 in Egypt had argued against
Severus of Antioch that the flesh of Jesus Christ was incorruptible
from the moment of his conception and not only after the resurrection. As his summary here suggests, Leontius looks upon Julian as
the Monophysite *par excellence*.

Finally, *CNE* 3.[41] Its title in the text: τῆς ἀπορρήτου καὶ
ἀρχοειδεστέρας τῶν Νεστοριανῶν ἀσεβείας καὶ τῶν ταύτης Πατέρων
φωρὰ καὶ θρίαμβος, adducing VOGPM.[42] *CNE* 3 is a diatribe—no
other word will do—against Theodore of Mopsuestia, to which Leontius appends a florilegium intended to prove that Theodore and,
before him, Diodore of Tarsus are the spiritual fathers of Nestorius.

To these preliminaries Leontius adds a third part: a final word
to the reader, begging his forgiveness for the faults of the piece, but
urging him not to boggle at the difficulty of the argument.[43] With
this, he—and we—pass on to *CNE* 1.

[39] Leontius' description: PG, 86, 1269B 13–D 12. For *CNE* 2 itself:
1316D 1–1358A 11, copied from *SpicRom*, X, 2, pp. 95–127. Again, the complete florilegium will be found only in Turrianus' Latin.

[40] PG, 86, 1269D 10–12. προσθεμένους VOGˣ θεμένους G. The title at
the head of *CNE* 2 itself is almost identical; adducing VO as if variants, we
find: *ante* πρὸς *add.* τοῦ αὐτοῦ V τοῦ αὐτοῦ ἀββᾶ λεοντίου λόγος β′ O.
ἐξ ἡμῶν] ἐκ τῶν ἡμετέρων VO.

[41] Leontius' description: PG, 86, 1271A 1–B 17.' For *CNE* 3 itself:
1357B 1–1396A 13, copied from AMai, *SpicRom*, X, 2, pp. 66–94. Again, the
complete florilegium only in Turrianus' Latin.

[42] PG, 86, 1271B 15–17. φωρὰ] φῶρα V φορὰ OGPM. The title at the
head of *CNE* 3 itself is similar. Before we turn to it, however, a note on the
title of *CNE* 3 in PM. As I have said just above, PM reproduce, first, that
portion of *CNE prol* which describes *CNE* 3, and second, *CNE* 3 itself.
PM therefore offer three titles to *CNE* 3. They are, in order: first, the title
set by the compilers of PM at the beginning of their excerpts from *CNE* 3;
second, the title of *CNE* 3 incorporated in the text of *CNE prol*, described
at the beginning of this note; and third, the title at the beginning of *CNE* 3
itself. It is this last form of the title which I adduce in what follows. The
title at the head of *CNE* 3, then, adducing VOPM as if variants to the title
reproduced in the text above: *ante* τῆς *add.* κατὰ ἀφθαρτοδοκητῶν. λόγος
τρίτος V. (κατὰ ἀφθαρτοδοκητῶν clearly belongs to the piece immediately
preceding *CNE* 3 in V, that is, *CNE* 2.) *ante* τῆς *add.* τοῦ αὐτοῦ σύνταγμα
περὶ O. ἀρχαιοειδεστέρας O. ταύτης : αὐτῆς O. φωρὰ V φορὰ OPM. *post*
θρίαμβος *add.* λόγος Γ′ O.

[43] PG, 86, 1272C 1–D 7.

III. *CNE* I

A. *Introduction*

1. The Organization of *CNE* I in the Manuscript Tradition

In his brief description of *CNE* I in *CNE prol* Leontius tells us of its scope and organization. "The first book," he says, "contains in a single treatise my answers and responses in brief to the contradictory and spurious speculation of both Nestorius and Eutyches, and in a word takes into account pretty nearly all of their criticisms. This same book I have divided into chapters, each containing, of course, the arguments which can be subsumed under it. Its title has been chosen as peculiarly appropriate to the end in view: ..." — and there follows the title.[44] Of the peculiar tactics which Leontius employs against his two mutually antagonistic adversaries here, we will say more later. Just now, we must see how he has organized the treatise.

"This same book I have divided into chapters ...," writes Leontius, but the reader of the copy of V in Mai and Migne looks for them in vain. Nonetheless, the manuscripts prove Leontius an honest man: VOG each distinguish seven chapters, each chapter itself introduced by an objection or *dubitatio* (ἀπορία) raised by Leontius' adversaries, to which he then responds.[45] These *dubitationes* are usually marked by *obeloi*, i.e., dashes. A close examination of the manuscripts produces the following outline, to which we shall frequently refer:

CNE I, prologue: PG, 86, 1273A 1–1276D 4
(Chapter) 1: 1276D 5–1280B 10. The *dubitatio*: 1275D 5–7
        2: 1280B 13–1284A 10. The *dubitatio*: 1280B 13–C 6
        3: 1284B 1–1285B 14. The *dubitatio*: 1284B 1–5
        4: 1285C 1–1289B 1. The *dubitatio*: 1285C 1–5

---

[44] *Ibid.*, 1269A 15–B 7.
[45] The first to describe the division of *CNE* I was JP Junglas, *LeontByz*, 22. His source was B, a copy of G. Later, R. Devreesse, *op. cit.*, 549–550, described the divisions in V.

5: 1289B 2–1293B 10. The *dubitatio*: 1289B 2–9[46]
6: 1293B 12–1297C 4. The *dubitatio*: 1293B 12–C 3
7: 1297C 5–1305D 2. The *dubitatio* (here a simple request that Leontius state his own position): 1297C 5–D 2
CNE 1, epilogue: 1305D 5–1308A 8.

2. The Argument of *CNE* 1

These are the bones of the book: a long argument in seven chapters sandwiched between a prologue and an epilogue. We ask next: how does that argument advance? Answer: in three steps. In the first chapter, Leontius summarily introduces the fallacy common to both his opponents: "If," they say, "you posit two natures of the one Christ; but if there is no nature without hypostasis; then there will be [in him] two hypostases, too."[47] Then, after a brief skirmish with his Monophysite,[48] he turns to the Nestorian and advances to the attack in the paragraph for which he is most famous.[49] "Hypostasis," he says, "is not the same as what is enhypostasized," that is, an enhypostasized nature.[50] Granted that hypostasis separates, that is, distinguishes the individuals of a single nature from one another; and granted too that such hypostases must be of the same number as their natures. Nonetheless, an hypostasis may also unite, that is, join different natures into a single individual; and then, of course, the hypostasis will never be of the same number as its natures. So it is in Jesus Christ; and so also—we stand at the threshold of the

---

[46] The manuscripts waver here: V seems not to know whether chapter five ends at 1293B 10 or earlier, at 1293A 5. Closer reading of the text nonetheless establishes that the passage 1293A 6–B 10 is not a *dubitatio* beginning chapter six, but rather an answer to Leontius' charge in chapter five (1292C 4–7) that the Monophysite asserts not both one *and* two natures, but only one. Replies the Monophysite: we do indeed assert only one nature, but in two senses! 1293A 6–B 10 therefore belongs to chapter five. I note that the Monophysite's speech here ends with τῆς ἐνώσεως at 1293A 9, not with τῇ φύσει ἕν at A 10, as PG suggests; here the manuscripts unanimously confirm the sense of the argument.

[47] PG, 86, 1276D 5–7: Εἰ δύο φύσεις ἐπὶ τοῦ ἑνὸς Χριστοῦ φατε, οὐκ ἔστι δὲ φύσις ἀνυπόστατος, δύο ἄρα ἂν εἶεν καὶ αἱ ὑποστάσεις.

[48] *Ibid.*, 1276D 11–1277C 12.

[49] *Ibid.*, 1277C 14–1280B 10.

[50] *Ibid.*, 1277C 14: Οὐ ταὐτόν, ὦ οὗτοι, ὑπόστασις καὶ ἐνυπόστατον, etc.

inner sanctum—the union of soul and body.[51] We must emphasize the point: for Leontius, the union of soul and body is the peculiar and proper paradigm of the union of Word with flesh. Indeed, with the paradigm *soul : body* = *Word : flesh*, Leontius has unmasked his artillery, for he will give the whole second part of the treatise, its very core, to a determined assault on the *dubitationes* of both those who reject the paradigm—the Nestorians, of course—and those who pervert its right use to their own lamentable ends—the Monophysites.

In the second part of *CNE* 1, then, we have to do with the union of soul and body as paradigm of the incarnation. Five *dubitationes* introduce five chapters, that is, chapters two through six. The first three, chapters two through four, reply to the criticism of the Nestorian; the next two, chapters five and six, answer the Monophysite.

Finally, in order to bring the piece to a fitting close, the seventh and last chapter abandons the way of *dubitatio* and *solutio*; for here the *dubitatio* of Leontius' adversaries simply asks him to review the issues so that the truth may appear,[52] and in fact serves him as occasion for a brief dissertation on the mode of the union, the τρόπος τῆς ἑνώσεως. The book closes with a short epilogue, after which Leontius introduces a long florilegium.

B. *CNE 1: the Prologue*[53]

Leontius' prologue to *CNE* 1 falls into two parts: first, a brief statement of purpose,[54] which passes into a sharp attack on "those now counted wise", mentioned above; and second, what we had best call a prefatory statement of the way in which he intends to attain that purpose.[55]

---

[51] *Ibid.*, 1280B 7–10: ῞Οπερ ἄν τις εὕροι καὶ ἐφ' ἑτέρων μὲν πραγμάτων, οὐχ ἥκιστα δὲ ἐπὶ ψυχῆς καὶ σώματος, ὧν κοινὴ μὲν ἡ ὑπόστασις, ἰδία δὲ ἡ φύσις, καὶ ὁ λόγος διάφορος.

[52] *Ibid.*, 1279C 5–D 1.

[53] *Ibid.*, 1273A 1–1276D 4.

[54] *Ibid.*, 1273A 1–C 5.

[55] *Ibid.*, 1273C 7–1276D 4.

INTRODUCTION

1. "Those Now Counted Wise"

[Since] the definition of [the terms] hypostasis and ousia, that is, prosopon and nature—for both [pairs mean] the same thing and each is [predicated] of the same thing[56]—remains confused and vague among those now counted wise, I have undertaken to elucidate and clarify [them] .....[57]

So Leontius begins; then, after an appeal for his readers' prayers, goes on:

Now they who now oppose us, they who have a single [and common] objection both to the good itself and to godfearing men, we are not unaware that just as they despise [the Fathers], so also [they despise] those of us who defend their teaching and hold it before us [as a model]; thereby unconsciously honoring us in the community of their contempt. These same people both make sport of divine matters and insult [true] theologians; and so what wonder that they scorn us too, nobodies that we are! of whom this alone is worthy of note, that they studiously neglect every virtue [lying] in [good] works, but rather command themselves to be wise, and are as it were sagacious by decree; and the mere wishing [for it] makes them cultured and cultivated; so that one of the wittier [among us] has appropriately nicknamed them σαπροφιλόσοφοι.[58]

---

[56] Against PG, 86, 1273A 2–3 and with Turrianus I read: φύσεως—ταὐτὸν γὰρ ἄμφω καὶ περὶ ταὐτὸν ἑκάτερα— etc. The οὐ inserted before A 2 ταυτὸν in V *secunda manu* finds no support in OG and anyhow, as Turrianus saw, ruins the sense. That hypostasis and prosopon, ousia and nature are synonyms is a commonplace in Leontius.

[57] PG, 86, 1273A 1–5.

[58] *Ibid.*, 1273A 10–B 9. I read B 8 σαπροφιλοσόφους with G against ἀκροφιλοσόφους V σαρκοφιλοσόφους O, if only because the readings of VO are hardly *bons mots*. Why then σαπροφιλόσοφοι? To reconstruct the humor of another age by speculation is an enterprise no less foolhardy than fascinating; but let us try. Leontius supposes here that the wisdom, σοφία, loved by philosophers implies ἀρετὴ ἡ ἐν ἔργοις (B 4), that is, works of practical asceticism; and he pours scorn upon those who worship, as the preachers say, with their words but not with their works. Now, the *locus classicus* for such a conviction is of course Matthew 7:17, where we read: "a sound tree cannot bear evil fruit, nor can a bad tree"— σαπρὸν δένδρον —"bear good fruit." Can it be that σαπροφιλόσοφοι are those lovers of wisdom, philosophers, who yet will have wisdom without the works of wisdom, that is, its fruit, and so are *bad philosophers*?

The σαπροφιλόσοφοι, then, pretend to an acumen in matters theological to which in fact they have no true and proper claim; for they press their claim—and press it successfully, it seems—not upon the evidence of the tradition, nor again with the testimony of good works, but rather by an unnamed authority in which they "command themselves to be wise and are as it were sagacious by decree." Now, who are they?

Marcel Richard has offered a convincing reply. "Those now counted wise," he suggests, can hardly be Leontius' adversaries in *CNE* I, that is, his Nestorians and Monophysites. To the contrary, Richard believes that they were Chalcedonians—but Chalcedonians inclined to interpretations of the formula of the Council very different from the interpretation of Leontius and the Origenists. More specifically, they were that group of Chalcedonians both Eastern and Western who had labored for the imperial condemnation of the Origenist party in 543; Chalcedonians, we might add, particularly sensitive to Monophysite charges that they were soft on Nestorianism, so that they were all the more anxious to purify their party of all elements liable to compromise it. "Hauts personnages," says Richard; and then explains who they must be. Leontius was a disciple of Nonnus, an Origenist, and in early 543 Origen had been condemned. "Bref, lorsque Léonce écrivait ces lignes sa pensée voguait bien au delà de son objectif immédiat, les Nestoriens et les Monophysites du Ier livre, jusqu'aux personnes influentes qui venaient de condamner Origène"—I add: or perhaps were just about to condemn him—"et par ricochet de jeter un blâme sur tant de Pères qui l'avaient admiré et suivi, de couvrir enfin d'opprobres le parti de l'abbé Nonnus: Ephrem patriarche d'Antioche, Menas patriarche de Constantinople, le diacre Pélage, apocrisiaire du pape Vigile, l'empereur lui-même, voilà quels étaient les Ἀκροφιλόσοφοι" — or, as I have suggested, the σαπροφιλόσοφοι.[59]

[59] MRichard, "Léonce ... origéniste?" *RevEtByz*, V (1947), 54–55. On the other hand, I cannot agree with Richard that "les hérésies combattues dans le Ier livre" are "très théoriques"; and I frankly doubt that Leontius and his contemporaries of Chalcedonian persuasion would have felt that the heresies in question represented "un danger pour l'orthodoxie ... à la fois trop général et trop lointain, pour qu'un polemiste chalcédonien puisse en parler avec une telle amertume"—that is, such as Leontius' "amertume"—"et

2. Leontius' Argument: Existence and Essence

With this, Leontius turns to the work at hand. The second part[60] of the prologue to *CNE* 1 begins by introducing Leontius' readers to his strategy: though Monophysites and Nestorians have very different ends in view, they use one and the same argument; and so Leontius will employ a single argument to refute them.[61] This common argument? We shall find it in the *dubitatio* of *CNE* 1.1. Meantime, Leontius continues his introduction by comparing the errors of his adversaries, Monophysites and Nestorians, with the errors of the heretics Sabellius and Arius; in short, by correlating the doctrine of God with Christology. We must look at this paragraph more closely.

a. *The first parallel*

Leontius' argument here[62] advances in two steps: two comparisons of the relations of the two sets of heretics. We begin by translating the first comparison in full.

> It must be understood that in respect of the *oikonomia*—that is, the incarnation—Eutyches stands in the same relation to Nestorius as in respect of *theologia* Sabellius to Arius; for these latter, too, by reason of their opposition to one another—literally, by reason of [arguments] opposed to one another—fell into a [single and] equivalent evil. [Sabellius] for the sake of the ousia confused the hypostases into a single hypostasis; while [Arius], for the sake of the hypostases, divided with them also the ousia. With [Nestorius and Eutyches], however, it is the other way around; for the former splits the natures into hypostases, while the latter mingles the natures into a [single]

---

comme une chose l'affectant personellement." We remember that in the period 531–536 the Chalcedonians in Constantinople were at close quarters with at least the Monophysites.

[60] PG, 86, 1273C 7–1276D 4.

[61] For this first paragraph (of two) of the second part of the prologue: *ibid.*, 1273C 7–1276B 11, summarized in 1276B 3–11.

[62] For the second paragraph of the second part of the prologue: *ibid.*, 1276B 12–C 14, followed by a brief conclusion (C 14–D 4) serving also to introduce the first chapter (D 5 ff.).

nature; and again, the former makes the hypostasis into hypostases, while the latter mixes the natures into a [single] nature.[63]
What is Leontius saying?

It must be admitted at once that in this first comparison or parallel, Leontius introduces a certain confusion: in his first statement of the parallel (B 15–C 2) he posits very explicitly *Eutyches* : *Nestorius* = *Sabellius* : *Arius*; while in his subsequent exposition of the parallel (C 3–8) he seems to posit *Sabellius* (C 3–5) : *Arius* (C 5–6) = *Nestorius* (C 6–7) : *Eutyches* (C 7–8). Can we resolve or reduce this confusion? We must, if we are to understand Leontius.

Let us ask first just where the confusion lies. Not, we see, in Leontius' primary distinction, for in each of his two statements of the parallel the terms of each pair are united and the pairs themselves distinguished by the same opposites, that is, *oikonomia* and *theologia*. Or, more simply, in each statement of the parallel, Eutyches and Nestorius, Sabellius and Arius, are always on the same side of the equation. On the other hand, the principle in each statement by which the terms of each pair are distinguished from one another seems to be different from the corresponding principle in the other statement; the proposition *Eutyches* : *Nestorius* = *Sabellius* : *Arius* implies a different relation between Eutyches and Nestorius (as also between Sabellius and Arius) from the relation implied in the proposition *Sabellius* : *Arius* = *Nestorius* : *Eutyches*. Here lies the confusion.

We must ask next, then, by just what two different principles Leontius distinguished the terms of each pair from one another in his two different statements. We find them both in Leontius' expansion of the parallel. The first principle: the pair of opposites σύγχυσις *(confusio)* : διαίρεσις *(divisio)*,[64] which we may for convenience reduce to its lowest common denominator, the notorious couple ἕν : πολλά, the one and the many. Clearly Leontius employed this pair in his first statement of the parallel: for, as in Christology Eutyches *confuses* the natures and Nestorius *divides* the natures of Christ, so in *theologia* Sabellius *confuses* the hypostases and Arius *divides* the three hypostases of God. On each side of the equation

---

[63] *Ibid.*, 1276B 12–C 9.
[64] *Ibid.*, C 4 συγχέων. C 5 συνδιαιρῶν. C 7 τέμνει. C 7 φύρει.

the pair *confusio* : *divisio* distinguishes the two heretics in question, and distinguishes them *in the same order*, *confusio* describing the first term and *divisio* the second. On the other hand, this pair of opposites does not explain the order of terms in Leontius' subsequent exposition of the parallel *Sabellius* : *Arius* = *Nestorius* : *Eutyches*.

Nevertheless, the exposition suggests a second pair of opposites by which to distinguish the terms within each pair: the pair of opposites ὑπόστασις : οὐσία (or φύσις, here its homonym), that is, *existence* : *essence*. Why does Sabellius confuse the three hypostases of God into a single hypostasis? διὰ τὴν οὐσίαν (C 4). For Sabellius, essence is prior to existence. Why does Arius divide the divine ousia? διὰ τὴν ὑπόστασιν (C 5), that is, in order that it may conform to the three hypostases; for Arius believes that existence, whether one or many, is prior to essence. In Christology, of course, Nestorius begins from the two natures of Jesus Christ because he holds to the priority of essence, while Eutyches takes his departure from the one Christ because he believes in the priority of existence. This pair of opposites, *existence* : *essence*, does not explain the order of terms in the first statement of the parallel (C 15–B 2), but may well explain the order of terms in the exposition of the parallel *Sabellius* : *Arius* = *Nestorius* : *Eutyches*.

Alas, both interpretations of this section cannot be right. If, as seems clear from the context, the second parallel (C 2–8) is really an exposition of the first (B 15–C 2) and not a second and utterly different parallel, Leontius must have been nodding: somehow he has reversed the order of terms in one side of the equation *(Nestorius* : *Eutyches)* either in his first statement of the parallel or in his exposition of it. Which reading shall we choose? Happily enough, we need not choose at all; for whatever the most likely interpretation of these lines, one thing is clear: by the end of these lines Leontius has fixed his attention on the opposites *hypostasis* : *ousia*. Indeed, in the next lines—introduced by an explanatory γάρ (C 9)—he will introduce still another equation, in which the pair of opposites *hypostasis* : *ousia* will serve not to distinguish terms within each of the two pairs compared, but to distinguish from one another the two pairs themselves.

b. *The second parallel*[65]

From his first parallel Leontius moves directly into his second: "for it is on the very principles"—προβλήματα: axioms?—"in which the Trinity is seen divided by an earlier age, that we find the *oikonomia* confused"—i.e., the two natures confused—"in later days; and it is [on the very principles] by which some nowadays divide the *oikonomia* that those [earlier heretics] confuse the divine nature." The parallel intended is clear; *Arius : Eutyches = Nestorius : Sabellius*. Each term of each pair, that is, each heretic, employs the same *problemata* as the other term of its pair, though of course in different ways. We ask then: what *problemata* do Arius and Eutyches have in common? What *problemata* Nestorius and Sabellius? Our first step must be to inquire what pair of opposites expresses the difference between the two sets of *problemata*, that is, the difference between the two pairs of heretics here equated.

Let us proceed by elimination. In the lines discussed above, we have found that Leontius employs three pairs of opposites: first, *oikonomia : theologia*; second, *confusio : divisio*, which we have reduced to the pair *one : many*; and finally, *hypostasis : ousia*. In this second parallel now, we see that the two sides of the equation cannot be distinguished by either of the first two pairs of opposites just mentioned. The reason? Because each pair of the equation, that is Arius and Eutyches, Nestorius and Sabellius, includes both terms of both of the first two pairs of opposites: for Arius, in the doctrine of God, divides, while Eutyches, in Christology, confuses; and so forth. Are then the pairs of the parallel distinguished by the pair of opposites *hypostasis : ousia*? Clearly they are: for just as both Arius and Eutyches begin with existence, that is, hypostasis, whether one or many, so also both Nestorius and Sabellius begin with essence, ousia, whether one or many. If then we go on to ask by which of the remaining two pairs of opposites Leontius distinguishes the terms of each pair, we must reply: by the pair *many : one*; for just as Arius begins with the many, that is, the three hypostases, but Eutyches with the one, that is, the single nature of Jesus Christ, so also Nestorius begins with the many, the two natures of Christ, and Sabellius with the one, the single nature of God.

Back then to our question: What *problemata* do Arius and Eutyches, Nestorius and Sabellius have in common? The parallel suggests that Arius and Eutyches will argue from existence to essence, but Nestorius and Sabellius from essence to existence. Is existence prior to essence or essence to existence? For Leontius, this is the ground common to the battles between Sabellius and Arius and between Nestorius and Eutyches. We shall see below that Leontius resolves the problem by asserting that essence is simultaneous with existence. *very imp*

C. *The Way Ahead*

With this, Leontius is ready to embark upon his argument, and we are tempted to follow him, if only because the first port of call, the first chapter, includes just those passages in which scholarship both ancient and modern has found Leontius' peculiar contribution to Christology, his definition of hypostasis. Nonetheless, as Marcel Richard reminds us so very frequently, with Leontius things are not what they seem.[66] The first chapter of *CNE* is, to be sure, a beginning, but such a beginning, I suggest, as can hardly be comprehended before the end. In fact, in so polemical a piece as *CNE*, the order of Leontius' arguments follows the course of the debate, not the logical development of his own system of thought. Unfortunately it is just the development of Leontius' own thought which we wish to recover here. We begin, therefore, with a resolute refusal to lose ourselves in the drift of the argument now before us. Instead, we must scour the arguments of Leontius for traces of the system of thought which it defends, discover its elements, analyze them, and put them in the order which the development of his thought demands. Only then will we be in a position to follow the course of the arguments in detail; this essay, alas, will not get so far.

In what follows, then, we leap over the piece to its last chapter, *CNE* 1.7, in which we shall find the *analysis of being* from which Leontius' further argument depends. Back then, in Chapter Three,

---

[66] E. g., MRichard, "Léonce ... origéniste?" *RevEtByz*, V (1947), 53: "Avec lui [Léonce] toutes les scènes se jouent le rideau baissé."

to *CNE* 1.4, in which we will learn of the ways in which the beings described in *CNE* 1.7 unite with one another. With this, we shall have fairly described the form of Leontius' Christology, and so turn, in Chapter Four, to look for the proper matter to fill that form. Now our search will lead us to the Christology of Evagrius of Pontus, in whom we shall find Leontius' spiritual master: indeed, the Jesus Christ of Leontius' Christology will prove to be identical with the Jesus Christ of Evagrius. Having thus united form and matter, we return, in Chapter Five, to Leontius' own work in order to resolve the problem, posed by *CNE* 1.1, which has most persistently interested Leontius' readers: Leontius speaks of a φύσις ἐνυπόστατος in Jesus Christ; but what is it? We hope to answer the question definitively, and so to establish the outline of the thought of Leontius of Byzantium on the person of Jesus Christ.

CHAPTER TWO

THE SEVENTH CHAPTER OF *CNE* I:[1] THE ἕνωσις κατ'οὐσίαν

I. THE *Dubitatio*[2]

With chapter six, Leontius has completed his defense of the paradigm *Word : flesh = soul : body*. In chapter seven he enters the third and last part of his argument, the most critical and the most perplexing: an analysis of the *mode of union* of God and man in Jesus Christ, that is, the τρόπος τῆς ἑνώσεως. We shall also hear echoes of his Christological formula, a ἕνωσις κατ'οὐσίαν.

The *dubitatio* itself tells us clearly that the treatise has entered a new and final stage. We hear no more of the proposition that there is no nature without hypostasis, no more of the union of soul and body. Indeed, in this last chapter, Leontius defends no specific proposition at all. Consequently, the *dubitatio* is not a proper *dubitatio* either: that is, an assertion of its adversaries that a certain proposition implies a certain contradiction or inconsistency. Instead, the *dubitatio* is a modest request that Leontius define and clarify the points at issue in the previous discussion in order that the truth of the matter may appear. In short, Leontius gives up the argument by *dubitatio* and *solutio* for simple exposition.

How does Leontius answer his adversaries' request? The issue, as the first words of the *dubitatio* suggest, is the *mode of the union*, the τρόπος τῆς ἑνώσεως. What is it? Leontius begins without delay. "The union of the divine nature [of Jesus Christ] with the human nature is described by some as according to ousia (κατ' οὐσίαν), by others as according to activity (κατ' ἐνέργειαν), and by others still as according to will (κατὰ γνώμην)."[3] To be sure, he continues, there are those who out of a manifestly hypocritical piety prefer

---

[1] For *CNE* I. 7, see PG, 86, 1297C 5–1305D 2.
[2] *Ibid.*, 1297C 5–D 2.
[3] *Ibid.*, 1297D 3–5.

23

to call the union "inexpressible,"[4] and will commit themselves to no other formula; but in fact, the only truly *inexpressible* union is the union κατ'οὐσίαν,[5] and so we pass on to the other, more serious formulae.[6] There follows the main body of the chapter in two parts: first, an attack upon the Christological formulae of the school of Antioch (itself unmentioned) and in particular upon the formula ἕνωσις κατ'ἀξίαν; and second, an exposition of the true and Orthodox formula, ἕνωσις κατ'οὐσίαν, which Leontius carefully distinguishes from the same phrase in the mouths of the Monophysites.

---

[4] *Ibid.*, 1297D 7–8, *passim.*

[5] *Ibid.*, 1300A 9–10.

[6] For the whole of this scathing excursus against those who call the union "inexpressible," see *ibid.*, 1297D 5–1300B 12. To whom is Leontius referring here? Almost certainly to Pseudo-Dionysius the Areopagite: 1297D 13–14 τῷ ἀρρήτῳ τὸ ρητόν seems to reflect Pseudo-Dionysius' *ep* 9, PG, 3, 1105C 15–D 5, in which he asserts that in the images of the scriptures (D 5) συμπέπλεκται τῷ ρητῷ τὸ ἄρρητον. Two further considerations support this hypothesis. First, I note that sixth-century readers of Pseudo-Dionysius would not have been without justification in summarizing Pseudo-Dionysius' Christology in the formula *inexpressible union*. Consider Pseudo-Dionysius' assertion about Jesus in *ep* 3, that "the mystery . . . in him (τὸ κατ' αὐτὸν . . . μυστήριον) . . . although spoken, remains inexpressible (καὶ λεγόμενον ἄρρητον μένει)" (*ep* 3, PG, 3, 1069B 6–11, and especially B 9–10). It is no surprise, then, that Pseudo-Dionysius describes both the "divine creation" (Θεοπλαστία) of Jesus and the "divine work" (Θεουργία) accomplished in him as "inexpressible," that is, ἄρρητος (*De divinis nominibus*, 2.9 [PG, 3, 648A 1–4], and 2.6 [PG, 3, 644C 9–14], respectively). The second consideration: by Leontius' times, Pseudo-Dionysius' work was so widely known that it might quite properly have been described as "commonplace and trite"—if indeed the Greek words in question do not mean "widespread."

Here a problem. Does not Leontius consider Pseudo-Dionysius one of the Fathers? *CNE* 1.4 (PG, 86, 1288B 11–C 1) quotes *De div. nom.*, 2.10 (PG, 3, 648C 6–7, with which compare 7.2, PG, 3, 869A 3–5), with approval; *CNE* 1.7 (PG, 86, 1304D 12–1305A 6) quotes *De div. nom.*, 2.4 (PG, 3, 641A 11–C 10); and at the very head of the florilegium of *CNE* 2 (V, p. 113; O, fol. 143ᵛ; see also Robert Devreesse, "Le florilège de Léonce de Byzance," *Revue des sciences religieuses*, X [1930], 569) stands a quotation from *De div. nom.*, 4.25 (PG, 3, 728B 8–10). How can Leontius elsewhere attack Pseudo-Dionysius? Time and space do not allow us more than simply to raise the question; but I suggest in passing—as I have publicly suggested at the symposium "Justinian and Eastern Christendom" at Dumbarton Oaks in Washington, D. C., on 4–6 May 1967 and before the meeting of the American Society of Church History at Nashville, Tennessee, on 26–27 April 1968—that, in one of its major aspects, the *corpus Dionysiacum* may be considered a critique of the doctrine of Evagrius of Pontus; among whose disciples, as we shall see, we must number Leontius of Byzantium.

II. The τρόπος τῆς ἑνώσεως: Leontius' Reply

A. *Against the Nestorians: A* ἕνωσις κατ'ἀξίαν?[7]

On the face of it, Leontius' criticism of the ἕνωσις κατ'ἀξίαν of the tradition of Antioch is hardly remarkable. It is indeed open to question, he begins, whether such a union is a true union at all;[8] but more wonderful still is that the very same theologians who are so chary of a confusion of natures should themselves confound the ἀξίαι proper to each nature into a single ἀξία of Jesus Christ;[9] as if ἀξία could be separated from its nature.[10] What then of the ἀξία of the saints, identical as it must be with the ἀξία of Jesus Christ if there is only one ἀξία? Shall we join it (and with it Jesus Christ and the saints) to the divine nature? Then we must suppose two natures in each of the saints, too;[11] and besides we must incorporate the saints into the Trinity as one of two, three, or four divine hypostases.[12] On the other hand, should we refuse to assign the ἀξία of

[7] PG, 86, 1300B 13–1301C 5. This very difficult passage may be rendered more nearly comprehensible than PG leaves it. A brief *apparatus vix criticus*: 1300C 1 ἂν] ὃν VOG. C 6 ἦ] ἡ VG εἰ O. C 7 ἐπεισί] ἐπεῖσι ed. C 10 *post* δίκαιον *distinxit* ed. C 11 *post* πραγμάτων *non distinxit* ed. C 12 ἀξίαι²] αξία VOG. D 1 ἦ¹] ἡ VOG. D 6 *post* εἴη *add.* <ἡ ἀξία> ed. D 9 *post* ἀξίας *add.* <οἱ ἅγιοι> ed. 1301A 8 μόνοις] μόνος VOG. To this I add two editorial speculations. The first: 1300C 5 *post* μετὰ *add.* <τὴν ἕνωσιν> — as the text seems to imply. I anticipate my argument enough to say that I interpret the passage in the light of the Christology of Evagrius of Pontus: the ὑπερφυὴς καὶ μόνη ἕνωσις is probably that of the νοῦς Jesus Christ with his flesh *after* (μετὰ) his μόνη καὶ πρώτη ἕνωσις as it were κατὰ θεωρίαν with the Word. The second: 1301B 4 μηδὲ VOG μηδεμίαν *ed.*; so as to bring the subject of the clause B 4–8 into agreement with A 15 κἀκείνας (i. e., A 14 ἐνεργείας and A 15 ἀξίας).

[8] PG, 86, 1300C 4–7.

[9] *Ibid.*, 1300C 7–14.

[10] *Ibid.*, 1300C 12–14, D 4–10. Note that Cyril of Alexandria had earlier argued against Nestorius that equality of honor does *not* unite natures. See Cyril of Alexandria, *ep 3 ad Nestorium*, in *ACO*, tome I, vol. 1, part 1 (Berlin-Leipzig, 1930) (item 6, paragraph 3), p. 36, ll. 13–15 and especially l. 15: οὐ γὰρ ἑνοῖ τὰς φύσεις [ἡ] ἰσοτιμία (PG, 77, 112B 8–11).

[11] PG, 86, 1300D 3–4.

[12] *Ibid.*, 1301A 15–B 4. Leontius does not specify just how many hypostases will result, but suggests two hypostases, I think, for those who will then identify nature with hypostasis, three for those who will identify the saints with the hypostasis of the Word, and four for those who will make the saints an hypostasis separate and distinct from the three hypostases of the Trinity.

Jesus and the saints to the divine nature, we shall then have to suppose that by their union with Christ they constitute a single, created Son, or else that like the saints Jesus Christ is Son in name only, that is, after the prototype of the divine Son.[13]

All this, again, is hardly worth writing home about. However, a closer examination of the argument reveals some startling details. After having established that "to the degree that [the saints] participate in the dignity [of the Word], they participate also in the nature of the Word,"[14] Leontius pauses to note that his adversaries might prefer to join "the rest of the saints besides Christ"[15] to some other person of the Trinity than the Son. We boggle a moment at the implication that Christ is merely one of the saints, but go on. Leontius has a ready answer. "Why is it," he asks, "that of the whole rational and blessed creation, both among angels as well as among men, full as it is of the grace of the [Holy] Spirit, which makes [them] gods and sons, [why is it that] he alone who took his appearance from the Virgin is both called God and Son of God in the Scriptures (and rightly so) and is worshipped by the whole rational nature?"[16] He who was born of the Virgin one of the λογικὴ καὶ μακαρία κτίσις, and that κτίσις composed of angels and men, who then worship him who is called God and Son of God? Yet lest we doubt that he means what he says, Leontius continues: "For these godless people must understand that even though the better portion of the variegated dispensation [of the creation] belongs rather to [those beings] nobler and more excellent than to [those] inferior [to them], nevertheless the grace of God's activity over all and the gift of dignity [and honor] are common to all."[17] Such an argument can only be addressed to someone who has suggested that "he who took his appearance from the Virgin" was

---

[13] *Ibid.*, 1301B 4–8. B 4 ὁμονύμως is used in the sense of Aristotle, *Cat*, 1a 1–2: ὁμώνυμα λέγεται ὧν ὄνομα μόνον κοινόν, ὁ δὲ κατὰ τοὔνομα λόγος τῆς οὐσίας ἕτερος . . . .

[14] PG, 86, 1300D 8–10.

[15] *Ibid.*, 1301A 2: τοὺς παρὰ τὸν Χριστὸν λοιποὺς ἁγίους.

[16] *Ibid.*, 1301A 5–11: Πῶς τοίνυν πάσης τῆς λογικῆς καὶ μακαρίας κτίσεως, ὅση τε ἐν ἀγγέλοις καὶ ὅση ἐν ἀνθρώποις, τῆς θεοποιοῦ καὶ υἱοποιοῦ τοῦ Πνεύματος χάριτος πληρωθείσης, μόνος ὁ ἐκ Παρθένου πεφηνὼς θεός τε ἐκλήθη καὶ Υἱὸς Θεοῦ ἐν τῷ λόγῳ καὶ κατὰ τὸν λόγον, προσκυνεῖταί τε παρὰ πάσης λογικῆς φύσεως;

[17] *Ibid.*, 1301A 11–15.

of a higher order than we and so of a different and superior dignity. Leontius' reply is as clear as could be wished. Jesus Christ is one of the rational creation, that is, of the order of angels and men. To be sure, Leontius is willing to concede that he is *one of the higher beings* of that order; but he hastens to emphasize that for all of his rank, Jesus Christ enjoys precisely the same dignity and honor as the rest of the rational creation. In short, the saints are joined to the Word and none other than the Word because one of the nobler of their number, born of the Virgin, has been called God and Son of God, that is, has been called by the names of the Word; even though the dignity of all is the same.

What follows is rather less alarming. Leontius goes on to pose the dilemma we have already described: since Jesus Christ and his saints—that is, ἡ λογικὴ κτίσις—possess a single ἀξία, to join Jesus Christ to the Word κατ' ἀξίαν is to add a created nature to the Trinity; while to distinguish him from the Word is to render him Son in name only and not in reality. The next question, then: how do we distinguish Jesus Christ from the saints? Leontius answers: "Since there is one [and only one] sonship by nature, from which is by participation every [other] sonship, this man, ἄνθρωπος, whom they [Leontius' adversaries] have made for themselves, must either participate in the sonship by nature, or in that by grace; that is, they must either join him to the Only-begotten as in a ἕνωσις κατ'οὐσίαν which communicates what is present in each nature to the other, too, or, if they cannot bear to believe the right and pious thing, they must openly and in all seriousness number him among the rest [of the saints]."[18] What that ἕνωσις κατ'οὐσίαν is, he will now explain, and when he has finished we shall see that even these last words have a sense very different from what we might expect.

B. *The* ἕνωσις κατ'οὐσίαν: *Against the Monophysites*[19]

Having disposed of the formula of the school of Antioch, Leontius next undertakes to explain the true and orthodox formula, a ἕνωσις κατ'οὐσίαν; and since the Monophysites too use the formula, he

[18] *Ibid.*, 1301B 8–C 2.
[19] *Ibid.*, 1301C 8–1305C 3.

takes the occasion to explain the difference between its right use and its perversion. As Leontius himself puts it in his brief introduction: "So that you may understand what the difference is between things united κατ'οὐσίαν but not altered, and things which by nature are altered in their union, what the species of the former is and what the result of the latter, let the distinction be made clear now."[20]

The argument advances in two steps. In the first, Leontius fixes upon πάντα τὰ ὄντα in order to analyze what he calls their essential relations, that is, their unions and distinctions from one another.[21] Second, when his analysis attains to the class of beings whose essential relations he calls "composite," he divides the class into two subclasses, and then goes on to demonstrate that the union of beings of the first subclass is the paradigm of the incarnation properly conceived,[22] but that the union of beings of the second subclass is a paradigm of the confusion taught by the Monophysites.[23]

1. The First Step: The Analysis of Being

Leontius' argument in this second part of chapter seven has been much read but little understood, and therefore must be examined in some detail. We translate the entire first step of his argument, his analysis of being. For easier comprehension, we present it in the form of an outline, and comment freely.

[20] *Ibid.*, 1301C 15–D 3. A problem here. The text: Ἵνα δὲ ἡμῖν γνώριμος ἡ διαφορὰ γένηται τῆς τῶν κατ' οὐσίαν ἡνωμένων καὶ μὴ τρεπομένων πρὸς τὰ ἐκ τῆς ἑνώσεως τρέπεσθαι πεφυκότα; for which the manuscripts show only one insignificant variant. Now what does the clause mean? As it stands, its logic is quite improper. The first τῆς seems to demand that we insert ἑνώσεως; but where? After τρεπομένων? But then a union is improperly compared to the elements of a union (τὰ ... πεφυκότα). After πεφυκότα? So as to read "the critical distinction (διαφορά) ... of a union of things united κατ' οὐσίαν and yet not altered [thereby], with things which by nature are altered by the union." However, this translation strains the sense of διαφορά and seems to err in reading πρός with the ἑνώσεως we have added, and not with διαφορά. Nor does the passage so translated find an echo in what follows. A better solution is simply to omit τῆς and translate as we have just above. Such a translation exactly describes the distinction with which Leontius will end in 1304B 1–1305C 4.
[21] *Ibid.*, 1301D 5–1304A 14.
[22] For the second part of the argument: *ibid.*, 1304B 1–1305C 3. For the first subclass: 1304B 4–1305A 15.
[23] *Ibid.*, 1305B 1–C 3.

a. *The essential relations of beings: unions and distinctions*

"All beings"[24]—so Leontius begins—"are joined to one another by [categories expressing] generality, and again are distinguished from one another by specific differences.[25] Neither in their unions do they confuse what is distinguished, nor in their distinctions do they separate what is united;[26] but if one must speak in paradox and after the manner of the Fathers, [all things] are united in such a way as distinguishes, and distinguished in such a way as conjoins."[27]

Our data, it seems, are properly speaking neither hypostases nor ousiai—hypostases and ousiai will make their entrance only in the next stage of the analysis—but *beings*, τὰ ὄντα. These beings stand to one another in what Leontius will soon call their "essential relations,"[28] that is, in unions with and distinctions from one another.[29] In more nearly classical terms, Leontius defines the essential relations of a being by means of the pair of opposites *like : unlike*, that is, ὅμοιον : ἀνόμοιον; though Leontius himself never uses these terms. These "essential relations," we may suppose, are called *essential* because they *define* the beings so related; and so we understand here that we have to do not with all possible relations whatsoever of any given being, but only with those relations in which that being is defined. We note in passing that it is not commonplace to define a being by its relations with other beings, rather than by an analysis of the being itself.

If a being is defined by its essential relations, we must suppose also that its essential relations are simultaneous both with the be-

[24] *Ibid.*, 1301D 5: πάντα τὰ ὄντα.
[25] *Ibid.*, 1301D 6–7: ... ταῖς καθ'ὅλου κοινότησι ... ταῖς εἰδοποιοῖς διαφοραῖς....
[26] *Ibid.*, 1301D 8 *post* ἑνώσεσι *add.* τὸ διακεκριμένον συγχέουσιν, οὐδὲ ταῖς διακρίσεσι VOG.
[27] *Ibid.*, 1301D 9–10: ἥνωνται διηρημένως καὶ διακέκρινται συνημμένως. Basil the Great, *ep* 38.4 (perhaps by Gregory of Nyssa; in SBasile, *Lettres*, I [Paris, 1957], 87, ll. 88–91), says this of the three hypostases of the Trinity. We shall see just below (1304A 2–8) that Leontius includes even these in "all things that are," πάντα τὰ ὄντα. Cf. Pseudo-Dionysius the Areopagite, *De div. nom.*, 2.4, PG, 3, 641B 2–3.
[28] PG, 86, 1304A 10–11: τὰς οὐσιώδεις ... σχέσεις.
[29] We recall that in *CNE* 1.4, PG, 86, 1289A 7–8, Leontius has already made mention of τῶν κατὰ τὴν διάκρισίν τε καὶ ἕνωσιν σχέσεων.

ing itself and with one another. Now Leontius mentions *two* such essential relations, that is, union and distinction; and so we conclude that each being as such is simultaneously united with *and* distinguished from other beings. Indeed, if unions and distinctions were not simultaneous, Leontius could hardly say that beings in their unions do not confuse what is distinguished, nor in their distinctions separate what is united.[30] In distinguishing union from distinction, then, Leontius is not dividing all beings into two classes, those defined by their unions and those defined by their distinctions. Rather he describes union and distinction as simultaneous modes in which every being is defined. Consequently, he will soon call these essential relations of a being its "twofold relation" to other beings, its διττὴ σχέσις.[31]

b. *The determination of the essential relations of beings:* ousia *and* hypostasis

However, the pair of opposites *union : distinction* cannot as such properly define a being. These essential relations must be determined by a second pair of opposites, which can answer the question: *in what* is X united to and distinguished from other beings? Leontius therefore continues:

"Now the definition of these unions and distinctions is twofold.

[I] Some things are united by species but distinguished by hypostases, while

[II] Others are distinguished by species but united by hypostases."[32]

In what follows we shall identify the two classes as class I and class II, respectively.

The pair of opposites, then, which determine the essential relations of a being—that is, define it—is the pair *hypostasis : ousia*; and the hypostasis and ousia of any being may therefore be defined

---

[30] Note that Leontius' second definition of hypostasis, PG, 86, 1280A 13–15, states that the beings united are united simultaneously: τὰ ἐκ διαφόρων φύσεων συνεστῶτα, τὴν δὲ τοῦ εἶναι κοινωνίαν ἅμα τε καὶ ἐν ἀλλήλοις κεκτημένα.

[31] *Ibid.*, 1304A 4–5.

[32] *Ibid.*, 1301D 10–1304A 1.

as the determinations of the essential relations of a being, that is, its likeness and unlikeness; and since its essential relations are simultaneous with one another, it follows that hypostasis and ousia are simultaneous too.[33]

If we may still hold Leontius to his earlier definitions of hypostasis as the expression of τὸ ἴδιον and ousia as the expression of τὸ κοινόν,[34] we may best interpret the pair of opposites *hypostasis : ousia* as the classical pair *other : same*.

There remains a problem, however: the relation of things of class I to things of class II. Do the two modes of determination described here constitute two *classes* of beings, so that any given being will belong to the one class or the other? To suggest an answer, we must anticipate our later argument.

In *SolArgSev*, as we shall see,[35] Leontius distinguishes between two states of certain beings, their ὅρος or τρόπος τῆς φύσεως, that is, their mode of nature, and their τρόπος τῆς ἐνώσεως, that is, their mode of union or combination. In the former state, it seems, each being is taken in and for itself; in the second state, in its combinations with beings of different nature.[36] Should then the beings in the second state be of such a nature as to preserve their natures intact even in their combinations—that is, should they be beings of class I, as we shall call them soon[37]—they will each exist in both modes; for though as combined each being exists in its mode of union, nonetheless as preserving its nature each being exists also in its mode of nature.

---

[33] For hypostasis and ousia as simultaneous determinations of the unions and distinctions of a being, see also *CNE* 1.4, PG, 86, 1288D 1–1289A 11.

[34] *Ibid.*, 1280A 8–10.

[35] See the commentary on PG, 86, 1936D 1 ff., *infra*, p. 54 ff.

[36] I note that the *union* of the phrase *mode of union* is not to be confused with the union described in the formulae *united as hypostasis* or *united as ousia*. In the former, union implies *combination* with a being of another nature. In the latter, union is that determination of the essential relations of a being which expresses the *likeness* of that being to other beings. To be sure we shall see that, for Leontius, these two kinds of unions are necessarily simultaneous, and more exactly, that every being in which hypostasis is really distinguished from ousia and its unions exists also in a mode of union with beings of other natures. Nevertheless, the two unions remain different and distinct.

[37] See the commentary on *CNE* 1.7, PG, 86, 1304B 1 ff., *infra*, p. 42 ff.

I suggest, now, that the two modes of determination described by Leontius in *CNE* 1.7 correspond exactly to the two modes discussed in *SolArgSev*: that things united as ousia but distinguished as hypostasis correspond to things in their mode of nature, and things united as hypostasis and distinguished as ousia correspond to things in their mode of union. Things of mode of determination I, then, will be, as it were, beings in themselves, and things of mode of determination II will be these same beings in their unions and combinations—unions and combinations, to be sure, in which the beings united preserve their natures intact.

Here, however, in order to avoid confusion, we must clearly distinguish *beings of class II themselves*, that is, beings of class I in their unions and combinations, from *the products of the unions* in which they combine. Every being in its mode of union is by definition united to at least one other being, and so forms a *tertium quid*. For convenience, we may call such a *tertium quid* or product a *subject*; for though it is not necessarily of the same ontological rank as the beings of class II which compose it, it is nonetheless a unity, and so also a proper subject of predication. Now, as we have defined them here, beings of class II are not these subjects; unless, of course, these subjects themselves be supposed to have entered into their modes of union. Rather class II comprises those beings which in their modes of union compose subjects.[38]

When we ask again then: does the distinction between these two modes of determination create two classes of beings, the answer

---

[38] I exclude subjects as such from class II because, as we shall see, Leontius' analysis of being does not number the relation of parts (here *beings*) to the whole (here *subject*) which they comprise among the *essential relations* of beings. *CNE* 1.4, PG, 86, 1288C 1–14 ff., establishes that, e. g., soul may be defined in its relation to other souls, as also body in its relation to other bodies—that is, as beings of class I; *or* soul and body may be defined in relation to one another—that is, as beings of class II; *or* finally, the subject man may be defined in relation to souls and bodies like the soul and body which compose him; but the soul and body which compose him, his parts, are never defined by the (*whole*) man they compose nor he by his soul and body. And rightly so! For, after all, his soul and body *are* a man, and he himself *is* his soul and body, so that, properly speaking, neither can *define* the other. In short, *CNE* 1.4 suggests that beings of class II are defined as such by their relations to *one another*, not by their relations to the *subject which they compose*; so that the subject, though implied in the definition of beings of class II, is not comprised by it.

must be that it does not. Indeed, only this interpretation of Leontius' distinction here can explain what follows. How so? In what follows, Leontius ignores beings of class II altogether in order to analyze beings of class I alone.[39] On the face of it, this is puzzling. Does he not intend to explain the union of Word and flesh in Jesus Christ? And are not Word and flesh in Jesus Christ beings in their modes of union—that is, beings not of class I but of class II? If now he turns to analyze beings of class I, can his analysis apply to beings of class II, too? The answer is simplicity itself. We shall see that Leontius derives all further distinctions in the *modes of union* of beings—distinctions upon which his whole Christology rests—from distinctions in their *modes of nature*. A being unites as it unites because it is what it is. Now if the mode of nature of a being determines the mode of union of a being, it can only be because the being in the mode of nature is one and the same with the being in the mode of union, that is, the same being in different modes—just as we have described them here.

There can be no doubt, then, that the distinction between beings of class I and beings of class II corresponds exactly to the distinction between beings in their mode of nature and beings in their mode of union.

c. *Simple and composite*

Leontius continues:

"Further, of [I] beings united in species but distinguished by hypostases

[A] Some possess [their] union and distinction as simple (ἁπλῆν), while

[B] Other [possess them] as composite (σύνθετον)."[40] Then, as it were aside: "However, about beings having their twofold relation

---

[39] This is the plain sense of PG, 86, 1304A 1–2, which reproduces the definition of beings of class I in 1301D 11–13.

[40] *Ibid.*, 1304A 1–4. Students questioning the rule *lectio difficilior* may ponder the note of FLoofs, *LeontByz*, 67, on this passage: "Den oben citierten Absatz vermag ich im vorliegenden Texte nicht zu verstehen, doch glaube ich ihn richtig deuten zu können, wenn ich 1304 A, Z[eilen] 1 u[nd] 2 die gesperrt gedruckten Worte für ausgefallen ansehe: καὶ τῶν ἡνωμένων μὲν τοῖς εἴδεσι, διῃρημένων δὲ ταῖς ὑποστάσεσι] καὶ τῶν ἡνωμένων ταῖς ὑποστάσε-

33

[of union and distinction] as a simple [relation], let us say nothing for now; after all, the detailed explanation of these [beings] is no part of the inquiry at hand, and besides escapes the understanding and training of the average person. However, about beings [having their twofold relation] as composition (κατὰ σύνθεσιν) or connection or mingling or union or however else one may please to call the essential relations of beings of different natures (ἑτεροειδῶν) [— about these beings] we must speak ...."[41]

Leontius is not altogether wrong in passing over the distinction which he makes here between simple and complex essential relations: it is, as he claims, of no importance for his argument. Nevertheless, we may well be curious as to just what beings are distinguished here and how they are distinguished. The answer, I think, is that a "being having its twofold relation [of union and distinction] as a simple [relation]" is a being in which its essence or ousia is *indistinguishable* from its existence or hypostasis; while a being having its twofold relation as composition is a being in which its essence or ousia is *distinguishable* from its existence or hypostasis.

This explanation of Leontius' distinction here will be rather more secure should we be able to suggest just which beings have their twofold relation as a simple relation; that is, which are the beings in which their essence is indistinguishable from their existence. Now in fact Leontius himself offers us an instance: none other than the three hypostases of the Trinity.

In *CNE* 1.4, Leontius finds it necessary to remind his Nestorian that the Word of God differs from the Father as hypostasis and not

---

σι, διηρημένων δὲ τοῖς εἴδεσι [τὰ μὲν ἁπλῆν ἔχει τὴν ἕνωσίν τε καὶ διάκρισιν, τὰ δὲ σύνθετον. Der Ausfall dieser Worte ist bei ihrer Ähnlichkeit mit den vorangehenden nicht auffällig. Der ziemlich simple Sinn der stelzbeinigen Sätze ist alsdann: "Ἕνωσις und διάκρισις kommt in zwiefacher Art vor: 1. ἕνωσις τοῖς εἴδεσι, διαίρεσις ταῖς ὑποστάσεσι, 2. ἕνωσις ταῖς ὑποστάσεσι, διαίρεσις τοῖς εἴδεσι. Im erstern Fall ist die διττὴ σχέσις, d.h. das Verhältnis der ἕνωσις und der διάκρισις, ein einfaches, im letztern Falle entstehen σχέσεις der Zusammensetzung ... [1304 A]." In his search for a "simpler Sinn," Loofs has completely confused Leontius' sense, identifying class A with class I and class B with class II. The manuscripts, of course, read with PG, and insist that classes A and B are subclasses of class I; and we shall soon see that this makes good sense.

[41] PG, 86, 1304A 4–11.

as nature, for the ousia of the Word is precisely the nature of God.[42] He adds, as it were: and the *whole* nature of God, too, for the Word is not as it were a part of a divine nature composed of Father, Son, and Holy Spirit, "for the nature of the Father and [the nature] of the Son and [the nature] of the Holy Spirit is not such as completes a whole,[43] as if [the nature were] more in the one [composed of three] than in [each of] the three. The Trinity is by nature precisely that which any one of those [hypostases] which are seen in the Trinity might be;[44] for [there is] not one perfect [whole] from three imperfect [parts], but from three perfect [wholes] one [whole, as it were] supraperfect and preperfect, as the great [Pseudo-]Dionysius said somewhere."[45]

Now, to say of the Trinity that it is "by nature precisely that which any one of those [hypostases] which are seen in the Trinity might be," is only to say of the Trinity that its essence or nature is one with its existence or hypostasis.[46] We add: the distinction

[42] *Ibid.*, 1288A 10ff., comprehensible only if with OG (against V) we read B 3 διδόασιν [οἱ Νεστοριανοί] τὴν ὡς ὑπόστασιν [σχέσιν], ἀγνοοῦντες ὅτι φύσις, etc. The general sense of this passage: since the Word is distinguished as hypostasis from his *Father*, he cannot be distinguished as hypostasis from his *flesh* too; but rather as hypostasis the Word will be related to the flesh in a relation *opposite* to his relation to his Father; so that as hypostasis he will be not distinguished from but united to his flesh.

[43] *Ibid.*, 1288B 9: οὐ ... συμπληρωτικὴ ἡ ... φύσις, etc.

[44] *Ibid.*, 1288B 11–13: Καὶ τοῦτο τῇ φύσει ἡ Τριάς, ὅπερ ἂν ἕν τι τῶν ἐν τῇ Τριάδι θεωρουμένων τυγχάνοι.

[45] *Ibid.*, 1288B 9–C 1. See Pseudo-Dionysius, *De div. nom.*, 2.10 (PG, 3, 648C 6–7), with which compare 7.2 (PG, 3, 869A 3–5).

[46] To say of the Trinity that its essence is identical with its existences is in effect to say also that God is *one in nature*, ἕν τῇ φύσει, as the Cappadocians and—*mirabile dictu*—Evagrius of Pontus argued. See René Arnou, "Unité numérique et unité de nature chez les Pères, après le Concile de Nicée," *Gregorianum*, XV (1934), 242–254, to which I refer the curious reader.

However, to say that God is one in nature is not to deny his three hypostases. What Leontius himself says of the Christological formula *one nature* holds true for the Trinity, too: οὐ γὰρ τὴν μίαν φύσιν ἐν εἶναι τῷ ἀριθμῷ (*CNE* 1.5, PG, 86, 1292C 9–10). As the opposite of *in number*, the phrase *in nature* rather indicates that the ousia of God is not *one* in such a way as to imply a synthesis of τὰ κοινά, as if the three persons were prior to the one ousia; nor again is any one of the hypostases of God *one* in such a way as to be only a case or instance of the divine nature, as if the ousia were prior to the three hypostases. In God each hypostasis has its oneness *by nature*, that is, by reason of its identity with a divine nature indivisibly one: just as any given man is capable of laughter by reason of being man by nature, so each hypostasis of the Trinity is one by reason of

implied here between beings in which essence and existence *are* and *are not* one at very least offers us a precedent for our identification of that distinction with the distinction between class A and class B, that is, between beings having their twofold relation as a *simple* relation and as a *composition*.

This granted, a problem appears.

The distinction between beings of class A and beings of class B is a distinction among beings of class I *as such*, and so it is as a being of class I, that is, as a being in its mode of *nature*, that each being of classes A and B is what it is. It is therefore with a certain surprise that we hear Leontius virtually identify beings of class B— that is, beings having their twofold relation as a composition—with *beings united to beings of different natures*, that is, with beings in their mode of *union*; for he speaks plainly of "beings [having their twofold relation] as composition, or connection, or mingling, or union, *or however else one may please to call the essential relations of beings of different natures* . . . ."[47] Is class II, that is, the class of beings in their modes of *union*, simply the same as class B, that is, the class of beings having their twofold relation as composition? If so, our analysis has all too clearly gone astray. I suggest, however, that Leontius is saying nothing of the kind. Rather we have here a first application

---

being God by nature, that is, one. On the other hand, the oneness of the nature is identical with the oneness of the Father who begets Son and Holy Spirit, for the divine nature proceeds from the Father in the Son and Spirit as from its source. The Trinity is, therefore, not one as the first of a series, that is, a many. Rather it is simply and absolutely one. In this light, by the way, the interpretation of this passage in JPJunglas, *LeontByz*, 90f., was not utterly absurd. "Die ἀπλῆ ἕνωσις," he wrote, "scheint uns nun eine Vereinigung aus *einfachen* Teilen zu sein, die ἕνωσις σύνθετος eine Vereinigung aus zusammengesetzten Teilen" (p. 90). Unfortunately, Junglas went on to identify the "simple union" of PG, 86, 1304A 4–8, with "die ersten, einfachen ἕνωσις der Dinge aus den vier Elementen" (p. 91), although in C 15–D 6 immediately below Leontius offers the union of fire to air and air to water as an example of the union of beings of a subclass of class B, and the union of water to earth as an example of the union of beings of another subclass of class B. Now class B comprises things having their twofold relation as a composition and not as a simple relation, so that Junglas' interpretation is impossible.

[47] The same association of *composite* nature with nature united to a different nature is implied also in *CapTrig* 14, PG, 86, 1904D 10–1905A 5 —although it must be admitted that Leontius' argument here is *ad hoc* and so does not necessarily establish the definitions of *simple* and *composite*.

of the principle we have discussed above: that the modes of nature of beings determine their modes of union. Nevertheless, it must be admitted that Leontius' words here are not easy to understand. What is he saying?

One thing he implies quite clearly: that beings which have their twofold relation—that is, of course, their mode of nature—as *composite* are *as such* and *necessarily* found also in their *mode of union*. This is as much as to say that every being which in its mode of nature finds its existence distinct from its essence is necessarily united to a being of another nature: existence distinct from essence must be united to another being.

Less clear, however, is whether Leontius believes the contrary true too; that is, that every being found in its mode of union is as such and necessarily a being of class B, that is, a being whose existence is distinct from its essence. A moment's thought and we must reject the proposition. In Jesus Christ, Word and flesh are present *in their modes of union*. The proposition then demands that the existence of the Word be distinct from his essence. However, we have found good reason to believe that the Word is a being of class A, that is, a being in whom his existence and essence are one. Therefore his entrance into his mode of union does not imply the distinction of his existence from his essence; and so the proposition is false.

If this is so, the distinction between the modes of union of beings of class A and beings of class B can hardly be other than this, that the former enter their modes of union as it were *of their own free will*—e.g., as the Word took flesh by grace—but the latter by reason of their very modes of nature, that is, *necessarily. Mirabile dictu*, we shall see below that the two subclasses of class B are first, the class of beings joined by a *divine decree*, and second, the class of beings joined by a *natural inclination* or drive, that is, modes of necessary union.

Nonetheless, we may speculate still further. May it not be that another distinction between the modes of union of beings which *are* and *are not* one in existence and essence is this: that the former unite only with beings which, like themselves, are one in essence and existence; while the latter unite only with beings which, like themselves, are not one in existence and essence? We note in passing that, since a being in its mode of union is by definition united to a being of a different nature from its own, this is as much as to suggest that class A comprises at least one other nature than that of the Trinity; and specifically, another set of beings one in essence and existence, to one of which the Word united himself.

Here, of course, we face precisely the objection which we ourselves have just employed. Is not the Word united to his flesh, and does not Leontius use both soul and body as examples of a subclass of class B, so implying that soul and body are beings in which essence and existence are distinct?[48] And if so, is not the Word in fact united to a being in which existence and essence are distinct, that is, against our speculation?

Nevertheless, such a criticism of our speculation will not hold. It rests upon a false assumption. This assumption? In Jesus Christ, the Word is found in his mode of union. Now, that a being enters its mode of union implies the existence of a being of different nature, to which the former being is united. Should we ask then what being it is whose existence is implied by the entrance of the Word into its mode of union, our critic assumes that we must reply: his flesh. Our critic assumes that it is in and by reason of his union with the flesh that the Word enters into his mode of union.

Now this assumption, as I have said, is false, and I add: the reason that it is false will reveal the skeleton in Leontius' closet!

Just above, we have distinguished the two or more beings which compose a subject from that subject itself. Let us fix upon that subject. Because a subject is a product of the union of at least two beings, the definition of a subject will always include three terms: one for the subject itself and one for each of the at least two beings composing the subject. The term for each of the two beings composing the subject assumes besides that there exists *outside* the subject a being like in nature to that being *in* the subject which the term designates. Only in this way will each of the beings which compose the subject be fully identified in the subject.

A warning here, however. Two beings may be united in a subject in either of two ways. First, the two beings composing the subject may unite *in each other*. Second, the two beings may each unite to a *third being* which existed even *before* the union, that is, a third being

[48] E. g., *CNE* 1.7, PG, 86, 1304B 9–10, discussed *infra*, p. 46.

which as it were appropriates two beings of different nature and so may be said to unite them. Such a being in its union with two such natures may also be called a *subject*, of course, for in its union with the natures which it has appropriated, it too enters into its mode of union. Nevertheless, both the subject which results from such a union and the mode of union itself are different from the subject and the mode of union which we have just described above.

First, the first subject described above comprises only the two beings which combine to form their product; while the subject of which we speak here comprises three beings, that is, two beings of different nature and the third being which unites them by itself appropriating each.

Second, the modes of union are different, too. In the first subject described above, the definition of either or any one of its components in the mode of union of that component necessarily comprises the other being or beings with which it is united, for both beings have as it were entered their mode of union only with and in the same moment as their union to one another. So soul in its mode of union necessarily implies body and body in its mode of union necessarily implies soul, because neither has its mode of union apart from the other.

Not so, however, in the second subject described above. Here the definition of neither of the extreme beings united necessarily implies the other. First, each of the beings appropriated by the mean being will enter its mode of union by reason of its union with the mean being and not by reason of its union with its extreme. Moreover, the union of one extreme with the mean does not as such compel the mean to unite with the other extreme and so to unite the extremes in itself. Today I have eaten an apple and a banana. I have united the apple and the banana by eating each. The apple and the banana may now be said to be united to one another; but, properly speaking, each is united to me, and it is only, as it were, after the union of each with me that they are united to one another. Besides, I could very well have eaten the apple without eating the banana at all. Therefore the definition of the apple in its mode of union now necessarily comprises me, but it does not necessarily comprise the banana.

Hence, there are two kinds of subjects in which beings of different nature are united. Two beings may be united *either* in one another *or* in a third being. In other words, the three terms comprised in the subject may represent *two* beings in their mode of union, or *three* beings.

Back then to our speculation. We speculated that the difference between the modes of union of beings which *are* and *are not* one in existence and essence is this: that the former unite only with beings which, like themselves, are one in existence and essence, while the latter unite only with beings which, like themselves, are *not* one in existence and essence. To this we objected that the Word, in whom essence and existence are one, did after all unite to his flesh, in which essence and existence are *not* one. Now, however, it seems that it need not be by reason of his union with his *flesh* that the Word enters his mode of union, but that it may be rather by reason of his union with a *third being*, which united Word and flesh by appropriating each. Therefore the union of Word with flesh in Jesus Christ does not as such invalidate our speculation: for they may have united not in one another but in a third being.

Still our speculation is not thereby saved. If we ask what sort of being this third being might be, it is clear that it must somehow both be and not be one in essence and existence: *be,* in order that it may unite with the Word, and *not be,* in order to unite to the flesh. We assume, of course, that neither Word nor flesh is such a being, that by their natures the Word is one in essence and existence and the flesh not one. Yet cannot the same be said of every being? Is there *any* being which somehow *both is and is not* one in essence and existence? If not, our speculation falls, for even if Word and flesh be supposed to unite in a third being, there will be no being to which both can unite.

Is there such a being then? We anticipate the argument of Chapter Four to say: there is indeed! He is Jesus Christ, the one unfallen *nous* of the Christology of the Origenist Evagrius of Pontus. More on Evagrius later. Enough for now to note that, for Evagrius, it is the property of *nous* as such that it may either persist in the vision of God or fall away from it; that is, as I propose to translate, either hold to the original unity of its existence with its essence or abandon it. *Nous both is and is not* one in essence and existence in that it may be either the one or the other. However, in a single case it is as it were both at once. For Evagrius, we know, Jesus Christ is the single *nous* of the whole intellectual world who has not fallen away from the Word; but he is also by God's grace joined to his flesh. In Evagrius' Christology, then, it is the *proprium* of Jesus Christ to be *the one nous united both to the Word and to the flesh*: to the Word because it is the nature of *nous* to unite to the Word, and to the flesh because the mercy of God towards Jesus Christ's fallen brethren demands that they have in the body of Christ a paradigm of the sense and purpose of the visible world, a revelation to men that God made the world as a ladder of contemplation by which men may so purify themselves that in the last judgement they may repossess the proper object of intellectual or essential contemplation, the Word.

Now, as a being simultaneously united to Word and to flesh, and simultaneously, as it were, *both one and not one in essence and existence*, Evagrius' *nous* Jesus Christ conforms to the requirements of our speculation astonishingly well—so well that there is nothing else for it: we must ask whether Leontius' Jesus is not Evagrius' *nous* Jesus, and to that question we shall turn in Chapter Four. For now, then, we lay our speculation aside, and that all the more readily because it will prove true. Yet before we go on with our analysis it is worth noting that if Leontius' Jesus is Evagrius' *nous* Jesus, we have the key to an otherwise puzzling ambiguity in Leontius' argument. We have argued above that Leontius' argument permits us to hypothesize two kinds of subjects in which beings of different natures can unite. Two beings, we said, may be united either in one another or in a third being, so that the three terms comprised in the definition of the resulting subject may represent either *two* beings in their mode of union or *three* beings. Now we notice that Leontius' statement of the problem takes no account of this distinction between subjects. Nor does his argument, as it stands, require such a distinction. After all, it pretends to be no more than a description of the union of two beings of different natures. Whether those beings unite in one another or in a third being seems irrelevant. Nevertheless, the distinction is not without interest, I think, for if Leontius' Jesus is Evagrius' *nous* Jesus, if the subject Jesus represents three beings, not two, then it is reasonably clear that Leontius has so constructed his argument as to dispense with the distinction—that is, so as to conceal from his Orthodox readers his true conviction: that Jesus Christ is not Word become flesh but Word and flesh each united to *nous*.

2. The Second Step: Two Paradigms of the Incarnation[49]

Leontius has just now distinguished between beings in their mode of nature and beings in their mode of union. He has gone on to assert, in effect, that in beings in their mode of nature hypostasis and ousia may be either indistinguishable (class A) or distinguishable (class B)—although he has clearly implied that all beings of class B as such exist also in their modes of union. Now he offers a second division of class I, and assigns to each of the two classes produced by the division its proper mode of union. Within class I, he says, there are a class of beings which even in their unions preserve "the definition of their being" and a class of beings which do not. We call these two classes class 1 and class 2, respectively. The unions of beings of class 1, we shall hear later,[50] are paradigms[51] of the union of Jesus Christ with God and man; but the union of beings of class 2 is a paradigm of the confusion of God and man in Jesus Christ which the Monophysites propose. Again we may let Leontius speak for himself.

"Now of beings which exist essentially (οὐσιωδῶς) and are united κατ'οὐσίαν,

[1] some even in their union preserve the integrity of the definition of their being, while

[2] others both confuse and obliterate it,[52] destroying τὴν ἀκρότη-τα τῶν ἡνουμένων"—literally, "the extremeness, the property of being an extreme, of each of the beings united."[53]

---

[49] PG, 86, 1304B 1–1305C 3.
[50] *Ibid.*, 1305C 3–12.
[51] *Ibid.*, 1305C 6–7: ὑποδείγματα.
[52] *Ibid.*, 1304B 3 *post* δὲ *add.* <αὐτὸν> *ed.* συγκεῖται] συγχεῖ τε VOG.
[53] *Ibid.*, 1304B 1–4: τῶν τοίνυν οὐσιωδῶς ὑπαρχόντων καὶ κατ' οὐσίαν ἑνου-μένων, τὰ μὲν κἄν τῇ ἑνώσει σώζει τὸν ἴδιον τῆς ὑπάρξεως λόγον, τὰ δὲ <αὐτὸν> συγχεῖ τε καὶ ἐξαφανίζει, τὴν ἀκρότητα [the opposite of μεσότητα] τῶν ἡνωμένων λυμαινόμενα.

Before going on to examine each class for itself, we must pause to consider the opening words of the paragraph: "Now, of beings which exist essentially (οὐσιωδῶς) and are united κατ'οὐσίαν...." What beings does Leontius mean? At first we assume that the formula is simply another definition of beings of class B, that is, composite beings; and that the definition stands here because we are about to subdivide class B. Not so, I believe. *Prima facie*, the formula in no way reflects the difference between simple and composite beings. It is rather, I suggest, a recapitulation of his definition of beings of class I, that is, things united as ousiai and distinguished as hypostases, beings in their mode of nature.

The simplest reason for believing so is that we shall see immediately below that the two classes of beings subsequent to the definition at the head of the division are comprised not by the definition of beings of class B alone, but by the definition of beings of the class comprising classes A and B, that is, by the definition of beings of class I. Not by the definition of beings of class B, I say, because one of the classes subsequent to the division, that is, class 1, includes a member of class A, that is, the Word; for Leontius insists that the union of the Word with his flesh is to be understood after the paradigm of unions of beings of class 1,[54] thus in effect assigning a being of class A to class 1. However, class 1 also includes beings of class B, too: e.g., soul and body.[55] Now, if one of the two classes subsequent to the definition at the head of the division at hand includes beings of both classes A and B, then the definition itself must be the definition of the class of beings comprising classes A and B; which is to say, must be the definition of class I. Therefore, "beings which exist essentially and are united κατ'οὐσίαν" are simply beings of class I, and we may add: the true sense of Leontius' division here seems to be that of beings of class I, *all* beings of class A (e.g., the Word) and *some* beings of class B (e.g., his flesh) preserve the definition of their own being even in their unions, while *some* beings of class B do not. Classes 1 and 2 are, therefore, not subclasses of

---

[54] *Ibid.*, 1305C 3–12.

[55] I call soul and body beings of class B because I suppose that all the beings included in Leontius' examples of beings of class 1, in PG, 86, 1304B 9ff., are also beings of class B.

class B, but, after the division of classes A and B, a second division of class I, that is, the class of beings in their mode of nature.[56]

The consequence of this interpretation is clear. That the definition of beings in their mode of nature stands at the head of the

[56] Nevertheless, it is not clear why Leontius defines beings of class I, in PG, 86, 1304B 1–2, just as he does. To be sure, the phrase "united κατ' οὐσίαν" copies the definition of beings of class I in 1301C 11–14 above; but what of the formula τῶν ... οὐσιωδῶς ὑπαρχόντων? Mr. Ronald Hathaway, sometime Junior Fellow at the Dumbarton Oaks Research Library and Collection, Washington, D. C., suggests that we must consider the possibility that Leontius taps the analysis of being developed by Proclus Diadochus and adopted, says Mr. Hathaway, by almost all Neoplatonic philosophers after him.

Proclus' most influential work was his *Elements of Theology* (ed. E. R. Dodds, 2d ed. [Oxford 1963]). In proposition 103 (*ibid.*, p. 92, ll. 13–29) and elsewhere, Proclus distinguishes what we may call the three states in which all beings are said to be in all other beings: τὸ ὄν, ἡ ζωή, and ὁ νοῦς (l. 13f.). He then goes on to describe the three modes in which each state may be related to the other two: κατ' αἰτίαν ... ἢ καθ' ὕπαρξιν ἢ κατὰ μέθεξιν (l. 17f.). Here we learn that in the state τὸ ὄν, the other two states, life and *nous*, are characterized by the mode καθ' ὕπαρξιν (l. 21f.), and are said to be present in τὸ ὂν ὄντως (l. 24) as ζωὴ οὐσιώδης καὶ νοῦς οὐσιώδης (l. 24f.). In short, in τὸ ὄν, life and *nous* are taken as *being*, so that their mode is the mode of being—that is, καθ' ὕπαρξιν or ὄντως—and the predicate assigned them is the predicate of being, οὐσιώδης. As such, another author might well have called them τὰ οὐσιωδῶς ὑπάρχοντα, especially if, like Proclus, that author meant to distinguish *beings as being* from *beings in their relations to other beings*, whether as cause or as participant. Now Leontius, I suggest, is just such another author, for his distinction between mode of nature and mode of union corresponds quite exactly to Proclus' distinction between τὸ ὄν on the one hand and ζωή and νοῦς on the other, and again between ὕπαρξις on the one hand and αἰτία and μέθεξις on the other.

Happily enough, we find a roughly similar borrowing in Pseudo-Dionysius the Areopagite, *De div. nom.*, 4.7, PG, 3, 704B 7ff. Here Pseudo-Dionysius clearly depends upon Proclus' analysis of being: the equivalents— as I take them—of the modes κατ' αἰτίαν, καθ' ὕπαρξιν, and κατὰ μέθεξιν appear in precisely that order (704B 7–8, 9, and 10ff., respectively). And more: Pseudo-Dionysius describes these ὑπάρξεις as οὐσιώδεις ὑπάρξεις (704B 9). To be sure, Pseudo-Dionysius seems to treat these οὐσιώδεις ὑπάρξεις as Proclus' ζωαί, since he supposes them creatures of God, their cause (704B 7–9; with which compare Proclus, *op. cit.*, p. 92, ll. 25–27). However, Pseudo-Dionysius is not inconsistent in calling them οὐσιώδεις, I suggest, for they stand at the head of the list of τὰ ὄντα (704B 9ff.), and so may be supposed as οὐσιώδεις to be τὰ ὄντα *as such*, that is, beings as *being*, and so distinct from their relations—relations which, by the way, Pseudo-Dionysius lists immediately thereafter in an order startlingly like the order of Leontius' analysis of being: Ἐκ τούτου [τοῦ αἰτίου, that is, God] πᾶσαι τῶν ὄντων αἱ οὐσιώδεις ὑπάρξεις (and here begins the list of relations) αἱ ἑνώσεις, αἱ διακρίσεις (compare PG, 86, 1301D 5ff. and especially 1301D 10–11: τῶν δὲ ἑνώσεων καὶ τῶν δια- κρίσεων, etc.), αἱ ταὐτότητες, αἱ ἑτερότητες (the equivalent of Leontius' οὐσίαι and ὑποστάσεις? [1301D 11–1304A 1], αἱ ὁμοιότητες, αἱ ἀνομοιότητες (reflected perhaps in Leontius' distinction between beings whose existence

44

division to follow, only confirms what we have said above: that the division itself, the distinction between two modes of union, derives from a distinction among beings in their modes of nature. Beings of classes I and 2 unite as they unite because they are what they are.

This interpretation of the formula "things which exist essentially and are united κατ'οὐσίαν" seems to conform perfectly with Leontius' account of the division that follows. All beings that enter unions, he assumes, possess a "definition of their being" or existence. In their unions, however, some preserve it, and others lose it. Now, the "definition of their being" can only be the definition of their existence as a being of class I, that is, their existence in their mode of nature. If so, and if the definition which stands at the head of the division must be a definition of that being with which both the classes now to be distinguished begin, then it follows that the formula "things which exist essentially and are united κατ'οὐσίαν"—which stands at the head of the division—must be, as I have suggested, the equivalent of the definition of beings of class I, that is, beings in their mode of nature or in "the definition of their being."

With this we are ready to begin our examination of classes I and 2.

a. *The Orthodox paradigm*

First, then, the mode of union of beings of class I. Leontius continues:

"Now as for the former"—that is, beings which preserve the integrity of the definition of their being even in their unions—"[their] relation [to one another], seen both with and in one another, produces from both of them a certain, single thing, and, as one might say, they render [it] one in number, while yet preserving the dif-

---

is *like* [class A] and *unlike* [class B] their essence? [1304A 1–15]), αἱ κοινω-νίαι τῶν ἐναντίων, αἱ ἀσυμμιξίαι τῶν ἡνωμένων (beings of class 2 and class 1 respectively?), etc.

Though this is Pseudo-Dionysius' only use of the phrase οὐσιώδης ὕπαρξις, its context is so like Leontius' own argument as strongly to suggest Leontius' dependence upon Pseudo-Dionysius or his master in this point, Proclus. In any case, it seems not unreasonable in the light of the evidence to take Leontius' οὐσιωδῶς ὑπάρχοντα as *beings as being*, or, in his own terms, beings in their *mode of nature*.

ference of their being in the sameness of the union."[57] There follow no less than six examples,[58] each proposing two extremes (the first and third terms of each paradigm in the list below) which are found united but unconfused in a mean (the second or middle term of each paradigm).

First, *soul* : *man* : *body*, the subject of chapters two through six.[59]

Second, an example from the realm of "simple and natural bodies,"[60] *fire* : *torch* : *wood*, followed by a brief monitory excursus.[61]

Third, *fire* : *air* : *water*, perhaps another example among "simple and natural bodies"; followed in any case by a second monitory parenthesis relegating the union of water and earth to the mode of confusion.[62]

Fourth, *separable quality X* : *ousia* : *separable quality Y*. Sense: utterly different qualities (here X and Y) appear in a single ousia without confusion. There follows an example from astronomy which I do not claim to understand fully.[63]

---

[57] PG, 86, 1304B 4–9. I translate the text as it stands, reading B 8 σώζοντα in apposition with the implied subject (neuter plural) of ἀποδείκνυσι; and yet I would willingly amend B 8 σώζοντα to σώζουσα, so as to read B 7–9: "[their] relation ... renders them one in number, while yet preserving ...," etc.

[58] *Ibid.*, 1304B 9–1305A 3. *Apparatus*: 1304D 2 ἢ δὴ V ἤδη OG *et ed.* 1305A 3 *post* φῶς *add.* οὔτε τι προσλαμβανομένης (προσλαβομένης G) τῶν ἑτέρων VOG. αὐτοῖς] αὐταῖς VOG.

[59] *Ibid.*, 1304B 9–10.

[60] *Ibid.*, 1304B 10–11.

[61] The whole: *ibid.*, 1304B 10–C 14. The excursus: C 9–14. For this example, see Cyril of Alexandria in *Excerpta graeca ex Cyrilli scholiis de incarnatione unigeniti, ACO*, tome 1, vol. 5, pt. 1 (Berlin–Leipzig, 1924–1925) (*appendix*), p. 221, ll. 17–32; PG, 75, 1377D 3–1380B 7 (*capitulum* 9). Compare *ACO, ibid.* (pt. 1), p. 226, l. 40-p. 227, l. 14, a fragment somewhat expanded in PG, 75, 1380D 3–1381B 9 (*capitulum* 11), which itself seems to represent the original of the fragment of the *scholia* in Latin in *ACO, ibid.*, p. 190, ll. 15–32. Leontius incorporates a part of the second passage cited (*ACO, ibid.*, p. 227, ll. 11–14; PG, 75 1381A 15–B 4—or so the version of V) into the florilegium of *CNE* 1 as (in Devreesse's numeration) number eighty-nine. Note that Leontius' fragment closes with the line which closes the Greek fragment of *ACO, ibid.*, not with the line which closes the Greek fragment of PG, 75, and the Latin fragment of *ACO, ibid.*—The edition of the *Scholia* in Cyril of Alexandria, *Epistulae tres oecumenicae* ..., ed. P. E. Pusey (Oxford, 1875), 498–579, cited here from Johannes Quasten, *Patrology* (3 vols. [Westminster, Maryland, 1950–]), vol. III (1960), 128, is not available to me.

[62] The whole: PG, 86, 1304C 14–D 6. The parenthesis, which anticipates the argument of 1305B 1–C 3, *infra*: 1304D 1–6.

[63] *Ibid.*, 1304D 6–11.

Fifth, *art* : *artifact* : *nature*; for so I interpret "art, which imitates nature."[64]

Sixth and last, an example borrowed from Pseudo-Dionysius the Areopagite, *torch* : *light* : *torch*.[65]

The sense of the argument so far is plain: the beings united in a true and Orthodox ἕνωσις κατ'οὐσίαν *both* preserve their integrities *and* yet are really united. Leontius combines these two propositions in his insistence that the natures united enjoy a *communicatio idiomatum*: for if the beings united do not remain what they are they cannot possess the *idiomata* assumed in a *communicatio idiomatum*;[66] and yet, without a *communicatio idiomatum*, they cannot be truly united.[67] Their relation—not they themselves, we note, but their relation—must be "seen with and in one another,"[68] that is, in each element in its integrity, for their relation is "an essential relation to one another of beings self-subsistent and capable of existing in and of themselves."[69] On the other hand, they must also, as it were, produce something "one in number,"[70] a genuine unity.

---

[64] *Ibid.*, 1304D 11–12.

[65] *Ibid.*, 1304D 12–1305A 3. See *De divinis nominibus*, 2. 4, PG, 3, 641A 11–C 10.

[66] PG, 86, 1304C 5–7: καὶ ἀντιδέδωκε θάτερον θατέρῳ τῶν ἰδιωμάτων ἐν τῇ μονίμῳ ἑαυτῶν καὶ ἀσυγχύτῳ ἰδιότητι μείναντα—in the second example, *fire* : *torch* : *wood*. Here the *communicatio idiomatum* is employed against the Monophysites.

[67] See the epilogue to chapter seven, *ibid.*, 1305C 15–D 2: καὶ μηδεμίαν κοινωνίαν ἢ ἀντίδοσιν ἐχούσας [τὰς φύσεις] ἢ ἀντιδιδούσας. Here Leontius uses the *communicatio idiomatum* against the Nestorians.

[68] *Ibid.*, 1304B 5–6: ἡ μετ' ἀλλήλων καὶ ἐν ἀλλήλοις θεωρουμένη σχέσις. Compare B 15, σὺν ἀλλήλοις δὲ καὶ ἐν ἀλλήλοις ὄντα in the second example, *fire* : *torch* : *wood*; D 8 ἐν ἀλλήλαις ... γίνονται in the fourth example, *separable quality* : *primary ousia* : *separable quality*, and, in the same example D 10 ἀλλήλαις ... κιρνάμεναι; and, above all, in *CNE* 1.1, 1280A 15, τὰ ... τὴν ... τοῦ εἶναι κοινωνίαν ἅμα τε καὶ ἐν ἀλλήλοις, explained in 1280B 4–7 ὡς τῆς θατέρου—a *tertium quid*—φύσεως καὶ οὐσίας μὴ καθ' ἑαυτὴν θεωρουμένης ἀλλὰ μετὰ τῆς συγκειμένης καὶ συμπεφυκυίας.

[69] *Ibid.*, 1304B 11–12: ἡ τῶν αὐθυποστάτων καὶ καθ' ἑαυτὰ εἶναι δυναμένων πρὸς ἄλληλα ποιὰ σχέσις in the second example. "Essential relation" here rather interprets than translates ποιὰ σχέσις, and means in effect "the relation in which each being is defined," a *definitive* relation. It will be remembered that for Aristotle a being was properly defined by its secondary ousiai, that is, its species and genus, but that species and genus themselves define τὸ ποιόν (Aristotle, *Cat*, 3b 19–20).

[70] PG, 86, 1304B 7: ἕν ... τῷ ἀριθμῷ, here, I think, the equivalent of "united in number," and opposed to τὰ διαφέροντα τῷ ἀριθμῷ in Leontius' first definition of hypostasis in *CNE* 1. 1, PG, 86, 1280A 12–13 (ὑποστάσεως δὲ ὅρος· ἢ τὰ κατὰ τὴν φύσιν μὲν ταὐτά, ἀριθμῷ δὲ διαφέροντα· etc.), with which

Should then Leontius' Monophysite object that two beings truly united cannot each retain its integrity, Leontius adds that they retain their integrity because neither possesses *affective qualities*.[71]

---

compare *CNE* 1.4, in 1288A 4–6 (τῷ μὲν γὰρ ἀριθμῷ πρὸς ἑαυτὰ διακρινόμενα, τῷ δὲ ὅρῳ πρὸς ἑαυτὰ συναπτόμενα), and *CNE* 1.5, in 1292C 9–10 (οὐ γὰρ τὴν μίαν φύσιν ἓν εἶναι τῷ ἀριθμῷ). In all these cases *number* is virtually a synonym of *hypostasis*. The same contrast in different terms in *CNE* 1.5, 1293A 9–10: οὐ ταυτὸν τὸ τῇ ἑνώσει ἓν λεγόμενον—i. e., the ἓν ... τῷ ἀριθμῷ of our passage—καὶ τὸ τῇ φύσει ἕν. This interpretation of our passage corresponds well with the passage in *SolArgSev* in which Leontius explains to his adversary that, in and of itself, number neither unites nor distinguishes, but that it unites and distinguishes only when it is applied to concrete beings in order to determine their relationships (PG, 86, 1918D 10ff., and especially 1920A 7–14). We recall that hypostasis too, both unites and distinguishes (e. g., *CNE* 1.1 in 1280A 12–15 *et passim*).

[71] PG, 86, 1305A 4–15, anticipated by 1304D 1–6. On this passage more *infra*. I note here only that Leontius' use of the formula *affective qualities* will prove to be that of Aristotle's *Categories*. In Aristotle, *Cat*, 9a 28–10a 9, we learn that of four genera of qualities, the third genus comprises *affective* qualities, ποιότητες παθητικαί. These affective qualities are *affective* in two senses. First, they are affective *not* as if that of which they are predicated had *been affected* or had *suffered* something, but rather as *producing an affect* in the senses, as whiteness has made white. Second, they are affective as the *results of an affect* in their subject, as whiteness in the face of a man may be the *result* of his having been frightened, that is, of his having been affected. A quality may be affective, in short, either as cause or effect; and it is this distinction which Leontius seems to have in mind when he contrasts active qualities with passive qualities in 1305A 6–12.

However, Leontius seems to tap other sources besides the *Categories* and its commentaries; for the commentaries—at least on the passage of the *Categories* just described—leave much of Leontius' argument unexplained. E. g., Aristotle and the commentaries oppose παθητικός to ποιητικός, not δραστήριος (A 7). Again, Aristotle and the commentaries do not distinguish the two modes of union of beings possessing affective qualities as does Leontius (1305A 6–8; A 8–12), much less use the term ἀντιπεπόνθησις. More important still, from Porphyry on the commentators on the *Categories*, associate the second class of affective qualities, those produced as results of affects or passions, with κρᾶσις, and indeed distinguish it in this from the first class (Porphyry, *In Categorias*, ed. Adolf Busse in *Commentaria in Aristotelem graeca*, IV, 1 [Berlin 1887], p. 130, l. 33–p. 131, l. 1; confirmed emphatically by the sixth-century commentator Olympiodorus of Alexandria, *In Categorias*, ed. Adolph Busse, *ibid.*, XII, 1 [Berlin 1902], p. 126, ll. 17–22, where I understand ὁ κατὰ φύσιν ὠχρὸς καὶ ὁ κατὰ φύσιν ἐρυθρός [l. 17f.] to possess their ὠχρότης and ἐρυθρίας as affective qualities of the first class, that is, as qualities *producing* affections upon the senses of others, and appeal to Aristotle, *Cat*, 9b 30–32). Leontius, however, seems to identify all beings with affective qualities with beings of class 2, that is, beings whose unions produce confusion, that is, κρᾶσις, and so seems to attribute κρᾶσις to the union of *both* classes of beings with affective qualities, and not only to the second class. Of course, the κρᾶσις of the commentators may well be very different from the one Leontius fears. Therefore, I cheerfully leave the question to those better informed.

Here an important point. In asserting that even in their unions beings of class 1 preserve their definition of being, Leontius preserves and defines *not one but two* relations of those beings: first, the relation of each being in the subject to the other beings of its nature (e.g., of the Word to the Father), and second, the relation of each being in a union to the other beings in the union; that is, of course, beings of another nature than itself.

First, he preserves and defines the relation of each being composing the subject to the other beings of its nature. This is to imply that each being in a subject is united to and distinguished from its ὁμοούσια by just that mode of determination in which each of them is united to and distinguished from every other: that is, they are all united as ousiai and distinguished as hypostases. This is the "definition of their being" which beings of class 1 always preserve, even in their unions. On the other hand, beings of class 2 in their unions always lose their definition of being, retaining neither that in which they are like their ὁμοούσια, nor that in which they are unlike.

Second, Leontius preserves and defines the relation of each being composing a subject to the subject itself. If in their unions beings of class 1 remain what they are, they cannot become identical with the subject they compose, for that subject also comprises at least one other being *ex hypothesi* of different nature. What then is the relation of these beings to their relations? Here Leontius employs a paradigm: the beings composing a subject are to it as extremes to mean.[72] Such a relation is a genuine union, and yet such a union

---

[72] In PG, 86, 1304B 3–4, we hear that the union of beings of class 2 destroys the ἀκρότης of the beings united, and in 1304D 4–5 that such unions end in "the change and alteration of the extremes (τῶν ἄκρων)." Now, since the unions of beings of class 1 are the opposites of unions of beings of class 2, we may suppose the former preserve the ἀκρότης of each ἄκρον, in short, that ἀκρότης is here the paradigm of ὁ ἴδιος τῆς ὑπάρξεως λόγος (B 2–3), in which each being in the relation perseveres. Further, where there are extremes, there must be a mean, and so the paradigm of the unions of beings of class 1 is the relation of a mean to two extremes.

Nevertheless, *caveat lector*! The extreme beings of this paradigm are not thereby simply identical with the two *natures* of, e.g., Jesus Christ. Not that they are not identical in fact. In fact, because the extremes by definition remain extremes and so preserve the definition of their being, they, as it were, adduce their ὁμοούσια and so also their ousiai. However, it is not for this that they are called *extremes*, but rather by reason of their relation to their mean, that is, the whole in which they exist.

also preserves, indeed presupposes, the integrity of its extremes. Leontius might have added that such a relation does not imply *time* either, for though the relation itself may come into being or pass away in time, all the beings in the relation, both mean and extremes, exist *simultaneously*.

b. *The Monophysite paradigm*[73]

Leontius' exposition of the union of beings of class 1 has twice anticipated his description of the union of beings of class 2,[74] and so we are not surprised at what follows:

> With these distinctions of ours in mind, we must understand that beings capable of transforming and changing one another, consisting [as each does] of things more than one in species and different in ousia, preserve no one of the beings united by a synthesis in its purity after the synthesis. Rather ⟨the synthesis⟩[75] mixes and confuses the properties of all and produces from all a hybrid species different from all; and there comes to be in the mixing a combination and confusion which leaves intact neither the peculiar properties of the hypostasis [of its elements] nor the common properties of their nature, but instead produces something different from these which is in nothing the same as[76] the [elements] from which it came into being.[77]

If then God and man are so united that neither preserves the identity of its nature even after the union, "then neither divine nor

---

Again, the extremes of this paradigm are not the extremes of the argument of *CNE* 1.4, in 1288A 10 ff., where the extremes are rather sets of essential relations, not the beings themselves which establish a relation. Nor again are the extremes of this paradigm the extremes implied by the paradigm of *CNE* 1.5, in 1292C 14 ff., for though the latter do indeed, as also the extremes of this paradigm, represent not ousiai but beings, they represent beings of the *same* ousia, as 1293A 4–5 concludes. Here, however, the extremes represent beings of *different* ousiai.

[73] *Ibid.*, 1305B 1–C 3.
[74] First, in the parenthesis to the third example, *fire : air : water, ibid.*, 1304D 1–6; and, again, at the very end of the section in 1305A 6–15, where he implies that beings of class 2 possess affective qualities.
[75] *Ibid.*, 1305B 5 *post* συγχέουσα *add.* ⟨ἡ σύνθεσις⟩ *ed.*
[76] *Ibid.*, 1305B 11 *post* ταυτὸν *add.* τῶν VOG.
[77] *Ibid.*, 1305B 1–11.

human nature will remain, but ⟨the union⟩[78] will produce another species of ousia by no means [identical to] these''[79]—which is blasphemous.

Again the point is unmistakable. Among beings of class 2, union means confusion: the disappearance of the elements united and the appearance of a *tertium quid*, an utterly new and different being possessing utterly new and different determinations of its essential relations; for this, of course, is the meaning of the phrase, ''a combination and confusion which leaves intact neither the peculiar properties of''—or ''the peculiar properties represented by''—''the hypostasis [of its elements] nor the common properties of their nature.''[80] This mode of union reflects the very nature of the beings themselves, for while beings of class I are united ''with and in one another'' and so persist, beings of class 2 are ''of such a nature as to transform and change one another'';[81] that is, to change one another into a *tertium quid*. Among such beings, of course, a *communicatio idiomatum* is impossible, for if in the moment of union the beings united themselves simply disappear, how much more so their *idiomata*.

Leontius' paradigm for the relations of these beings in their unions is the relations of two causes to their effect—again three terms. This relation, of course, implies time, for, since the moment in which the causes unite to form the result is itself not time, the causes and their effect can be comprehended only in a *before* and *after*, that is, in time. Causes as causes and effect as effect cannot be simultaneous.

c. *The two modes of combination: an analysis*

So much then for Leontius' distinction of the modes of combination of beings of classes I and 2. It is none too clear. We ask therefore: does his distinction between these two modes of combination find an echo elsewhere in his work, from which we may expand his

[78] *Ibid.*, 1305C 1 *post* ἀποτετέλεκεν *add.* ⟨ἡ ἕνωσις⟩ *ed.*
[79] *Ibid.*, 1305B 14–C 1.
[80] *Ibid.*, 1305B 8–10: οὔτε τὸ ἰδιάζον τῆς ὑποστάσεως οὔτε τὸ κοινὸν τῆς φύσεως φυλάξασα.
[81] *Ibid.*, 1305B 2: τὰ... ἀλλοιωτικὰ ἀλλήλων καὶ μεταβλητικά, echoing 1304D 4–6, τὴν ἐκ τῆς ἀντιπεπονθήσεως γινομένην τῶν ἄκρων μεταβολὴν καὶ ἀλλοίωσιν. This quality of beings of class 2 is doubtless associated with the affective qualities proper to them (1305A 6–15).

account? The answer: it does indeed. We first compare his distinction here with his brief analysis of change and movement in *CNE* I.2, and second, develop his distinction between beings united and not united by reason of their affective qualities.

(1) Leontius' analysis of motion

In *CNE* I.2[82] Leontius is defending the paradigm *Word : flesh = soul : body* against a familiar objection: the Word, says his Nestorian, exists before his flesh, but the soul does not exist before its body; and so the paradigm does not hold.[83] Replies Leontius: but the definition of a being defines it only in its present state, not in its subsequent states. "Otherwise," he continues, "none of the [class of] things which come into being [and pass away] would be susceptible of a definition of its being what it is (ὅρον τοῦ εἶναι ὅπερ ἐστίν), since none [of them] persist; for things which come into being and pass away all change (μεταβάλλει) into all others."[84] The similarity of the changes of "things which come into being and pass away" with the combinations of beings of class 2 in *CNE* I.7 is striking. Both are defined as changes (μεταβολαί);[85] and in the change, each of the elements of the former loses its "definition of its being what it is," while each of the elements of the latter gives up its ἴδιος τῆς ὑπάρξεως λόγος,[86] so that something utterly new and different comes into being. Plainly "things which come into being and pass away" are at least very like beings of class 2.

Moreover, Leontius' next words expand the parallel. "For that matter," he adds, "all the rational ousiai, which are susceptible of increase and decrease according to [their] virtue (ἀρετήν) and are seen now in one state, now in another (τὸ νῦν μὲν οὕτως, νῦν δὲ ἐκείνως ἔχειν), [they] too are [always] seen in motion (ἐν κινήσει); for to remain in the same state is not a property of the created nature— [that is,] if 'but you are the same' is properly said of God alone."[87]

---

[82] *Ibid.*, 1280B 14–1284A 10.
[83] *Ibid.*, 1280B 14–C 6.
[84] *Ibid.*, 1284A 1–4.
[85] With *CNE* I.2, *ibid.*, 1284A 3, μεταβάλλει, compare *CNE* I.7, μεταβολὴν καὶ ἀλλοίωσιν, with which see also 1305B 2.
[86] *Ibid.*, 1304B 2–3.
[87] *Ibid.*, 1284A 4–10. See Ps. 101:28, LXX (102:28, Heb.).

"All the rational ousiai," it seems, are very like beings of class 1; for, while in their combinations the latter preserve "their proper defini- tion of their being," the motions of the former seem to change not their being itself but only their state and disposition, and more exactly, the degree of their *arete*.

Finally, the parallel may be expanded, I think, to include Leon- tius' distinction between unions of beings of classes A and B, too, that is, his distinction between unions simple and composite; for just as he distinguishes class A, simple beings, from class B, compos- ite beings, and then redivides class 1 into beings which do and do not preserve in their unions their proper definitions of being, so in *CNE* 1.2 he distinguishes God from beings "in motion," and sub- divides beings in motion into beings "susceptible of increase and de- crease according to [their] virtue" and "things which come into be- ing and pass away." Beings united *in simple unions*, which we have already identified with the Trinity, therefore, include beings *not in motion*, that is—in *CNE* 1.2 Leontius is explicit—God; and beings united in composite unions include beings *in motion*.

(2) Affective qualities or a divine decree?

We have already noticed in passing that in his account of unions in which each of the beings united preserves its definition of being Leontius further defined these beings as *not having affective qualities*;[88] implying thereby that beings which lose their definitions of being in their unions *do* have affective qualities, and that their having them is the reason of their losing their definitions of being. We examine this distinction more closely in hope of discerning its sense.

Let us begin by asking: just what are affective qualities? We assume, of course, that beings joined by reason of them lose in their unions their definitions of being; but what are these affective quali- ties in themselves?

Our first clue lies in Leontius' examples of unions of beings of class 1, that is, of beings which do *not* have affective qualities. His second, fourth, fifth, and sixth examples seem to appeal to distinc- tions rather logical than ontological; but the first and third are

[88] *Ibid.*, 1304B 9–10.

unions of real and existent beings: the union of soul and body to form man—for so I understand the phrase ὁ καθ'ἡμᾶς ἄνθρωπος[89]—and the unions of at least three of the four elements.[90] More important still: Leontius speaks of these two examples elsewhere, too.

Soul and body on the one hand, the four elements on the other: we know why and how they are *not* united—that is, they are *not* united by reason of affective qualities—but we do not learn in *CNE* I how they *are* united. We do not seem to be the first to have posed the question, for in *SolArgSev*, Leontius' defense of *CNE* I against the attack of an apologist for the formulae of Cyril of Alexandria, Leontius answers it.

In the section of *SolArgSev* now in question,[91] Leontius again faces the charge that to assert two natures in Jesus Christ is also to assert two hypostases.[92] His reply is to distinguish the ὅρος φύσεως (elsewhere τρόπος τῆς φύσεως[93] or λόγος τῆς φύσεως[94]) from the λόγος οἰκονομίας[95] (elsewhere λόγος τῆς ἑνώσεως[96] or τρόπος τῆς ἑνώσεως[97])—plainly intending to expound the classical distinction between *theologia* and *oikonomia*. Now, he says, it is unthinkable that God should be joined to man by the definition of his nature,[98] that is, that the incarnation should be not "the condescension of [his] love for man, but a *natural* conjunction of the Highest with the lower."[99] It will therefore be only in the *oikonomia* that God and man will be joined. He then goes on:

> Indeed I am so far from saying that God the Word has his union with our [humanity] by reason of the definition of [his] nature, that I refuse to assert that even the human soul suffers its conjunction with its [own] body by reason of its nature [and] apart from the divine power (ἄνευ τῆς θείας δυνάμεως).

[89] *Ibid.*, 1304B 10.
[90] *Ibid.*, 1304C 14–D 6.
[91] Neither Leontius nor the manuscripts distinguish chapters in *SolArgSev*, but the section now in question clearly begins with PG, 86, 1936D 1.
[92] *Ibid.*, 1936D 9–10.
[93] *Ibid.*, 1937D 8–9.
[94] *Ibid.*, 1940B 13.
[95] *Ibid.*, 1937A 3–4.
[96] *Ibid.*, 1937D 1.
[97] *Ibid.*, 1940B 12, C 7.
[98] *Ibid.*, 1940A 10–B 3.
[99] *Ibid.*, 1940A 12–14. With A 13–14, φυσικὴ ... ἡ συνάφεια, compare B 1, φυσικῇ τῇ προσάλληλα ὁλκῇ.

But why speak of man's soul? Since I would say that not even the compounding and mixture[100] of the elements occur in this way in any absolute sense and by reason of [their] nature alone, but that they are brought into order and harmony rather by a divine decree [much] mightier than [their] nature (λόγῳ δὲ μᾶλλον θείῳ καὶ τῆς φύσεως κρείττονι).[101]

Why and how is soul joined to body and the elements to one another? Not by their affective qualities, but by a "divine power" or a "divine decree, [much] mightier than their nature." Soul and body, element and element join to one another not by a natural and necessary conjunction, that is, by reason of the definition of the nature of each, but by the will of God, that is, by reason of the divine *oikonomia*, the τρόπος τῆς ἑνώσεως. The application to *CNE* 1.7 is almost self-evident. Why do beings of class 1 preserve the definitions of their being even in their unions? Why do they not, as beings of class 2, combine to form new and different ousiai and hypostases? Because they are united to one another not by nature but only by divine decree. Again, this is surely why Leontius can attribute to "simple or physical bodies the [essential] relation to one another of beings self-subsistent and capable of existing in and of themselves."[102]

Beings of class 1, then, which in their unions preserve their definitions of being, are joined by a divine decree according to the mode of union; while beings of class 2, by implication, are joined by their affective qualities, that is, as it were, by their definitions of being, the mode of their natures, a natural inclination towards one another, so that in their unions they lose their identities.

And yet, before we pass on, we pause again to raise a question. Leontius tells us that Word is joined to flesh, soul to body, and element to element not by a natural attraction of the one for the other but by *a divine decree*. In pursuing the sense and motive of that decree—Leontius, of course, says nothing about its sense and motive—we shall see that the movement of the soul is an increase and decrease *according to virtue*. The question then: is it possible

[100] *Ibid.*, 1940B 9, πρᾶξιν] κρᾶσιν VO.
[101] *Ibid.*, 1940B 3–12.
[102] *CNE* 1.7, PG, 86, 1304B 10–12. "[Essential] relation" translates ποιὰ σχέσις.

that the decree joining soul to body has as its motive and measure the virtue of the soul; that the decree joining the elements to form a body for the soul composes those elements into a body proper to the virtue of its soul; that the Word is joined to the flesh in Jesus Christ in order that other rational ousiai may see in the flesh a paradigm of the virtue which they must attain in their own bodies? Idle speculation, perhaps; yet just such a doctrine was current in Leontius' own circles, and we shall soon see that Leontius himself is simply translating it.

(3) The structure of beings of class 1: change and persistence

In the two sections immediately above, we have identified Leontius' distinction between beings of class 1 and beings of class 2; first, with his distinction between beings which move only by increase or decrease and beings which come into being and pass away, and second, with his distinction between beings united to other beings of different ousia by a divine decree and beings united to other beings as it were by their natures. A third parallel may be deduced. Both in his analysis of soul and in a cursory description of the four elements—all beings of class I, we remember—Leontius seems to distinguish in all *two components*, one of which admits of motion and change, the other of which persists and endures. Now if we may suppose that beings of class 2 do not preserve their integrities in their unions because their structure is different from that of beings of class 1, we will be able to describe the difference between the two classes more exactly still.

(a) *The structure of the soul.* We begin by reporting Leontius' description of the soul in *CNE* 1.3, then go on to analyze it, adducing also *CNE* 1.6.

1. Leontius' psychology. In the *dubitatio* of the third chapter, Leontius' Nestorian is continuing his attack on the paradigm *Word* : *flesh* = *soul* : *body*. The soul, he argues, "is circumscribed in the body, and undergoes affections (πάθη) and endures afflictions."[103] To

103 *Ibid.*, 1284B 1–3.

56

use the union of soul and body as paradigm of the incarnation is therefore "to make [the Word] passible and circumscribed (παθη-τὸν καὶ περίγραπτον)."[104] Leontius' reply foreshadows the argument of *SolArgSev* described just above:

> Now if [it is] *by nature* [that] the Word is passible or under-goes circumscription in place, then he will be so in and of him-self, but not because of [his] union with [his] passible and, circumscribed body; and so he will be [capable of] suffering and circumscription even should he not [in fact] suffer nor be circum-scribed. If, on the other hand, [it is] by nature [that] he is unchangeable and uncircumscribed and impassible, then even should he come to be in a body, he would preserve the proper definition of his impassibility and unchangeability (τὸν ἴδιον τῆς ἀπαθείας καὶ ἀτρεψίας λόγον).[105]
> So also with the soul, for the soul too does not suffer [affec-tions] simply because it is in a body; else [the soul] too will be visible and will die[106] and would suffer all the rest that the body suffers. However [the soul] does not suffer [affections] be-cause it possesses them in its essence (οὐσιωδῶς) as receiving them from God, but [rather] it suffers [them] as having [in it-self] affective powers or faculties (παθητικὰς δυνάμεις), which it takes with it even when it departs from the body . . . ; the soul suffers in an absolute sense (ἁπλῶς), as receiving affective pow-ers conformed to what is good for it; though it suffers somatic affections too [that is,] from its mixture with the body to which it is bound and [from] the properties of the places in which it dwells; for though it is by its nature that it suffers in an abso-lute sense, it is susceptible of such [somatic] affection[s] also.[107]

Just now it is with Leontius' description of the soul that we con-cern ourselves. Two points are of special interest.

First, the affections of the soul are of two kinds. The one kind it owes to its own nature, the other kind to the body in which it dwells. Hence the soul will have or suffer affections even when it departs

---

[104] *Ibid.*, 1284B 5.
[105] *Ibid.*, 1284B 9–C 2. B 13 *post* παθητὸς *add.* καὶ VOG.
[106] *Ibid.*, 1284C 14 *post* ὁραθήσεται *add.* καὶ τεθνήξεται VOG.
[107] *Ibid.*, 1284C 10–1285A 3.

from its body.[108] This distinction, we note, is a parallel of Leontius' distinction in *SolArgSev* between τρόπος φύσεως and τρόπος ἐνώσεως: the soul will always have affections of its own, that is, in its mode or definition of nature; but in its union with the body, that is, in its mode of union, it may suffer affections aroused by the body, too.

Whence come the affections of the soul which are *not* from the body, we shall learn later.

However, it is a second point I emphasize just now: Leontius' clear distinction between the soul itself and its affective qualities.

Although the affections proper to the soul belong to it by nature—πάσχει ... διὰ τὸ πεφυκέναι πάσχειν, as Leontius puts it[109]— it does not possess even these natural affections as it were "in its essence (οὐσιωδῶς) as receiving [them] from God, but [rather] it suffers [them] as having [in itself] affective powers or faculties (παθητικὰς δυνάμεις), which it takes with it even when it departs from the body"[110]—affective powers which Leontius then immediately describes as "conformed to what is good for" the soul.[111] The soul, then, "has"[112] or "receives"[113] certain affective powers; and they are "conformed to what is good for it." Just below, we shall hear besides that the soul may "befoul"[114] them. In brief, the soul is distinct from its affective powers in that the soul determines whether they shall do their work *according to* or *contrary to* their nature, *for* or *against* the "good" of the soul. We had heard that the affections of the soul are not determined and defined, for the soul "does not suffer [its affections] because it possesses them in its essence as receiving them from God."[115] Rather, affections as such are determined by the affective powers. Now, however, we learn that the affective powers in turn are determined by the soul itself. Leontius even tells us how.

---

[108] *Ibid.*, 1285D 10–13.
[109] *Ibid.*, 1284C 12–13, with which compare 1285A 2–3.
[110] *Ibid.*, 1284C 15–D 3.
[111] *Ibid.*, 1284D 11–12: παθητικὰς πρὸς τὸ αὐτῇ [τῇ ψυχῇ] συμφέρον συναρμοσθείσας δυνάμεις.
[112] *Ibid.*, 1284D 2: ἔχουσα.
[113] *Ibid.*, 1284D 12–13: λαβοῦσα.
[114] *Ibid.*, 1285B 1–2.
[115] *Ibid.*, 1284C 14–D 1.

First, and as it were in passing, Leontius offers the examples of the demons and the spirits in hell to whom Christ preached, in order not only to prove that souls have affective powers and suffer affections even apart from the body, but also to establish that the affective powers of the soul may act in violation of their own nature.[116]

On the other hand, Leontius describes quite explicitly what the affective powers do when the soul determines them *according* to their nature. In the next line of *CNE* 1.3 he tells us:

> The soul may suffer divine [affections?] even according to [the will of?] God,[117] [yet suffers them] in no way by reason of the body—for how [could it]? since [the body] often strives against [the soul? God?]—but [rather] by reason of itself and its own nature. The appetitive [faculty] (τοῦ ... ἐπιθυμητικοῦ) strains passionately toward God; the spirited [faculty] (τοῦ ... θυμοειδοῦς) braces itself firmly (ἀρρενωπῶς) and steadily supports the appetitive faculty; [and] the cognitive [faculty] (τοῦ ... λογιστικοῦ) receives unshaded [its] immaterial reflections and is integrally (ἑνοειδῶς) illumined. Indeed, it was well said by a certain divinely wise man from those [gone] before us —Evagrius of Pontus— '[that there is] one desire [which is] good and eternal, the [desire] which strives for the true *gnosis*.' For [on the other hand,] when [the soul] befouls its powers, it falls into evil and ignorance; yet it does not have its evils from its body, even if some of them are brought to pass by means of the body.[118]

In all its perceptions, then, the soul stands before a choice: affections there must be, but is the soul to receive them in its affective powers as the nature of those powers and its own good prescribes; or contrary to their nature and against its own good? If the former, its affections are good and healing; if not, they are evil and blinding.

---

[116] *Ibid.*, 1284D 3–8.

[117] *Ibid.*, 1285 A6–7: πάσχει δ'ἄν καὶ κατὰ θεὸν τὰ θεῖα. A 6 δ'ἄν V δὲ O δὲ ἄν G. A 6–7 κατὰ θεόν *om.* Ὁ *scholium in locum manu recentiori* γράφεται πάσχει δὲ καὶ τὰ θεῖα· τὸ δὲ κατὰ θεὸν ἑρμηνεῖα (?) τοῦ τί θεῖα G. The scholiast of G forgets that the clause alludes to II Cor. 7:8–11, the theme of which is ἡ ... κατὰ θεὸν λύπη opposed to ἡ ... τοῦ κόσμου λύπη. Does Leontius borrow the phrase from Pseudo-Dionysius, *ep* 4 (PG, 3, 1072B 13–C 2)?

[118] PG, 86, 1285A 6–B 4.

Here, however, an excursus, for the passage just quoted answers a question which we could not answer before: whence come the affections of the soul which are not from the body? To be sure, Leontius is hardly at pains to elaborate, but his description of the natural and proper activity of the affective powers of the soul leaves little room for doubt: all three affective powers strain toward what can only be called the *vision of God*. Indeed, the highest of them, here τὸ λογιστικόν, has as its proper stimuli τὰς ἀύλους ἐμφάσεις, "immaterial reflections,"[119] by which, it seems, it attains a state of illumination.[120] Whence these immaterial reflections? Even if *from* the body, they cannot be *of* the body. First, they are after all *immaterial*, and the body is as material as can be. Second, these "immaterial reflections" are surely identical with the "divine affections"—literally, τὰ θεῖα—which the soul suffers "according to [the will of?] God," that is, κατὰ θεόν;[121] and these "divine affections," we hear, the soul suffers *"in no way by reason of the body ... but [rather] by reason of itself and its own nature."*[122] Plainly, then, their source is divine.[123] But more—and with this we conclude our excursus. If we can indeed identify Leontius' "immaterial reflections" with his "divine affections," and if the soul suffers its divine affections "in no way by reason of the body ... but by reason of itself and its own nature," then these divine affections and immaterial reflections will be the true good of the soul as according to its nature. However, it is the highest element of the soul alone which seems to receive the immaterial reflections, and so it will be in its highest element alone that the soul will receive its true good. Can it be then that the *nature* of the soul resides in its highest element; that the other two faculties are in some sense *not* of its nature? We shall soon see that Leontius seems to believe just that.

We return then to our argument.

---

[119] *Ibid.*, 1285A 12.
[120] *Ibid.*, 1285A 13–14: τοῦ δὲ λογιστικοῦ ... ἐνοειδῶς ἐλλαμπομένου.
[121] *Ibid.*, 1285A 6–7, discussed above.
[122] *Ibid.*, 1285A 7–9.
[123] The same conclusion is implied in a note to PG, 86, 1285A 12–14, reprinted at the foot of column 1286, in which Turrianus suggests that the phrase "immaterial reflections" alludes to—as I understand him—Rom. I :20, τὰ γὰρ ἀόρατα αὐτοῦ [τοῦ θεοῦ] ἀπὸ κτίσεως κόσμου τοῖς ποιήμασιν νοούμενα καθορᾶται, ἥ τε ἀΐδιος αὐτοῦ δύναμις καὶ θειότης.

2. The two components of the soul. In all its perceptions, we have noticed, the soul stands before a choice: to determine its affective powers for or against its own good. We ask now: where in the soul does this principle of judgement, this *liberum arbitrium*, lie?

We pick up the thread that leads to the answer by noting that Leontius identifies the affective powers of the soul in the passage just quoted with the three faculties of the soul: appetitive, spirited and cognitive. Now this same analysis of the soul appears in *CNE* 1.6 also, in a passage in which Leontius formally divides man into soul and body, then soul into οὐσία λογική and ποιότης ἀσώματος, and, finally, "incorporeal quality" into just the three elements listed in *CNE* 1.3—except that in *CNE* 1.6 he calls the cognitive faculty τὸ ἡγεμονικόν.[124] This *incorporeal quality*, then, which comprises the three powers of the soul, can it be the seat of choice and change in the soul?

We begin by recalling that we have earlier identified beings of class 1, that is, beings which even in their unions preserve the definition of their being, with "all the rational ousiai" of *CNE* 1.2, beings "which are susceptible of increase and decrease according to [their] virtue, and are seen now in one state, now in another."[125]

Next, we recall the passage from *SolArgSev* in which Leontius distinguishes within each being of class 1 a "definition" or "mode of nature" and a "definition" or "mode of union," in the latter of which it is united to other beings without losing the former.[126]

Now these two passages suggest that in all beings of class 1 (and so in all souls) there are *two components*: the first, an element admitting change, the second, an element persisting throughout the change. We ask: *in the soul*, does not the first component find its equivalent in the *incorporeal quality* of the soul; and the second component its equivalent in the *rational ousia* of the soul? The incorporeal quality of the soul will then express the *state* of the rational

---

[124] *Ibid.*, 1296C 9–11. Immediately below he raises and then begs off the question "whether [all] these are in the soul as *parts* or as *powers* (δυνάμεις); for some say one, and others the other"; so that here too the three elements of the soul are called *powers*. Compare *CNE* 1.3, *ibid.*, 1284D 1, D 12, 1285B 2.
[125] *Ibid.*, 1284A 4–7. See p. 52 f.
[126] *Ibid.*, 1937A 2 ff. See pp. 31 f., 54.

ousia, will be that element both bearing and determining the susceptibility of the rational ousia to "increase and decrease according to its virtue," that element in which the rational ousia is "seen now in one state, now in another," the element of a being in which its "mode of union" resides, and finally—to return to the question at hand—the component in which the affective powers of the soul, themselves parts of its incorporeal quality, are determined to be good or evil, and with them their affections. In short, the incorporeal quality of the soul possesses the *power of choice* of the soul.

On the other hand, the rational ousia of the soul will be that component persisting through change, preserving its "definition of being" or "nature" throughout the various determinations of the incorporeal quality of the soul, and in short will be that being of which the determinations of the incorporeal quality are predicated.

(b) *The four elements*. Granted then that the soul possesses two components, one admitting change and the other persisting throughout change. It may be objected, however, that these two components characterize soul only as soul, not soul as being of class 1. The only satisfactory reply will be to discover the same two components in other beings of class 1 also.

What, for instance, of the four elements, fire, air, earth, water? Leontius offers them too as examples of beings that preserve their definition of being in their unions,[127] and besides in *SolArgSev* he expressly associates the four elements with soul as beings joined to other beings not by reason of affective qualities but by a divine decree.[128] Now, does each of the elements comprise two components also—the equivalent of the rational ousia and incorporeal quality of the soul?

The answer is probably *yes*. In the same anthropological excursus in *CNE* 1.6 in which Leontius lists the parts of the soul, he lists also the parts of the body,[129] concluding: "... and ... the bones and

[127] *CNE* 1.7, PG, 86, 1304C 14–D 1 ff.
[128] *SolArgSev*, PG, 86, 1940B 3–12 and especially B 7–12.
[129] *CNE* 1.6, PG, 86, 1296D 5–1297A 2. On D 5–9, see Aristotle, *Parts of Animals*, II. 1, ed. and trans. A. L. Peck, Loeb Classical Library (Cambridge, Massachusetts, 1937), 106 ff., and the brief but useful note of A. L. Peck in Aristotle, *Generation of Animals*, ed. and trans. A. L. Peck, Loeb Classical Library (London, 1943), xlviii f.

tissues and sinews ... [are divided] into the four elements, and these into matter and form (εἰς ὕλην καὶ εἶδος).''[130] We shall certainly fall little short of the truth in supposing that in any one of the four elements form and matter function just as rational ousia and incorporeal quality in the soul. It will then be by reason of matter that an element unites with other elements, and in the union changes; and by reason of its form that it will persist throughout its changes as their subject.

We may conclude, then, that every being of class 1 comprises two components, one in which it changes, the other in which it persists throughout its changes.

Here we pause for another excursus. We have just now identified the part of the soul bearing its mode of nature as its *rational ousia*, that is, οὐσία λογική. This rational ousia we may associate with "all the rational ousiai" of *CNE* 1.2, beings "which are susceptible of increase and decrease according to [their] virtue, and are seen now in one state, now in another."[131] This, of course, is as much as to identify rational ousiai with souls; for to the question, what *is* a soul, and what is its *nature*, we should have to reply that a soul is a rational ousia.

Yet, we have met something very like these rational ousiai earlier in *CNE* 1.7, in the beings of what Leontius calls "the rational and blessed creation"[132] or "the rational nature,"[133] beings who seem also to include the saints.[134] Indeed, it seems all but certain that these beings are the same as our rational ousiai here. The sole objection: as we have seen, Leontius identifies Jesus Christ—"him who took his appearance from the Virgin," as Leontius calls him[135]—as one of the beings of this rational nature, and, more exactly, as the single one of those beings who is worshipped by his peers, implying that Jesus Christ enjoys this honor not by reason of an ἀξία or nature superior to that of his peers, but by reason of his union with the Word.[136]

---

[130] PG, 86, 1296D 7–9.
[131] *Ibid.*, 1284A 4–7.
[132] *Ibid.*, 1301A 6.
[133] *Ibid.*, 1301A 11.
[134] *Ibid.*, 1301A 2.
[135] *Ibid.*, 1301A 9.
[136] *Ibid.*, 1301A 5–B 4. See p. 26f.

Is Jesus Christ a *soul*, then, and different from other souls only by reason of his union with the Word? So it seems, and we may indeed go on to observe first, that his union with the Word may imply, as we have suggested, that like the Word, Jesus Christ is a being of class A, that is, a being in whom his essence is indistinguishable from his existence; and second, that if his difference in this from other souls does not lie in his nature, that is, in his *rational ousia*, it can only lie in his *incorporeal quality*, so that the question then arises: how is the incorporeal quality of Jesus Christ different from the incorporeal quality of any other soul? Alas, the answer must await our examination of Leontius' source.

(c) *Two different structures of being.* Back then to the argument. We have just concluded that every being of class 1 comprises two components, one in which it changes, the other in which it persists throughout its changes. We must go beyond this. I suggest now that this further definition of beings of class 1 will help us also to describe their difference from beings of class 2; for beings of class 1 preserve their definitions of being in their unions because they comprise two elements, and beings of class 2 lose their definitions of being in their unions because they do not comprise two elements, but in effect only one.

How so?

First, we must assume with Leontius that beings of both classes are in motion, that is, are changing.[137]

Second, we know that the changes proper to beings of one class are different from the changes proper to the others. This is so first in the act of change itself, for we have identified the change of beings of class 1 as an increase and decrease,[138] but the change of beings of class 2 as a coming into being and passing away.[139] However, the different changes produce different products too. Changes of

---

[137] *CNE* 1.2, where we have identified the beings mentioned in PG, 86, 1284A 1–4 with beings of class 2, and the beings of 1284A 4–10 with beings of class 1. See our discussion, *supra*, p. 52 f.

[138] *CNE* 1.2, PG, 86, 1284A 5: τὸ μᾶλλον καὶ ἧττον—said here only of "all the rational ousiai" (A 4–5), but certainly to be applied also to each of the four elements. See p. 62 f.

[139] *Ibid.*, 1284A 4: τὰ ἐν γενέσει καὶ φθορᾷ.

beings of class 1 produce no new ousiai, but changes of beings of class 2 produce not only new ousiai, but also new hypostases.[140]

Now I suggest that the reason of the difference of the changes is that in beings of class 1 the ousia of the being is distinct from that principle in the being which, as it were, allows the being to change, while in beings of class 2 such a distinction is impossible, except for a logic attempting to reconstruct the process of change. In beings of class 2, ousia and the principle of change are identical. If then change be assumed—and, as we have noticed, Leontius assumes it—then in its unions with beings of another nature it is impossible that a being of class 2 should not lose its nature; for that in it which changes in its encounter with the other being is, so to speak, identical with its very nature.

Again, this is almost certainly the reason that Leontius calls the qualities of beings of class 2 *affective* qualities;[141] for, as Aristotle's definition of affective qualities requires, they either work an affect upon the being with which their own being unites, or are the consequence of an affect worked in their own being by another being,[142] or both, the balance of affections depending upon the relative potency of the beings united.[143] In contrast—and here of course we enter an hypothesis pure and simple—the qualities of beings of class 1 may perhaps be called ποιότητες ἀπαθεῖς, *non-affective* qualities or *impassible* qualities. Not, to be sure, that in their unions with other beings these non-affective qualities do not give and receive affections;[144] but that the affections given and received do not determine the ousiai of the beings united; so that, as Leontius puts it, they preserve their definitions of being even in their unions.[145]

---

[140] *CNE* 1.7, PG, 86, 1305B 5–11.
[141] *Ibid.*, 1305A 4–15 and especially A 6.
[142] Aristotle, *Cat*, 9a 28–10a 9, described and discussed on p. 48, note 71, *supra.*
[143] PG, 86, 1305A 8–12.
[144] E.g., the *communicatio idiomatum* in Jesus Christ. We are reduced to speculation here because Leontius does not expand his psychology so far as a theory of perception.
[145] We may safely suppose that Leontius contrasts the *affective* qualities of beings of class 2 to the *incorporeal* qualities of beings of class 1; e.g., the incorporeal quality of the soul mentioned in PG, 86, 1296C 10, and discussed both *supra* and *infra*. Affective qualities will then be the qualities of *bodies*, an hypothesis which corresponds perfectly to the evidence so far adduced. To this it may be objected that the definition of the quality of

Hence the difference between beings of class 1 and beings of class 2 seems to reflect a difference in structure: the former consist of two elements, an ousia and a principle of change; while the latter consist of only one element, which comprehends both its ousia and principle of change.

III. The Union κατ'οὐσίαν: A Summary

It is time that we gather up the threads of our account. In the beginning of the chapter, Leontius undertook to explain just what the ἕνωσις κατ'οὐσίαν really is, and specifically how the true Orthodox ἕνωσις κατ' οὐσίαν differs from its perversion among the Monophysites. This difference Leontius finally describes as the difference between unions of beings of class 1, which even in their unions preserve their definition of being, and unions of beings of class 2, in which the beings united are "confused" into a *tertium quid*. However, the way to this happy end has been long and hard. Beginning with πάντα τὰ ὄντα, Leontius has had to traverse an entire *analysis of being*. This analysis is indeed indispensable for the understanding of Leontius' Christology in general, but for the history of Christian doctrine its chief interest is that in it Leontius offers the sole complete and satisfactory account of his interpretation of the critical terms of the Christological formula of the Council of Chalcedon: hypostasis and ousia. We may summarize Leontius' analysis of being in four steps.

---

the soul as *incorporeal* cannot be applied to beings of class 1 *as such*; for though the four elements are beings of class 1, their qualities can hardly be supposed *incorporeal*. I reply: *non liquet*! An element is not a body, but a component of body, as Leontius clearly implies in *CNE* 1.7, PG, 86, 1304B 11–12, in which he speaks of ἡ τῶν αὐθυποστάτων καὶ καθ' ἑαυτὰ εἶναι δυναμένων ... σχέσις—lines which in context clearly describe the four elements. Now, if the elements are capable of existing apart from the bodies which they compose, they and their qualities are, strictly speaking, *incorporeal*. This, of course, is not to deny that the qualities of the elements are *immaterial*; but that is another question, for in Leontius, I suggest, *incorporeal* defines *not* the mode of, say, visibility, by which elements might be distinguished from souls, but rather the mode of *change*. Now in their mode of change Leontius explicitly unites souls and elements, emphasizing that they change in the same way: for as beings capable of independent existence, they both preserve the definitions of their beings in their changes —and in this, I suggest, are *incorporeal*.

First, says Leontius, all beings are simultaneously united by what they have in common and distinguished by that in which they differ. These unions and distinctions are the essential relations of each being.

Second, these unions and distinctions are further determined as hypostases or ousiai, so that all beings are either united as ousiai and distinguished as hypostases (class I), or united as hypostases but distinguished as ousiai (class II). Adducing *SolArgSev*, we have identified class I as the class of beings in their mode of nature, and class II as the class of beings in their mode of union. In what follows, then, Leontius analyzes beings in their mode of nature. However, his analysis of their modes of nature proves also to describe their modes of union, for all distinctions among modes of union derive from corresponding distinctions among modes of nature.

The third and fourth steps offer two different divisions of beings of class I.

The third step distinguishes beings of class I into beings of classes A and B, that is, beings which have their essential relations as *simple* (class A) or as *composite* (class B). This distinction we have identified with the distinction between beings which *are and are not one* in existence and essence. However, we notice besides that Leontius seems to assume that all beings of class B as such exist not only in their modes of nature but also in their modes of union; although, to be sure, not every being in its mode of union proves also to be a being of class B: e.g., the Word. This important qualification has led us to two conclusions about the modes of union of beings of classes A and B. First, the former enter into their modes of union, as it were, *of their own free will*, but the latter, only by *necessity*. Second—though here we are frankly speculating—beings of class A unite only with other beings of class A, and beings of class B only with other beings of class B. The consequence is that in order that the Word, a being of class A, may unite with his flesh, a being of class B, we must suppose the existence of a third being able to unite with both; in short, a being of *both* classes A *and* B, that is, a being *both one and not one* in essence and existence; and this being we believe we have found in the *nous* Jesus Christ of the Christology of Evagrius of Pontus.

The fourth step offers a second division of beings of class I. With this division, Leontius attains his immediate purpose: to distinguish between the Orthodox and the Monophysite interpretations of the ἕνωσις κατ'οὐσίαν; and it is for this reason that we have earlier called this the second step of the argument. In their unions, Leontius says, beings of class I either preserve their definition of being (class 1) or they do not (class 2). Those that preserve it, preserve it because they do not have affective qualities, and those that lose it, lose it because they do.

This division we have identified with three other distinctions in his work.

First, we have identified it with the distinction in *CNE* 1.2 between beings the movement of which is an increase and decrease, and beings which move in a coming into being and a passing away.

Second, we have identified it with the distinction of *SolArgSev* between beings united to others by a divine decree in a mode of union preserving the definition of nature of each, and beings united by their very natures themselves, that is, in a "natural conjunction" and by "natural attraction."

Third, we have identified the distinction with the distinction implied in both *CNE* 1.3 and 1.6 between beings comprising a component admitting change and a component persisting throughout change, and beings composed as it were of one component only; and we have besides identified the two components of the former, first, in the soul as its incorporeal quality and rational ousia, and second, in each of the four elements as its matter and form.

With this we end our account of the seventh chapter. There remains only for Leontius to exhort the reader to comprehend the integrity which God and man preserve in Jesus Christ on the analogy of these examples;[146] and so he brings chapter seven to a close.

---

[146] PG, 86, 1305C 3–D 2, and especially C 5–7.

Chapter Three

THE FOURTH CHAPTER OF *CNE* I: ἕνωσις καθ᾽ ὑπόστασιν AND ἕνωσις κατ᾽ οὐσίαν

In the last chapter of *CNE* I Leontius has offered us his analysis of being. The occasion of that analysis, as we have seen, is the attempt of the Monophysites to pre-empt the formula ἕνωσις κατ᾽οὐσίαν for their own Christology; an attempt which leads Leontius to remind his readers of the true and Orthodox sense of the formula by means of an analysis of the modes in which a being may unite with another being of a different nature.

Now, at the end of *CNE* 1.7, we have heard Leontius adjure us— as we have put it—to comprehend the integrity which God and man preserve in Jesus Christ on the analogy of the examples which *CNE* 1.7 has set before us. A harsh exhortation indeed! For, though Leontius expressly intends in *CNE* 1.7 to elucidate the Orthodox union κατ᾽ οὐσίαν, he never bothers even to define it. What is the union κατ᾽ οὐσίαν? We learn well enough which of the beings described in his analysis of being are united as ousiai: i.e., beings of classes I and 1. Alas, of the union in which they are united, the union κατ᾽ οὐσίαν itself, we hear nothing. Yet we should like to know: how can beings both of like and of unlike natures be ousiai, and above all: how shall we apply such a union to the union of Word and flesh in Jesus Christ? For, to mention only one difficulty, if hypostasis and ousia are two distinct and different determinations of the essential relations of being, how can Leontius describe the ἕνωσις κατ᾽ οὐσίαν as a ἕνωσις ὑποστατική too?[1] To be sure, Leontius' analysis of being raises quite as many questions as it answers.

---

[1] In the introduction to the florilegium of *CNE* I, PG, 86, 1308C 8 f., Leontius speaks of τῇ κατ᾽ οὐσίαν ὑποστατικῇ ἑνώσει.

However, all these questions and many others Leontius has in effect answered in an earlier chapter, *CNE* 1.4, but because he does not introduce his answers there with the analysis of being necessary to understand them, their sense and significance are easily overlooked. Besides, the argument of chapter four is difficult to the point of despair, a despair both reflected and compounded in the peculiar frequency of errors in the manuscript and editorial traditions. In short, a jungle; but a jungle through which we must cut our way if we hope to attain to Leontius' Christology.

We turn then to *CNE* 1.4 to learn how Leontius applies the ousia and hypostasis of *CNE* 1.7 to the union of Word and flesh in Jesus Christ. We begin with a brief introduction to the chapter, then advance to the argument itself.

I. *CNE* 1.4: The Sense of the Argument

In chapters two and three of *CNE* 1 Leontius has been defending the paradigm *Word* : *flesh* = *soul* : *body* against the attacks of his Nestorian. In *CNE* 1.4, however, the Nestorian changes the direction of his attack, and demands in effect that Leontius concede that to distinguish two perfect natures in Jesus Christ is as much as to distinguish two hypostases. "If," the Nestorian argues, "the hypostasis of the Word is perfect, and the [hypostasis] of the man which he assumed is perfect too, but [if also] the Word remains unchangeable[2] and his flesh, too, is preserved unalterable, how then is it not [proper and] pious to affirm two hypostases in Jesus Christ, since neither of the two [hypostases] is confused [with the other]?"[3]

Alas, a full account of Leontius' reply would detain us too long. Suffice it to say that Leontius proposes to prove that a *perfect* godhood, that is, a perfect set of the properties proper to the divine nature, may be predicated not only of the Word in his *mode of nature* but also of the Word in his *mode of union*; which is as much as to say that a perfect set of the properties proper to the divine nature may be predicated of the subject Jesus Christ, even though he possesses a perfect set of the properties proper to the nature of man

[2] PG, 86, 1285C 3 ἀναλλοιώτως] ἀναλλοίωτος VOG.
[3] *Ibid.*, 1285C 1–5.

too. How this can be, Leontius now undertakes to explain. His argument advances in two steps: analyses first of the two relations of beings, and then of the three syzygies which result from those relations.

However, before passing on to the argument, we pause to note that to call Jesus Christ perfect in godhood is as much as to say that, by reason of the presence of the Word in him, he is united to the Father as ousia and distinguished from the Father as hypostasis; that is, is as much as to say that the subject Jesus Christ is united to the Father κατ'οὐσίαν, as also to his flesh. As in *CNE* 1.7, we are pursuing a ἕνωσις κατ'οὐσίαν. We shall see that, in defining it, Leontius also defines a ἕνωσις καθ' ὑπόστασιν.

II. *CNE* 1.4: THE ARGUMENT ITSELF

A. *The Two Relations of Beings*[4]

Leontius opens the argument proper by distinguishing between two sets of names: "for," he says, "of the names [of things], some indicate the *nature* of the subjects [of which they are predicated], while others signify the *relations* of the things."[5] Now the first set of names certainly denotes beings in their *mode of union*. However, since it is of Jesus Christ that Leontius will speak, and since, besides, Jesus Christ is a subject joining two beings in their *modes of union*, it is only natural that Leontius passes over the first set of names in order to discuss the second. He continues, therefore:

> Now, the κοινωνία—that is, the ἕνωσις or point of union —of the relations (τῶν σχέσεων) of [things of] *different* natures (τῶν ἐτεροειδῶν) will be found the contrary (ἐπαλλάττουσαν) [of the κοινωνία of the relations] of beings of the *same* nature (τὰ ὁμοειδῆ); for [it is] in [just] those [points] which things of the same nature have in common (κοινωνοῦσι) with things of different nature that [things of the same nature] differ from one another; and [it is] in [just] those [points] by which they are distinguished from things different in nature that they are

---

[4] *Ibid.*, 1285D 7–1288C 1.
[5] *Ibid.*, 1285D 7–9.

joined to one another. Since [it is] *by number* (τῷ ... ἀριθμῷ)
—that is, *by hypostasis*—that they are distinguished from one
another, [it is] by this that they are united to things of different
nature;[6] but [since it is] *by definition* (τῷ ... ὅρῳ)—that is,
by ousia—that they are joined to one another, [it is] by this[7]
that they are distinguished from things of different nature.[8]

On reading this passage, we suspect at once that the *relations*
which Leontius describes here are the "twofold relation" or "essential relations" of *CNE* 1.7; suspect besides that the *points in common* and *points of difference* here are identical with the simultaneous
determination of these essential relations as hypostasis and ousia;
and suspect finally that "beings the same in nature" and beings
"distinguished from one another *by number* and joined to one another
by definition" will soon appear in *CNE* 1.7 as beings of class I, that is,
beings united as ousiai and distinguished as hypostases. Indeed, the
very next lines vindicate our suspicions. "[There are], then," continues Leontius, "two relations seen in the same Word: one in which the
Son possesses [his] sameness with the Father, and another in which
the Son is distinguished from him. The [former] is indicated by the
term *nature*, while the [latter] is signified by the name *hypostasis*."[9]

There is no doubt of it. We have here a foreshadowing of that
analysis of being which will appear in all its colors only in *CNE* 1.7.
Here, however, Leontius will apply this still shadowy analysis of
being to *the hypostasis and natures of Jesus Christ*. Knowing his
analysis of being as we do, we shall be able to perceive quite clearly here his definitions of the ἕνωσις καθ' ὑπόστασιν and ἕνωσις
κατ' οὐσίαν.

B. *The Three Syzygies*[10]

Having established first, that every being possesses *two relations*,
one of likeness and one of unlikeness, and second, that these two

---

[6] *Ibid.*, 1288A 5 *post* διακρινόμενα *add.* τούτῳ (τούτῳ *om.* VO) τοῖς ἑτερο-
ειδέσι συνάπτεται (συνάπτονται G) VOG.

[7] *Ibid.*, 1288A 6 *post* συναπτόμενα *add.* τούτῳ G.

[8] *Ibid.*, 1285D 9–1288A 7.

[9] *Ibid.*, 1288A 10–B 1.

[10] *Ibid.*, 1288C 1–1289B 1, that is, to the end of the chapter.

relations are determined in every being as either hypostasis or ousia, Leontius now advances abruptly to the analysis in Jesus Christ of what we must call the relations of these relations. The argument advances in three steps. In the first, Leontius describes the three syzygies, or pairs of relations produced by the union of Word with flesh, in order to relate them to one another.[11] Second, he applies the three syzygies to his paradigm of the incarnation, the union of soul with body, in order to establish the essential relations of the beings within each syzygy.[12] Finally, he uses the essential relations of the third syzygy of the paradigm to explain the relation of the subject Jesus Christ to God the Father and to other men, that is, to explain the ἕνωσις κατ'οὐσίαν.[13] Our argument requires only that we describe the first step, from which in any case the other two are derived.

1. The Union of Word with Flesh

We begin with Leontius' own words.

"Indeed," he says "[as there are] six relations before us [now]: two [that is, one] of the Father to the Word and [one] of the Word to the Father; two [that is, one] of the Word to the flesh and [one] of the flesh to the Word; and two [that is, one] of Christ to us and [one of Christ] to the Father[14]—so there come to be three general syzygies,"[15] that is, three pairs or sets of determinations of essential relations.

We note at once that the first pair mentioned here describes the essential relations of beings of class I, that is, beings of like nature,

---

[11] *Ibid.*, 1288C 1–14.
[12] *Ibid.*, 1288C 15–1289A 2.
[13] *Ibid.*, 1289A 3–B 1.
[14] Both sense and the evidence both of PG, 86, 1288D 5f., *infra*—where *post* D 5 ἁπλῶς *add.* σῶμα καὶ πρὸς VOG—and D 13–14, *infra*, urgently require that for 1288C 6 ἡμῶν πρὸς αὐτὸν we read—as we have translated—πρὸς τὸν πατέρα; the reading of VOG in PG being, I suppose, an unconscious attempt to conform C 6 to the patterns of C 3 "and of the Word to the Father," and of C 4f. "and of the flesh to the Word." The correction also offers the only hope of correlating this passage with the argument of 1289A 3–B 1 *infra*.
[15] PG, 86, 1288C 6f.: τρεῖς γίνονται καθολικαὶ συζυγίαι. For the whole of the passage just translated: 1288C 1–7.

beings united as ousiai (κατ' οὐσίαν) but distinguished as hypostases, or beings in their *mode of nature*. The second pair introduces two beings, Word and flesh, in their *modes of union*, and so describes the essential relations of beings of class II, that is, beings united as hypostases and distinguished as ousiai. This of course is the ἕνωσις καϑ' ὑπόστασιν. The description of the third pair describes the relation of the subject to each one of the ὁμοούσια of the beings that compose it; that is, in Jesus Christ, the relation of Jesus Christ to the Father and to the human nature of other men, ourselves, to both of whom Jesus Christ is said to be ὁμοούσιος. Of this relation *CNE* I.7 has had nothing to say, but we shall soon see that it is this relation which Leontius expresses in the formula ἕνωσις κατ'οὐσίαν which *CNE* I.7 was meant to expound.

Three pairs or syzygies, then. Now Leontius advances to a puzzling argument: in brief, *he compares the relations of the beings within each pair to the relations of the pairs among themselves*. Again we let Leontius speak, but here we shall not hesitate to gloss him even more frequently than before.

2. The ἕνωσις κατ'οὐσίαν

Three pairs or syzygies, he has said. Now he continues, "the first relation of the syzygies"—he means the relations of the terms within the first syzygy and so the determinations of the essential relations of beings *united as ousiai but distinguished as hypostases*; e.g., the Trinity—"is the same as [the relation of] the third [syzygy or pair as such] to the first [syzygy or pair as such]."[16] The sense, though crabbed, is unmistakable: just as the *terms* of the first syzygy are united as ousiai and distinguished as hypostases, so also the first and third *syzygies as such* are united as ousiai and distinguished as hypostases.

a. *The intent of the argument*

Less obvious than the sense of Leontius' argument is the answer to the question: *what is its intent and purpose?* Of what good is it to

[16] *Ibid.*, 1288C 7 f.

Leontius to prove that the relation of the Word to God the Father is, *as relation*, ὁμοούσιος to the relation of Jesus Christ to the Father, as also to the relation of Jesus Christ to other flesh?

The answer is, in brief, that Leontius is using this argument to prove that *Jesus Christ as subject is united* κατ' οὐσίαν *both to God the Father and to other flesh*: whence Leontius will have proved to his Nestorian that Jesus Christ possesses a perfect set of the properties proper to the divine nature while possessing also a perfect set of the properties proper to the human nature.

How does Leontius prove this? His argument employs or implies three syllogisms.

The first syllogism begins with the *major premise* that the extremes resemble one another in that in which they are both opposed to the mean.[17] The *minor premise* is that the first and third syzygies are extremes of the mean or second syzygy.[18] Conclusion: the first and third syzygies resemble one another in that in which they are opposed to the mean or second syzygy.

The second syllogism has its major premise in the conclusion of the first syllogism, adds as minor premise that that in which the first and third syzygies are opposed to the mean or second syzygy is *the relation to one another of the terms in each syzygy*, and concludes

---

[17] *Ibid.*, 1288C 9 f. says so explicitly.

[18] This premise Leontius simply assumes. That he can simply assume it is puzzling. Puzzling, too, is that Leontius argues from the relations of the syzygies themselves to the relations of the beings composing the syzygies. No doubt Leontius believed the assumption valid for just the same reasons which led him to adopt the method of argument. Can it be that Leontius is influenced here by the triads of the analysis of being in Proclus Diadochus, *Elements of Theology*, proposition 103 (ed. and trans. E. R. Dodds, 2d ed. [Oxford, 1963], p. 92, ll. 13–29)? As we have suggested (*supra*, p. 44, note 56), that analysis might have been transmitted to Leontius by Pseudo-Dionysius. On the other hand, Evagrius of Pontus, whom we shall soon identify as the source of Leontius' Christology, himself suggests that the relation of soul to body in man somehow reflects the union of the *"nous nu"* to the Word in contemplation. (N. B.: the phrase *"nous nu"* I borrow from A. Guillaumont's French translation of Evagrius, cited immediately below; the Greek behind the Syriac behind the French was probably ψιλὸς νοῦς.) See EvagPont, *KephGn* ("édition critique de la version syriaque commune [that is, S1] et édition d'une nouvelle version syriaque, intégrale [that is, S2], avec une double traduction française"), 2.5 (S2; no Greek): "Le corps de ce qui est est la contemplation de êtres, et l'âme de ce qui est est la science de l'Unité." Perhaps then Leontius owes even his analysis of being to Evagrius.

that the terms of the first syzygy are therefore related to one another just as the terms of the third syzygy.

The third and last syllogism takes as its major premise the conclusion of the second syllogism, adds as minor premise that the relation of the terms of the first syzygy, that is, of God the Father and God the Word, is that they are united as ousiai and distinguished as hypostases,[19] and so concludes that the terms of the third syzygy too are united as ousiai and distinguished as hypostases. Now since the terms of the third syzygy are the subject Jesus Christ, God the Father, and the flesh of other men, Leontius is saying in effect that *Jesus Christ is united to God the Father and other flesh as ousia and distinguished from them as hypostasis*, a perfect ἕνωσις κατ' οὐσίαν; QED!

If then it be objected that Leontius only *implies* a union κατ' οὐσίαν here, that he does not draw this conclusion explicitly, we reply that he will be explicit enough just below.[20] In the third step of his argument[21] Leontius expressly says that Jesus Christ "as a whole is hypostasis in respect to the Father by reason of [his] godhood [together] with [his] manhood, and an hypostasis as a whole in respect of ourselves [together] with [his] godhood by reason of his manhood."[22] Now, since *hypostasis* here plainly is the equivalent of *whole*, and since it is *as a whole* that man, the paradigm of Jesus Christ, is *distinguished* from other souls and other flesh in step two

[19] A premise expressly stated in the application of the syzygies to the paradigm *soul : body* in PG, 86, 1287D 6–8.

[20] I grant, however, that the application of his conclusion here to the paradigm *soul : body* in the second step of the argument (PG, 86, 1288C 15–1289A 2) in 1288D 13–1289A 2 is anything but lucid and can be understood only in the light of the third step just below. The text of the second step seems firm, alas: 1288D 14 *post* ψυχὴν *add.* ὡς VOG is the only significant correction. I suggest, however, that the relation (1289A 2 σχέσιν) of 1289A 1 f. is the relation of ψυχὴ ἁπλῶς (other souls) and σῶμα ἁπλῶς (other flesh) to their ὁμοούσια among the parts of man (1289A 1 τὰ ἑαυτοῦ μέρη), that is, to man's own soul and flesh, respectively. This relation, of course, is the relation of beings united as ousiai but distinguished as hypostases. I suggest besides that 1289A 2 αὐτά refers not to μέρη but to ψυχὴ ἁπλῶς and σῶμα ἁπλῶς. Just how 1289A 2 δευτέραν ... κοινωνίαν is to be understood, I am not certain, but the parallel in A 3 ff. seems to require that it mean a union κατ' οὐσίαν.

[21] PG, 86, 1289A 3–14.

[22] *Ibid.*, 1289A 5 f., where A 5 *post* ἄκροις *add.* <ὡς> *ed.* ὅλως VG ὅλος O *et manu recentiori* G *ed.* *post* πρὸς *add.* τὸν πατέρα διὰ τὴν θεότητα μετὰ τῆς ἀνθρωπότητος· καὶ ὑπόστασις ὢν <ὡς> ὅλος (ὅλως VG) πρὸς VOG.

76

just above,[23] we must conclude that *hypostasis* here is the determination in which Jesus Christ is *distinguished* from God the Father and from other flesh; whence it follows that it will be *as ousia*, κατ' οὐσίαν, that Jesus Christ will be *united* to God the Father and to other flesh. The same conclusion is to be drawn from the lines immediately following: "Since the relations of both distinction and union are opposite [one another],[24] [Jesus Christ] is known as having the [one set of] relations to himself by reason of his [own] parts"—that is, the union of Word and flesh, which are united in and to Jesus Christ as hypostases and distinguished from him[25] and from one another as ousiai—"and possesses the [other set of] relations to both the Father and us by reason of the likeness of [his] parts to the extremes."[26] Now, if Word and flesh are united as hypostases and

---

[23] *Ibid.*, 1288D 14–1289A 1.

[24] *Ibid.*, 1289A 7 f., repeating 1285D 9–1288A 1, *supra*.

[25] *Ibid.*, 1289A 8 πρὸς ἑαυτόν parallels A 9–10 πρὸς τὸν πατέρα καὶ ἡμᾶς. The phrase is unexpected. Of the relations of Word and flesh *to one another* we have heard much, but nowhere else in our analysis has Leontius tried to describe the relations of Word and flesh *to Jesus Christ*. Yet, the phrase πρὸς ἑαυτόν plainly implies that the relation of each part of Jesus Christ to the other part is also the relation of each part to Jesus Christ himself. I ask: can it be that Leontius has let his guard fall for a moment, and given us here a glimpse of the *nous* Jesus Christ of the Christology of Evagrius of Pontus? If the subject Jesus Christ results from the union of Word and flesh not in a third being but *in one another*, to speak of the relations of Word and flesh to Jesus Christ is absurd, for Word and flesh *are* Jesus Christ. However, if Word and flesh are united only in a *third being*, a *nous* called Jesus Christ, then not only will it be possible to speak of the relations of Word and flesh to Jesus Christ, but we can define those relations quite exactly: Word and flesh will be united *to Jesus Christ* in precisely that mode of determination in which they are united *to one another*; for they are united to one another only in Jesus Christ. So the Word will first be united to the *nous* Jesus Christ as hypostasis and distinguished from Jesus Christ as ousia, and only then be joined to the flesh, which also is united to Jesus Christ as hypostasis and distinguished from him as ousia. How else then can Word and flesh be united in Jesus Christ than as hypostases? Or how else can they be distinguished from him than as ousiai? Now this, of course, is just what Leontius says.

If this interpretation is correct, Leontius offers us here a nearly formal statement about the nature of the union with God enjoyed by pure *nous* in its vision of God: the vision of God unites *nous* to Word in a union καθ' ὑπόστασιν. This, of course, is only what we would expect. How so? We need only, as it were, reverse Leontius' argument in *CNE* I: if the *nous* Jesus Christ is united to the Father κατ' οὐσίαν as to a being ὁμοούσιος to the Word, it follows that the *nous* Jesus Christ must be united to the Word himself καθ' ὑπόστασιν.

[26] *Ibid.*, 1289A 7–11.

77

distinguished as ousiai, and if the relation of Jesus Christ to the Father and us is, as Leontius clearly implies, the opposite of the relation of Word to flesh, then it follows that Jesus Christ is united to both Father and us as ousia and distinguished from Father and us as hypostasis.

The intent of the argument here is plain, then. Leontius means to establish that Jesus Christ is joined both to God the Father and to other flesh in a union κατ' οὐσίαν; and this he proves by proving that the relation of Jesus Christ to God the Father and to other flesh is identical with both the relation of God the Father to God the Word and the relation of the flesh of Jesus Christ to ourselves.

b. *The presupposition of the argument*

However, it must be admitted that, as it stands, the argument just described presupposes a proposition which will appear only later in *CNE* 1.7: that is, that in the subject Jesus Christ the Word and flesh which compose him do not lose their identities in a *tertium quid* neither Word nor flesh, but rather remain what they are, preserving what Leontius will soon call their *definitions of being*. Why is this proposition a presupposition of our argument? Simply because the subject Jesus Christ, composed of Word and flesh, is united κατ' οὐσίαν to God the Father only by reason of the persistence of the Word in his mode of nature even in his mode of union to the flesh in Jesus Christ. The Word incarnate in Jesus Christ is and remains ὁμοούσιος τῷ πατρί and so, as it were, bears the subject Jesus Christ, which comprises him, into exactly the same unity with the Father and the Holy Spirit which he himself, the Word, enjoys: a union κατ' οὐσίαν.[27] Nevertheless, that the Word and flesh each pre-

---

[27] This is clearly implied in Leontius' assertion in PG, 86, 1289A 5f., that Jesus Christ is "as a whole, hypostasis in respect to the Father *by reason of [his] godhood,*" that is, the Word, "[together] with [his] manhood, and an hypostasis as a whole in respect to ourselves [together] with [his] godhood *by reason of [his] manhood,*" that is, his flesh. The godhood *by reason of which* Jesus Christ is here distinguished from the Father as hypostasis—and so by implication united to the Father κατ' οὐσίαν—is, of course, the godhood or definition of the divine nature which the Word in Jesus Christ preserves even in his union with his flesh.

I note in passing that *CNE* 1.4 in general and this sentence in particular completely disprove the charge of MRichard, "LéonceJér et LéonceByz,"

serves its definition of being in its union with the other is a proposition tenable only by reason of the analysis of being of *CNE* 1.7. The argument of *CNE* 1.4, then, presupposes the analysis of being in *CNE* 1.7.

3. The ἕνωσις καθ' ὑπόστασιν

So much, then, for the union κατ' οὐσίαν. We pick up Leontius' argument where we left it, and find that the very next line introduces the union καθ' ὑπόστασιν!

We have heard Leontius argue that "the first relation of the syzygies is the same as [the relation of] the third [syzygy or pair as such] to the first [syzygy or pair as such],"[28] and have found therein a union κατ' οὐσίαν. The next line expands the argument to the middle term, the second syzygy. It reads: "and the second [relation of the syzygies"—that is, the relation of the terms of the second

---

MélScRel, I (1944), 60 f., that "dans l'*Adversus Nestorianos et Eutychianos* pas une seule fois [Léonce] ne se demande si la nature humaine du Christ n'était tout de même pas individuelle. Dans l'*Epilysis* [*SolArgSev*], qui est si visiblement une réponse aux critiques soulevées par son premier livre, il est bien obligé d'aborder cette question, de confesser, d'assez mauvaise grâce d'ailleurs, que l'humanité assumée par le Verbe était individuelle et d'expliquer pourquoi cette nature individuelle n'est pas une hypostase au moins relativement au Verbe."

Yet what is it to say that Jesus Christ is "an hypostasis as a whole in respect of ourselves [together] with [his] godhood by reason of his manhood," if not to say that "la nature humaine du Christ" is "individuelle?" But this is only to reiterate the main point of *CNE* 1.4: that in respect both of God the Father *and other flesh*, Jesus Christ is united as ousia *and distinguished as hypostasis*. Therefore, it is by no means "d'assez mauvaise grâce" that Leontius asserts in *SolArgSev*, PG, 86, 1916D 4 ff., that "l'humanité assumée par le Verbe était individuelle." He has said so all along. In *SolArgSev* he is simply repeating that what distinguishes the flesh of Jesus Christ from other flesh is *not the Word to which that flesh is united but rather the essential relations proper to the flesh itself*, just as he has argued earlier, in *CNE* 1.4, that God the Word in Jesus Christ is not distinguished from God the Father and God the Holy Spirit by reason of the flesh which he assumed, but by reason of his own and proper essential relations to Father and Spirit (e.g., 1288B 1–3, with the revisions offered above). In short, as man, Jesus Christ is different from Peter by exactly the same principle in which Peter is different from Paul; and Jesus Christ as Word is different from the Father by exactly the same principle in which the Father is different from the Holy Spirit. A philosopher would say that, for Leontius, each nature comprises the principle by which the beings which participate in it are individuated.

[28] PG, 86, 1288C 7 f.

syzygy—"is the same as the relation of the third syzygy] to the
middle [syzygy]."²⁹ The sense here: just as the second syzygy itself
is united to the third (and first) as hypostasis and distinguished
from them as ousia, so also the terms of the second syzygy are
united as hypostases but distinguished as ousiai. In brief, Word and
flesh are united in a union καθ' ὑπόστασιν.

The argument implied, of course, roughly parallels the argument
for the union κατ' οὐσίαν, but the reader will easily bear that we
reduce it to the final syllogism. Given that the first and third
syzygies are opposed to the mean or second syzygy in the relation
to one another of the terms in each syzygy; given besides that the
relation of terms of the first and third syzygies is that they are
united as ousiai and distinguished as hypostases; then it follows that
the relation of the terms of the second syzygy, that is, of Word
and flesh, is that Word and flesh are *united as hypostases and distinguished as ousiai*—a union καθ' ὑπόστασιν. Precisely the same
conclusion appears in the application of the argument to the paradigm *soul : body*. Here we hear that "soul," that is, the paradigm
of the Word, "is distinguished from its [own] body," that is, the
paradigm of the flesh, "in the difference of nature[s], but is *united
[to its body]* in the definition of hypostasis."³⁰ And though the third
step immediately following concludes an argument meant, as we have
said, to establish that the union of Jesus Christ to the Word is a
union κατ' οὐσίαν, we have already noticed that it mentions the
union καθ' ὑπόστασιν also; that is, in asserting that "[Jesus Christ]
is known as having [one set of] relations to himself by reason of his
[own] parts," the Word and the flesh.³¹

If then the subject Jesus Christ is united to God and other flesh
in a *union* κατ' οὐσίαν, the union of Word and flesh which composes
the subject Jesus Christ is a *union* καθ' ὑπόστασιν. A union καθ' ὑ-
πόστασιν, we may add, which predicates of itself a simultaneous
union κατ'οὐσίαν, and so must comprise the presupposition of the

---

²⁹ *Ibid.*, 1288C 8 f.: δευτέρα δὲ ἀπὸ τῆς μέσης; which demands that we read
[ἡ] δευτέρα δὲ [σχέσις οὕτως ἔχει ὡς ἡ τρίτη συζυγία]—words to be supplied from
C 8 οὕτως ἔχει ὡς ἡ τρίτη [συζυγία] (*supra*, p. 74)—ἀπὸ τῆς μέσης [συζυγίας].
³⁰ *Ibid.*, 1288D 9–11.
³¹ *Ibid.*, 1289A 8 f., commented *supra*, pp. 76–78, with note 25.

union κατ' οὐσίαν: that in their union, Word and flesh yet preserve their definitions of being.[32]

III. Conclusion

Where now do we stand? In the last two Chapters we have taken two steps toward the understanding of Leontius' Christology.

First, from his analysis of being in *CNE* 1.7 we have obtained what we may call his *formal definitions* of ousia and hypostasis: ousia and hypostasis are simultaneous determinations of those rela-

---

[32] With a full account of Leontius' unions κατ' οὐσίαν and καθ' ὑπόστασιν before us, we have wherewithal to reply to the assertion of Marcel Richard that in the second chapter of *SolArgSev* (PG, 86, 1917D 10 ff. and especially 1921A 4–B 4) "nous voyons Léonce l'ermite reconnaître sans raison bien apparente qu'un être peut être distinct à la fois par la nature et par l'hypostase. Cette concession a dû lui coûter, car elle compromettait assez sérieusement une démonstration de son Ier livre" ("Léonce . . . origéniste?" *RevEtByz*, V [1947], 59).

A pity that Richard does not locate that demonstration; for in fact nowhere in *CNE* I or elsewhere does Leontius assert that a being as being *cannot* be "distinct à la fois par la nature et par l'hypostase." Leontius does indeed imply that in any *one* of its modes, e.g., in its mode of nature, a being cannot be distinguished *both* as ousia *and* as hypostasis. Such is surely the sense of the first lines of Leontius' analysis of being in *CNE* 1.7 (PG, 86, 1301D 10–1304A 1): "Now, the definition of [these] unions and distinctions is twofold. *Some* things are united by species but distinguished as hypostases, while *others* are distinguished by species but united as hypostases." However, Leontius' beings need not exist *in one mode only*. They may exist in *two modes*, a mode of nature and a mode of union. Let us posit a being in *both* its modes; e.g., the Word, which in his *mode of union* with the flesh yet preserves his *mode of nature* also. What follows? *Pace* Richard, the Word incarnate in Jesus Christ is indeed distinguished *both* as hypostasis *and* as ousia. *As ousia* the Word is distinguished from the being of different nature with which he has united, and *as hypostasis* he is distinguished from his ὁμοούσια in the Trinity. Which is to say: as ousia, the Word is distinguished in his mode of union, but as hypostasis he is distinguished in his mode of nature.

So *CNE* 1.4. Does *SolArgSev* say otherwise? Not at all, as Richard himself would admit. *SolArgSev*, 1921A 4 ff., reiterates *CNE* 1.4. In *SolArgSev* Leontius argues that ousia and hypostasis *distinguish* (and unite) *in different ways*. When it distinguishes, ousia distinguishes as by τὸ διάφορον (1921A 13 f., B 2–5), but hypostasis as by τὸ κεχωρισμένον (1921A 5 f., B 1–2) or τὸ διῃρημένον (1921A 14). Why is the way in which ousia distinguishes different from the way in which hypostasis distinguishes? Plainly because ousia and hypostasis distinguish the being of which each is predicated from different things. To be sure, *this horse* and *this cow* and *this man* may, as Leontius assumes, be distinguished *both* as hypostases *and* as ousiai (1921A 10–13). This means only that, e.g., *this* horse is distinguished *as ousia* as a member of the

tions of beings which Leontius calls their *essential* relations, that is, the *unions* and *distinctions* of beings. These formal definitions of ousia and hypostasis are given us in the course of an analysis of being which carefully relates the definitions of beings in themselves, that is, in their modes of nature, to the two ways in which the same beings unite with beings of a different nature in their mode of union: in their unions with beings of different natures, some beings preserve the definition of their being, others lose it.

Second, in our account of *CNE* 1.4, we have learned how Leontius applies this analysis of being to the three terms comprising his Christ: Word, flesh, and Jesus Christ himself. In Jesus Christ, we hear, Word and flesh are united as hypostases, that is, in a union καθ' ὑπόστασιν, so that the Christ in whom they are united is united to their ὁμοούσια as ousia, that is, is united κατ' οὐσίαν *both* to Father and Holy Spirit *and* to other flesh. More specifically, we have learned that both Word and flesh are beings of class I (beings united in species but distinguished as hypostases, i.e., beings in their mode of nature); that the Word is also a being of subclass A (simple beings or beings whose existence is identical with their essence), while the flesh is also a being of subclass B (composite beings, the existence of which is *not* identical to their essence); and, finally, that both Word and flesh are beings of subclass 1 (beings which even in their unions preserve their mode of nature, i.e., the defini-

---

genus *horse* from all members of the genus *cow*; a distinction in which *this horse* stands in its mode of union or, so to speak, mode of comparison; while their distinction as hypostases distinguishes this horse *from other horses* and this cow *from other cows*, respectively, that is, in their mode of nature or mode of definition. *SolArgSev* here simply repeats the argument of *CNE* 1.

In short, the argument of *CNE* 1 is completely consistent with that of *SolArgSev* on this point: a being in any *one* of its modes cannot be distinguished *both* as hypostasis *and* ousia, but a being in *two* modes can be distinguished as hypostasis in one mode and as ousia in the other.

Nonetheless, to avoid confusion I note that this conclusion holds only for the beings which compose Jesus Christ, and not for the subject Jesus Christ himself; for Leontius predicates the distinction between mode of nature and mode of union only of Word and flesh, and never of Jesus Christ. As subject, Jesus Christ cannot be distinguished both as hypostasis and as ousia. How could he be distinguished as both? To be sure, he is distinguished as hypostasis from the ὁμοούσια of the Word and flesh which unite in him; yet, how will the subject Jesus Christ be distinguished *as ousia*? For, as Leontius insists, there is no *species*, that is, no *ousia* of Christ (*CNE* 1.5, PG, 86, 1292A 10 f.).

tion of their being). With this we have what we may call the *formal Christology* of Leontius.

Now it may be asked: why are the definitions obtained here called *formal*? The answer is: because they as yet remain distinguished from their proper *matter*. How so? Consider first what we have just called Leontius' *formal Christology*. That Christology teaches us that Jesus Christ comprises three terms: God the Word, his flesh, and Jesus Christ himself. Now, who the Word is and what the flesh is, is as clear as can be; e.g., we have no difficulty whatsoever in locating them in Leontius' analysis of being. But what of the term Jesus Christ? In fact, Leontius has so far offered nothing like an unambiguous definition of the third term of his Christology. So far we have been able to do no better than to speculate that it is identical with the *nous* Jesus of Evagrius of Pontus. However, that speculation is far from proved, not least because it reposes upon the apparent necessity that there exist for Leontius a being who is *not* easily read into his analysis of being, that is, a being of both class A and class B, a being whose existence both *is* and *is not* identical with its essence. Yet, until we can identify the term Jesus Christ with a certain being in Leontius' analysis of being, the Christology defined in part by the term Jesus Christ will necessarily remain *formal*; and *a fortiori* the same holds for what we have called the *formal definitions* of ousia and hypostasis. Alas, form as yet remains distinguished from matter.

Here of course our next mission, for the filling of the forms just described will occupy our next two chapters. In Chapter Four we will learn exactly who is the being Jesus Christ of whom Leontius predicates unions both κατ᾽ οὐσίαν and καθ᾽ ὑπόστασιν. Then, in the light of the conclusions of this chapter, Chapter Five will try to win for the formal definitions of ousia and hypostasis some small part of their proper matter in Christ by describing what Leontius calls an *enhypostasized nature*, a φύσις ἐνυπόστατος.

CHAPTER FOUR

LEONTIUS OF BYZANTIUM AND EVAGRIUS OF PONTUS

The question is: who is the Jesus Christ of Leontius' Christology; and more exactly, where does he stand in Leontius' analysis of being? We have a candidate, we know: the *nous* Jesus Christ of Evagrius of Pontus. To be sure, his claims are not strong. As we have said at the end of the last chapter, he does not easily find a place in Leontius' analysis of being. Nonetheless, his candidacy deserves consideration, and to that consideration we now turn.

Let us begin by asking how we shall proceed to assess the claims of Evagrius' *nous* Jesus. The answer is clear. If we are to win a place for him in Leontius' Christology, but cannot find him in Leontius' analysis of being, then we must find him elsewhere. Besides, wherever else we may find him, the evidence for him there must so clearly attest the *nous* Jesus Christ as Leontius' own Jesus Christ that we are authorized to ignore the silence of the analysis of being concerning him. Now in fact we shall be able to fulfill these requirements. Evagrius' *nous* Jesus will prove to be Leontius' Jesus, too. However, before we turn to the proof itself, we offer two prologues, the first describing the evidence that assures us that Leontius knew and admired Evagrius, the second describing the Evagrius whom Leontius knew.

I. Two Prologues

A. *The First Prologue*: *Evagrius in Leontius*

It seems to have been Leontius himself who first gave reason to believe that he was a disciple of Evagrius of Pontus, for in *CNE* 1.3 he interrupts an exposition of the true function of the soul's faculties to comment: "Indeed it was well said by a certain divinely wise man from those [gone] before us [that there is] one desire [which is] good and eternal, the [desire] which strives for the true gnosis"[1]—a nearly literal quotation of a sentence from Evagrius' *Kephalaia gnostica*,[2] which with Leontius' all too complimentary notice of the author is reason enough to ask: just how did Leontius stand to Evagrius?

From Leontius' own centuries we have, it seems, two answers.

The first answer is that of *an unknown scholiast* to the manuscript tradition. To this scholiast we owe a scholium to the passage just quoted. The scholium identifies the man of whom Leontius speaks: περὶ εὐαγρίου.[3] The same scholiast is almost certainly the author of a second scholium too; this to the passage in *CNE* I *prol*, in which Leontius first calls his Nestorians and Eutychians ἐναντιοδοκῆται Writes Leontius: "a pious and divine man named them well, when he called both of them ἐναντιοδοκῆται;"[4] and just how much Leontius feels himself in the debt of his anonymous friend, he will show in his title to *CNE* I: τῆς ... ἐναντίας δοκήσεως, etc.[5] Who is that friend? Replies the scholiast: περὶ τοῦ αββᾶ νόννου φησί.[6] And who is Nonnus? No doubt of it.[7] Nonnus is the spiritual leader of the Origenist monks in Palestine of whom Cyril of Scythopolis[8] tells

---

[1] PG, 86, 1285A 14–B 1: καὶ καλῶς εἴρηταί τινι τῶν πρὸ ἡμῶν ἀνδρὶ θεοσό-φῳ, εἰς πόθος ἀγαθὸς καὶ αἰώνιος, ὁ τῆς ἀληθοῦς γνώσεως ἐφιέμενος. *Apparatus*, adducing VOG: τινι τῶν πρὸ ἡμῶν *om.* O.

[2] EvagPont, *KephGn*, 4.50, the Greek of which is known only from Leontius. Leontius' quotation here seems to follow exactly the bowdlerized Syriac translation S1. The more accurate S2 adds, in A. Guillaumont's translation: "et on dit qu'il est inséparable du *nous*."

[3] *Apparatus*, adducing VOG: περὶ ευαγρίου V εὐαγρίου *sed manu recentiori et in operibus Leontii unica* G *om.* O. I speculate that the scholium of G was posted to it from V.

[4] PG, 86, 1273C 9–1276A 2: καλῶς γὰρ αὐτοὺς εὐλαβὴς καὶ θεῖος ἀνὴρ οὕτω κέκληκεν, ἐναντιοδοκήτας ἑκατέρους καλέσας....

[5] *CNE prol, ibid.*, 1269B 8–10, discussed in our Chapter One, *supra*, p. 10.

[6] *Ad* PG, 86, 1273C 9–1276A 1 *scholium in margine* περὶ τοῦ αββᾶ νόννου φησί VG *sed manu recentiori* G *om.* O.

[7] This in spite of the objection of WRügamer, *LeontByz*, 62 f., that "Nonnus ein ebenso wie Leontius unter den palästinensischen Mönchen öfters vorkommender Name ist." The links between Leontius and Nonnus about to be described identify Nonnus quite positively.

[8] Cyril of Scythopolis (*ca.* 523-*ca.* 558), a younger contemporary of Leontius, was a Palestinian monk who wrote the lives of the saints who established and led the monasteries of Palestine in the fifth and sixth centuries: e.g., Euthymius and Sabas. Cyril himself worked vigorously for the Orthodox side in the Origenist controversy in Palestine and incorporated much of the

us in his *Vita Sabae* and *Vita Cyriaci*:[9] Nonnus, twice called the advocate of the doctrine of Evagrius![10]

Of the sense and intent of the scholiast there can be little question. He is telling us that the theologian Leontius is an Origenist;[11] for who but an Origenist would quote Evagrius of Pontus as "a certain divinely wise man," or describe Evagrius' disciple Nonnus as a "pious and divine man," much less emphasize that he has borrowed his argument from Nonnus?[12]

With his mention of Nonnus, the scholiast in effect introduces us to a second witness to Leontius' Origenism: Cyril of Scythopolis. Nonnus is by no means the only Origenist named by Cyril. He reports besides that Nonnus' chief lieutenant in the controversies in Palestine was *a certain monk Leontius*[13] who, says Cyril, also shared the doctrines of Evagrius.[14] A mere coincidence, now, that the theologian Leontius accused by the scholiast of being an Origenist should bear the same name as Nonnus' chief disciple in the account of Cyril of Scythopolis? Hardly, and all the less so as the theologian Leontius will be found harboring the Christology of Evagrius. The scholiast doubtless knew—or at very least believed—that the theologian Leontius was himself the disciple of Nonnus; and if he is to be trusted, we may safely identify the theologian Leontius with the Leontius of

---

story in his life of Sabas, on which see the note immediately below. Among the *bêtes noires* of this piece is a certain Origenist monk Leontius of Byzantium.

[9] For complete references, see ESchwartz, *KyrSkyth*, 274 f., *s. v.* Nόννος. Schwartz's work embraces both an edition of the text of Cyril's lives of the saints and a long historical essay. In what follows, the pagination after citations of Cyril's work (CyrScyth, *VSabae*, *VCyriaci*, etc.), is, of course, that of the edition of Schwartz.

[10] CyrScyth, *VSabae*, p. 124, ll. 25–29; *VCyriaci*, p. 230, l. 26 f., which refer to p. 229, l. 7 ff.

[11] So also MRichard, "Léonce ... origéniste?" *RevEtByz*, V (1947), 34.

[12] That is, the argument that the Nestorians and Eutychians partake of a single error, a δόκησις conceived in opposite ways; whence they are ἐναντιο-δοκῆται.

[13] CyrScyth, *VCyriaci*, p. 230, l. 29 f.: [Νόννος ...] Λεόντιον τὸν Βυζάντιον ὑπουργὸν ἔχων καὶ ὑπέρμαχον καὶ συναγωνιστήν. It is Leontius who leads the assault of the Origenist monks of the New Laura upon the Grand Laura (*VSabae*, p. 190, ll. 7–29). Indeed, Leontius seems to have entered the New Laura as a disciple or perhaps an associate of Nonnus (*ibid.*, p. 176, ll. 12–15).

[14] CyrScyth, *VCyriaci*, p. 230, l. 29 f., to be read with p. 229, ll. 7 ff. and especially p. 230, ll. 11–14.

the *Vita Sabae* and the *Vita Cyriaci*. With this, of course, we have in Cyril of Scythopolis as it were a second witness that the theologian Leontius was an Origenist.

Here an objection. May not the scholiast simply be copying Cyril? Not likely. About Nonnus' stand in the christological controversies, Cyril offers no single hint; indeed, says no more of Nonnus' disciples Leontius, Domitianus, and Theodore Askidas than that they pretended to support the faith of the Council of Chalcedon.[15] The scholiast, on the other hand, knows that Nonnus called the Nestorians and Eutychians ἐναντιοδοκῆται; whence it follows that he taps a source other than Cyril. We add: a source so well-informed on at least certain points of Nonnus' thought that we can only suppose him to be Nonnus' contemporary.[16] The scholiast therefore is himself or reproduces an independent witness that Nonnus and Leontius were Origenists and disciples of Evagrius.

May we not then simply take it for granted that Leontius is an Origenist? Not, it seems, if we are to demonstrate that generous regard for the opinions of one's elders and betters so admired in young scholars; for, in fact, the relatively unambiguous evidence just adduced has made very much less headway among modern students of Leontius than might be expected. The reasons are not far to seek. It is only recently that the full scope of the thought of Evagrius of Pontus has been revealed;[17] and even Leontius has been taken either as a later interpreter of Cyril of Alexandria,[18] or a "Vermittlungstheologe,"[19] or an Origenizing intellectual counter-

---

[15] On Leontius, CyrScyth, *VSabae*, p. 176, l. 15 f.; on Domitianus and Theodore, *ibid.*, p. 188, l. 28-p. 189, l. 1.

[16] So also MRichard, "Léonce ... origéniste?" *RevEtByz*, V (1947), 34.

[17] That is, in A. Guillaumont's publication in 1958 of the full and unexpurgated Syriac translation of *KephGn* (EvagPont, *KephGn*), which he calls S2 (*supra*, Chap. Three, note 18). Earlier, in 1947, MRichard, "Léonce... origéniste?" *RevEtByz*, V (1947), 35, could reduce the Origenistic controversy of the sixth century to "des luttes autour d'une bibliothèque. Ce que l'on reprochait aux origénistes, c'étaient d'abord leurs lectures." So defined, of course, Origenism could hardly be identified, much less described.

[18] E.g., FLoofs, *LeontByz*, 71: " ... unser Verf[asser] vertritt eine möglichst zur alexandrinische Theologie zurücklenkende Orthodoxie. Das ist der bleibende Eindruck, den all seine Ausführungen hinterlassen." Most recently Werner Elert, *Der Ausgang der altkirchlichen Christologie* (Berlin, 1957), 61–64, *passim*, has said the same.

[19] JPJunglas, *LeontByz*, 148: "Leontius ist Vermittlungstheologe, der cyrillische und antiochenische Anschauungen in sich aufgenommen hat."

feiter, whose attack on Monophysites and Nestorians in *CNE* 1 is at bottom no more than "un trompe-l'oeil," a facade, merely "le cadre obligatoire de tout exposé christologique," which he has therefore "adopté tout naturellement."[20] Now, however, we are better advised. Evagrius has been rescued from the shadows, and Leontius stands revealed as a theologian of formidable gifts and clear and distinct opinions. Time now to turn to Evagrius himself and, afterward, to show in the rest of this Chapter that Leontius' Christology conforms to that of Evagrius not only, as it were, in its axioms, but also in its corollaries; in short, that the charge of Cyril of Scythopolis and the scholiast is in all points just and proper.

B. *The Second Prologue*:
The Heilsgeschichte of Evagrius of Pontus

For Evagrius, the history of salvation may be described as having three phases. We consider them in order.[21]

[20] MRichard, "Léonce ... origéniste?" *RevEtByz*, V (1947), 55. On p. 35 Richard notes besides that "il est bien exact qu'il n'y a guère à attendre, pour le sujet qui nous occupe"—that is, the Origenism of Leontius—"d'une étude doctrinale des traités de Léonce"—a judgement which the pages following will prove quite untenable.

[21] The following account of the *Heilsgeschichte* of Evagrius of Pontus generally depends upon AGuillaumont, *KephGn*, 15-170 ("Introduction: les *Kephalaia Gnostica* d' Évagre le Pontique" [pp. 15-43], and "Première Partie: Évagre et les controverses origénistes chez les Grecs" [pp. 45-170]). Guillaumont bases his analysis upon a newly discovered Syriac translation of the *Kephalaia Gnostica* (S 2). In 1958 he produced an edition of this translation together with a more critical edition of an earlier Syriac translation (S1) which had been edited in 1912 by Wilhelm Frankenberg: see WFrankenberg, *EuagPont*, 48-422. Hereafter we cite them only as EvagPont, *KephGn*, S1 or S2. In his monograph of 1962, Guillaumont summarizes the conclusions of his earlier studies on the text of the *KephGn*: the translator of S1 (Wilhelm Frankenberg's text) had, says Guillaumont, purged the original of its Origenism; it is the slightly later S2 which preserves Evagrius' own thought (AGuillaumont, *KephGn*, 22-31 ["Le texte"]. Beside the works which Guillaumont notices here, see Antoine and Claire Guillaumont, "Évagre le Pontique," *Dictionnaire de spiritualité ascétique et mystique*, eds. M. Viller et al., IV [Paris, 1961], 1734-1744). In short, Guillaumont's monograph adduces new evidence proving that Evagrius was even more radical an Origenist than previously supposed; and so his work virtually supersedes earlier descriptions of Evagrius. For an excellent survey of the state of the literature before the Guillaumonts' work, see Johannes Quasten, *Patrology*, III (Westminster, Maryland, 1960), 169-176. In what follows, then, we follow Antoine Guillaumont, although our argument will often carry us into rather greater detail than he offers.

LEONTIUS AND EVAGRIUS

1. Phase I: The First Creation

In the beginning, before God made the visible world, there were only God and the intellects or *noes*.

a. *God the Trinity*

For Evagrius, God is, of course, the Trinity: Father, Son, and Holy Spirit. Just as Athanasius and the three Cappadocians describe him, God is three persons in one nature; and Evagrius emphasizes that he is one not in number but in nature.[22]

b. *The intellects*

With God is his first creation, a world of eternal[23] and incorporeal[24] intellects, created for the knowledge of God.[25] These intellects Evagrius also calls *logikoi*, "la nature raisonnable,"[26] "all

[22] EvagPont *sub* BasMag, *ep* 8.2, in SBasile, *Lettres*, I (1957), 23–25. See especially l. 19 f. on p. 24. Basil's *ep* 8 is almost certainly by Evagrius of Pontus. See Robert Melcher, *Der 8. Brief des hl. Basilius, ein Werk des Evagrius Pontikus*, Münsterische Beiträge zur Theologie, eds. Franz Diekamp and Richard Stapper, Heft 1 (Münster in Westphalia, 1923).

[23] EvagPont, *KephGn*, 3.33 (S2; no Greek), referring to I Cor. 15:53 f.: "Le nom d' 'immortalité' fait connaître l'unité naturelle du *nous*, et *le fait qu'il est éternel* [fait connaître] son 'incorruptibilité'" (emphasis mine).

[24] Evagrius explicitly says that the *nous* as such is incorporeal: *ibid.*, 1.74 (S2; no Greek): "La lumière du *nous* se divise en trois, à savoir: en la science de la Trinité adorable et sainte, en *la nature incorporelle* qui a été créée par elle, et en la contemplation des êtres" (italics mine). Compare 3.13 (S2; no Greek): "... le *nous* incorporel voit la Trinité sainte en ceux qui ne sont pas des corps." Hence Evagrius says in 1.46 (S2; no Greek) that "le *nous* est délivré de la forme et de la matière," and implies in 2.11 (S2; no Greek) that *nous* is not "constitué des quatre éléments." We shall learn besides that for Evagrius the salvation of a *nous* inhabiting a body is the abolition of that body. See, for example, 2.62 (S2; no Greek): "Quand les *noes* auront reçu la contemplation qui les concerne, alors aussi toute la nature des corps sera enlevée, et ainsi la contemplation qui la concerne deviendra immatérielle."

[25] *Ibid.*, 1.50 (S2; no Greek): "Tout ce qui a été produit a été produit pour la science de Dieu...." So also 1.89 (S2; no Greek): "Toute la nature raisonnable"—that is, of the intellects—"a été naturellement faite pour être, et pour être connaissante, et Dieu est la science essentielle."

[26] A brief study of the occurrences of the words *raisonnable* (adjective) and *logikoi* (substantive) in Guillaumont's translation of the *KephGn* (*N. B.*: a translation into French of a Syriac translation from the Greek) establishes two points. First, with perhaps two exceptions, Evagrius uses these terms

the rational creation,"[27] and "the rational creatures."[28] It is because they are incorporeal that Evagrius calls them the *first* creation, for the *second* creation will be the creation of bodies proper to intellects which have fallen from God.[29]

That *nous* is creature distinguishes it from God in its very being. "L'incréé," Evagrius says of God, "est celui à qui, *parce qu'il est par son essence*, il n'y a rien qui soit antérieur;"[30] whence it follows that because the *nous* does indeed have something anterior to him, the *nous* does *not* exist by reason of its essence. This same difference Evagrius clearly identifies with the difference between beings which *are* and *are not* susceptible of opposition; to which indeed he lends the emphasis of the first sentence of his first century. "Au Bien premier," he says, "il n'est pas d'opposé, parce que c'est dans son essence qu'il est le Bien, et qu'à l'essence il n'est rien qui soit opposé;"[31] adding in the very next sentence that "l'opposition est dans les qualités, et les qualités sont dans les corps; l'opposition donc est

---

only of the intellects. Second, he uses them of three distinct sets of intellects: *first*, of the intellects in their pristine unity with God (2.80, 3.22, 4.1, 4.58, 6.20, 6.75, all *logikoi*, and 6.85, "la nature raisonnable;" plus all mentions of "la science qui concerne les *logikoi*" in 2.2, 2.4, 2.17, *passim*); *second*, of the intellects after their fall from unity with God and their assignment to bodies as angels, human souls, or demons (1.13, 2.76, 3.7, *passim*, of *all* orders of fallen *noes*; plus all mentions of "l'âme raisonnable" in 1.37, 1.59, 1.67, *passim*); and *third*, of all intellects whatsoever, whether fallen or unfallen (1.3, 1.63, 1.64, *passim*).

[27] EvagPont *sub* BasMag, *ep* 8.2, in SBasile, *Lettres*, I, 25, l. 51: πᾶσα ἡ λογικὴ κτίσις. That Evagrius means by this the world of intellects is beyond all reasonable doubt.

[28] EvagPont *sub* BasMag, *ep* 8.9, in SBasile, *Lettres*, I, 33, l. 5: ἕκαστον τῶν λογικῶν κτισμάτων.

[29] EvagPont, *KephGn*, 4.58 (S2; no Greek): "Dieu, quand il créa les *logikoi*, n'était en rien; mais quand il crée la nature corporelle et les mondes qui en proviennent, il est dans son Christ." Compare 6.20 (S2; no Greek): "Avant le mouvement"—that is, the fall—"Dieu était ... créateur des incorporels ...; après le mouvement, il est devenu créateur des corps ...."

[30] *Ibid.*, 6.5 (S1 and S2; no Greek; italics mine). "L'incréé" cannot be the *noes*, for in 4.58 (S2; no Greek) Evagrius expressly asserts that "Dieu ... créa les *logikoi*." Even of the *nous* Jesus Christ he says that "c'est *avec sa genèse*, en effet, que le Verbe Dieu aussi a résidé en lui" (6.18 [S2; no Greek]; italics mine). To be sure, such a *genèse* has not been preceded by a *destruction* (6.9 [S2; no Greek]); but that is not to say that "il n'y a rien qui soit antérieur" to it (6.5).

[31] *Ibid.*, 1.1 (S1 and S2). For the Greek see JMuyldermans, *Evagriana* (not available to me).

dans les créatures."[32] That "les qualités sont dans les corps" seems nevertheless not intended to mean that the *incorporeal noes* are incapable of such an opposition, for Evagrius at once assures us that "tout ce qui a été produit, ou bien est susceptible d'une opposition"—he is referring to the intellects—"ou bien a été constitué d'une opposition"[33]—words clearly defining the body. It is plainly because of their susceptibility to opposition that the intellects cannot be said to exist by reason of their essence.

The translation of Evagrius' words here is beyond doubt. God exists by reason of his essence, and so in him existence and essence are one. The intellects may indeed possess their existence and essence as one in their *unité* with God; and yet, even in that *unité*, they possess what Evagrius will call a susceptibility or *receptivité* allowing them to fall from that *unité*; for they are "susceptible d'une opposition." Their essence may be, but is not *as such*, identical with their existence.

So much then for God and the intellects in their pristine and proper state.

2. Phase II: The Second Creation

a. *The Fall*

The contemplation of God which the intellects of the first creation enjoyed, demanded a spiritual concentration on their part in which they did not in fact persist; and so it was that all but one fell from their original and immobile state into a "mouvement." This fall, Evagrius emphasizes, cannot be attributed to the God with whom they had hitherto been united, but is the fault of the intellects themselves. We have already heard his explanation: "Ce n'est pas l'Unité qui, à part soi, se met en mouvement; mais elle est mise en mouvement par la réceptivité du *nous*, lequel, par sa négligence,

---

[32] EvagPont, *KephGn*, 1.2 (S1 and S2). For the Greek, JMuyldermans, *Evagriana*.
[33] EvagPont, *KephGn*, 1.4 (S1 and S2). For the Greek, JMuyldermans, *Evagriana*. Compare 1.64 (S2; for the Greek, JMuyldermans, *Evagriana*): "Toute nature raisonnable, en effet, est susceptible d'une opposition." See also 5.62, to be mentioned shortly.

détourne d'elle son visage et, par le fait d'être privé d'elle, engendre l'ignorance," that is, becomes soul of a body.[34] Hence Evagrius can also call this movement "le mouvement de la liberté."[35]

b. *The oikonomia of God*

All intellects but one fell, as we have said; and the single *nous* who did not fall but remained in union with God[36] is the *nous*[37] who in the body which he was later to assume is called Jesus Christ. It was through this *nous* Jesus Christ that God set about restoring Christ's brothers to their original blessedness. This *oikonomia* of God advanced in two steps: the creation of the visible order and the incarnation of the *nous* Jesus Christ.

(1) The second creation: intellect transformed

In their negligence, the *noes* had fallen from that vision of God proper to them, and so were utterly estranged from him. The first step in their rehabilitation was therefore to provide them with a new and different object of contemplation, by means of which they might, as it were, reascend to God. This new object of contemplation was the visible world, the *second creation*. A passage in Evagrius' apology to his friends in Caesarea puts it very sharply: "Mais parce que notre esprit, qui était devenu épais, a été attaché à la terre, qu'il est mêlé à la boue, et qu'il est incapable de se fixer sur une contemplation directe, pour cette raison, conduit comme par la main par les

---

[34] EvagPont, *KephGn*, 1.49 (S2; no Greek). Compare 3.22 (S2; no Greek): "Le mouvement premier des *logikoi* est la séparation du *nous* d'avec l'Unité qui est en lui," commented in 3.27 (S2; no Greek) immediately below. See also 3.28 (S2; no Greek): "L'âme est le *nous* qui, par négligence, est tombé de l'Unité et qui, *par suite de sa nonvigilance*, est descendu au rang de la *praktiké*" (italics mine).

[35] *Ibid.*, 6.75 (S2; no Greek).

[36] E.g., *ibid.*, 1.77 (S2; no Greek): "et le *nous* est le Christ, *qui est uni à la science de l'Unité*" (italics mine). Compare 3.1 and 3.2 (S2; no Greek).

[37] Hence, *ibid.*, 2.2 (S2; no Greek), Evagrius says that "*dans la science qui concerne les logikoi*, nous avons été instruits au sujet de sa [Jesus Christ's] substance" (italics mine); and again in 2.22 (S2; no Greek) asserts that "la nature raisonnable (fait connaître) celle du Christ." The *logikoi* and "la nature raisonnable," of course, are the *noes*. See also 1.77, quoted *supra*, note 36.

beautés parentes de son corps, il considère les activités du Créateur, et dès maintenant il apprend à connaître ces causes à leurs effets, afin que, s'étant ainsi accru peu à peu, il ait un jour la force de s'approcher de la divinité elle-même, toute nue."[38] This new world God created in and through Jesus Christ: "Dieu, quand il créa les *logikoi*," that is, the first creation, "n'était en rien; mais quand il crée la nature corporelle et les mondes qui en proviennent," that is, the second creation, "il est dans son Christ."[39]

The second creation introduces us to Evagrius' doctrine of the human soul: soul is *nous* in its fallen state, or more exactly still, *nous* in the body by means of which its fallen state is to be repaired. "L'âme est le *nous* qui, par négligence, est tombé de l'Unité et qui, par suite de sa non-vigilance, est descendu au rang de la *praktiké*,"[40] where *praktiké* designates the life of a *nous* in a non-spiritual body.[41]

---

[38] EvagPont *sub* BasMag, *ep* 8.7, in SBasile, *Lettres*, I, 30–31, ll. 37–44. I borrow the translation of Yves Courtonne *in loc.* EvagPont, *KephGn*, 4.62 (S2; no Greek), is equally emphatic: "Il est nécessaire au *nous* d'être instruit soit sur les incorporels, soit sur les corps, ou bien de voir simplement les objects: c'est là, en effet, sa vie. Mais il ne verra pas les incorporels, quand il sera souillé dans sa volonté, ni les corps, quand il sera privé de l'*organon* qui lui montre les choses sensibles. Que donneront donc à l'âme morte, pour la contemplation, ceux qui méprisent le Créateur et calomnient aussi notre corps-ci?" On the providential uses of the body, see besides *ibid.*, 4.60, 4.76, 4.83, and 4.85. I note in passing that these sentences more than suffice to refute the charge of the first anathema of Justinian, *Edictum contra Origenem* (543), in *ACO*, III (Berlin, 1940), p. 213, l. 15f., that the Origenists believed that the fallen *noes* were united to bodies as punishment, τιμωρίας χάριν—unless τιμωρία here means help or succour, or unless Justinian has another Origenist than Evagrius in mind.

[39] EvagPont, *KephGn*, 4.58 (S2; no Greek). Compare 2.2, 3.6—to which compare 3.11—and 3.9. In 4.57, Evagrius argues that his miracles prove Jesus Christ to be creator. Note, however, that 5.81 establishes that *any* "*nous* nu" might be creator, for as "*nous* nu" it possesses "la science essentielle" and so is called God.

[40] *Ibid.*, 3.28 (S2; no Greek).

[41] Properly speaking, Evagrius' *praktiké* is the first of three stages of the reascent of the Christian to God: in *praktiké*, the soul overcomes the passions of the body by means of the virtues. See, e.g., in PG, 40, EvagPont, *CapPrac*, 1 (1221D 1–3), 50 (1233A 15–B 1), 53 (1233B 11–C 11), 59 (1236A 4–8). By extension, however, Evagrius uses the term to distinguish the life of men, that is, of *noes* in material, non-spiritual bodies, from the life of angels. Hence, he contrasts "le corps *praktikon*" to "le corps spirituel" in *KephGn*, 1.11 and 3.45, to which compare 1.13 and 3.48. The soul inhabiting such a body is therefore "l'âme *praktiké* (2.6, 2.46) or "l'âme du *praktikos*" (4.63). More on *praktiké infra*.

(2) Redemption: the incarnation of the *nous* Jesus Christ.

The second step in the restoration of the fallen intellects is the appearance among them of Jesus Christ. We ask who he is and what he does.

First, who he is. Properly speaking, Jesus Christ is the one unfallen *nous*, who by the grace of God has taken flesh while yet remaining in that essential union with God proper to *"nous* nu."[42] This flesh he takes, as we shall see, in order to reveal God, and not because he himself has fallen as his brothers have fallen. In his union with God, the *nous* Jesus Christ is unique, and so Evagrius can introduce sentences describing him with the formula "Il y en a un qui ...":[43] "Il y en a un seul qui est adorable, celui qui uniquement a l'Unique."[44] Jesus is unique also in this, that he alone of all intellects has been united both to God and to flesh at the same time.

Now what does this *nous* Jesus Christ do for us? What is his mission, or, in traditional terms, what is his work?

Here a *caveat* is in order. We will find in Evagrius only the faintest traces of the traditional doctrine of the work of Christ, that is, the atonement.[45] Evagrius never emphasizes, as, *exempli gratia*, Athanasius, that in Jesus Christ the Word assumes flesh in order that he may suffer in it and so take our sins upon himself.[46] The reason why is not far to seek. The goal of the atonement taught by Athanasius is the immortality and incorruptibility of the body in its resurrection.[47] Not so Evagrius. Of immortality and incorruptibility he speaks indeed, but not of an immortality of the body. Evagrius speaks of the immortality proper to an essentially incorporeal *nous*.[48] The traditional doctrine of the atonement is not that of Evagrius.

[42] E.g., EvagPont, *KephGn*, 1.77, 3.1, and 3.2 (all S2; no Greek), cited *supra*, p. 91, with notes 36 and 37.

[43] E.g., *ibid.*, 2.24, 2.37, 2.41, 2.43, 2.53.

[44] *Ibid.*, 2.53 (S1 and S2; no Greek).

[45] E.g., *ibid.*, 1.90 (S1 and S2; no Greek).

[46] E.g., Athanasius, *De incarnatione* [*verbi dei*], 8.4 (ed. F. L. Cross, Texts for Students, No. 50 [London, 1939], p. 12, l. 31-p. 13, l. 13).

[47] *Ibid.*

[48] E.g., EvagPont, *KephGn*, 1.58, 1.64, and especially 3.33 (S2; no Greek): "Le nom d' 'immortalité' fait connaître l'unité naturelle du *nous*; et le fait qu'il est éternel (fait connaître) son 'incorruptibilité'. Le premier

Then what is the work of Evagrius' Jesus Christ? Here the ground is rough and unexplored; but just for that reason an hypothesis will be all the more useful.[49] The mission of Evagrius' Jesus, I suggest, is to reveal the true purpose and sense of the visible creation: not only why God made it in the beginning, nor only to what end God is directing it now, but above all the path through it which the fallen *nous* must follow if he wishes to attain final blessedness. We have noticed above that God made the visible creation through Jesus Christ as a sort of temporal ladder by which fallen intellects might reascend to their original dignity—a ladder, we shall see, which they joyously abandon once it has brought them to their goal. However, the purpose of the creation is not unambiguously manifest to all. In its flesh, the fallen intellect cannot even be trusted to know its own nature, much less to recognize the perversion of it. Nor again does the world itself declare its end so clearly that its inhabitants can see and embrace it without hesitation. By no means! Therefore it is necessary that God himself declare the sense of it all through just that power by whom he made the world at first: the *nous* Jesus. Therefore, "l'héritier du Christ est celui qui connaît les intellections de tous les êtres postérieurs au premier jugement"[50]—that is, the first judgement after the fall, after which the first world was made— and so again "'le cohéritier du Christ' est celui qui arrive dans l'Unité"—that is, the henad of the intellects—"et se délecte de la contemplation avec le Christ."[51] The work of Jesus Christ is the revelation of the order of the world made by God in order to save us, and the true heirs of Jesus Christ are those whose use it as it was meant to be used.

Now, how does Jesus Christ reveal the purpose of the world? First, we must notice a presupposition of Evagrius' doctrine of Christ: that the terms *intellect* (νοῦς), *soul* (ψυχή), and *body* (σῶμα) not only designate what we may call the parts of the human being but also

---

nom, la science de la Trinité l'accompagne; et le second, la contemplation première de la nature."

[49] The following paragraphs are my own free exegesis of Evagrius' doctrine of *contemplation*, or more precisely, *contemplations*. Consequently, I dispense with detailed documentation, and that with all the better conscience because we will make little use of this section in what follows.

[50] EvagPont, *KephGn*, 4.4 (S2; no Greek).

[51] *Ibid.*, 4.8 (S1 and S2; no Greek).

represent moments of the ascent to the knowledge of God; indeed, moments of the knowledge of God itself. So, in the *locus classicus* for this doctrine, his letter to Melania, Evagrius can call *nous* the *body* of the Word and Holy Spirit as revealing Word and Spirit in its actions, and Word and Spirit in turn, the *soul* of the Father as revealing the Father in their actions.[52] With this, the mission of the *nous* Jesus Christ in the flesh can be fully explained. Plainly, the incarnation simply extends the system of revelation into the visible world inhabited by fallen intellects: the body of Jesus Christ reveals the soul of Jesus; the soul reveals its *nous*—Jesus himself; the *nous* Jesus reveals the Word; and the Word reveals the Father. The system extends as far as the body for the best of all possible reasons: taken from one of us and visible to all of us, the body of Jesus Christ reveals the true purpose and sense of the creation even to the worst of sinners among us, those who see not with the eyes of the spirit but with the eyes of the flesh alone. For these, Jesus' birth from a virgin, the miracles of his ministry, his cross, and his resurrection all serve to establish the authority of the way of transformation which he taught: the opening of the eyes of the spirit in the contemplation of the visible creation and the subsequent ascent of the soul to God by the ladder of contemplations. However, Jesus teaches too that our ascent is not an ascent of contemplation alone, but one of transformation also; for the progress in contemplation of each being is rewarded in an ascending series of worlds by a series of new and ever purer bodies. The proof? Jesus' own transformations, not only in his transfiguration but also, indeed chiefly, in his resurrection.[53] In short, in and by his flesh, the *nous* Jesus Christ summons all men, in each of whom lies hidden a *nous* exactly like Jesus, to imitate the life and death of his flesh, and so to attain the honor and glory to which they lead—an honor and glory precisely identical with that of Christ. For in the end, as we shall see, every difference between ourselves and Jesus Christ will be obliterated.

[52] E.g., EvagPont, *ep. ad Melaniam*, in WFrankenberg, *EuagPont*, p. 615, l. 38-p. 617, l. 1. Compare EvagPont, *KephGn*, 2.5 (S2; no Greek): "Le corps de ce qui est est la contemplation des êtres, et l'âme de ce qui est est la science de l'Unité. Celui qui connaît l'âme est appelé âme de ce qui est, et ceux qui connaissent le corps sont nommés corps de cette âme."
[53] E.g., EvagPont, *KephGn*, 1.90 (S2; no Greek).

3. Phase III: ἀποκατάστασις

We ask next: just what is this way of transformation? We begin as what we are, sinful intellects fallen from our pristine communion with God. We come to the end of the way as *"noes* nus," pure intellects utterly devoid of material bodies and so once again possessed of the vision of God. This end is the ἀποκατάστασις. The journey advances through three stages.

a. *The present world: the Christian life*

The Christian of the present world is bound to a body which strictly defines and limits the reascent to God demanded of him. These limits, however, are neither arbitrary nor unjust, for the nature of the body which each *nous* has received from this world is perfectly conformed to the sin in which he first fell from the vision of God before the worlds were made. Therefore, the tasks and trials which his body sets him are precisely the tasks and trials with which he must begin the long and arduous purification of his *nous*.

How does the Christian undertake this purification? We know, first, that the Christian consists of *nous*, soul, and body, and, besides, that each of these is a revelation of the one just above it: "Le *nous* enseigne l'âme, et l'âme le corps ...."[54] His purification, then demands a stage corresponding to each of the three. First, the Christian must purify his body, that is, master its passions. With mastery of the body, he attains ἀρετή or virtue. Next, he must master the passions of the soul, including the *nous*. With this he attains ἀπάθεια. The mastery of his passions both somatic and psychic so purifies his intellect that he is able to see the *logoi* of the cosmos, i.e., recognize the cosmos for what it is, a *Heilsanstalt*, a ladder of contemplations leading to the vision of God. With this he

---

[54] *Ibid.*, 2.56 (S2; no Greek). The sentence ends: "et seul 'l'homme de Dieu' connaît l'homme de science." In a note to this sentence, Guillaumont adduces Deuteronomy 33:1: "This is the blessing with which Moses *the man of God* blessed the children of Israel before his death." However, neither here nor in his monograph does Guillaumont attempt to explain the connection. I suppose that "l'homme de science" is he who himself *"enseigne le nous,"* that is, Jesus Christ. "L'homme de Dieu," then, will be the one who prophesied Jesus Christ, that is, Moses.

is ready for the last stage: the proper work of the *nous*, the vision of God itself. These three stages Evagrius calls πρακτική, φυσική, and θεωρητική: the first, πρακτική, by reason of the πράξεις required to beat down the passions of the body; the second, φυσική, by reason of the contemplation of the order of nature which attends it; the last, θεωρητική, by reason of the θεωρία or vision of God which defines it. In all this, however, there is no ecstasy properly so called, for even in the vision of God the Christian is not swept up into another order of being but remains both what and where he is.

b. *The succession of worlds to come*

For Evagrius, we say, there is no true ecstasy, but add at once: for Evagrius, this is not to say that the virtue or evil of the soul does not work a transformation of its very being; only that such a transformation will not be completed in *this* world. Indeed, there lies before the soul the possibility of a long, though not infinite, series of worlds, each preceded by a *judgement* and a new *creation*: a judgement in which Jesus Christ destroys the old world and assays the ascent or descent of the *noes* inhabiting it; then a creation in which Jesus Christ gives each intellect the body which its conduct in the previous world deserves. Evagrius resolves ecstasy into eschatology.

c. *The end of the worlds and the restoration of the intellects*

The weary *nous* may nonetheless hope for peace at the last. The series of new creations is not infinite, but has an end. The series of judgements concludes with a *last judgement*, after which all worlds vanish and there remain only the monad, God the Trinity, and the henad, the whole reconstituted set of intellects, now again united to the Father through the Son and in the Holy Spirit. Among these *noes*, of course, is the *nous* Jesus Christ, with whom now all *noes* are equal. But then was not this the whole purpose of the work of Jesus Christ?

So the *Heilsgeschichte* of Evagrius.

LEONTIUS AND EVAGRIUS

II. THE PROOF

In the two prologues just finished we have established that Leontius knew and admired Evagrius, and described the Evagrius whom Leontius knew. Now we return to the question which our prologues were intended to introduce: is the Jesus Christ of Leontius' Christology the *nous* Jesus Christ of the Christology of Evagrius of Pontus? The answer is *yes*; and in this second part of our chapter, we try to prove it. The proof falls into two parts. The first, part A, contains the proof itself; the second, part B, as it were applies it, that is, introduces the proposition proved, first, into Leontius' analysis of being, and second, into his Christology.

A. *The Proof Itself*

First then the proof itself. We divide it into two parts. In the first, we try to prove a syllogism establishing a high probability that Leontius' Jesus is Evagrius' *nous* Jesus; and in the second, we confirm the probability from Leontius' own testimony.

1. A Syllogism

Now, how shall we begin? The surest and simplest proof that Leontius' Jesus is Evagrius' *nous* Jesus would be the explicit testimony of Leontius himself. It is hardly necessary to say that Leontius offers no such evidence, and hardly difficult to suppose why: the Christology of Evagrius is as blatantly heretical as any ever. At best, we may hope that *if* Leontius is a disciple of Evagrius he will sometime have let down his guard, will sometime have furnished us evidence not direct but indirect. And so it will prove to be. However, in the study of history, *allusions* all too often are *illusions*. Indirect evidence is of value in comparisons only where comparisons are authorized, that is, only if it confirms and informs a previously established congruence of the elements compared. We ask then: is there such a congruence between the thought of Leontius and the thought of Evagrius? Our answer: *yes*. There is congruence indeed. Leontius' *doctrine of man* will prove to be virtually identical with

99

that of Evagrius, and more specifically, the *soul* of Leontius' anthropology will prove identical with the *nous* of Evagrius' doctrine. Hence, our syllogism: if the soul of Leontius' anthropology is the *nous* of Evagrius' cosmology; and if, further, one of Evagrius' *noes* is Jesus Christ; then is it not at least highly probable that one of the souls of Leontius' anthropology is Jesus Christ—that Leontius' Jesus is Evagrius' *nous* Jesus?

Plainly, it is our major premise that demands proof: is it true that the soul of Leontius' anthropology is the *nous* of Evagrius' cosmology? It is, I think; and I propose to prove it by a brief comparison of the doctrines of Evagrius and Leontius on the union of soul with body. Let us consider three points: first, the true and proper relations of soul and body; second, the power which unites them; and finally, the nature and function of the soul in its union with the body.

a. *The union of soul and body: according to or against their natures?*

A general characteristic of Evagrius' *nous*-soul is that it is joined to a body *both according to and against* its nature. *Nous qua nous, nous* as such, *"nous nu"* is not and cannot be joined to body, for if joined to a body it cannot see God as God meant it to see him.[55] So far as *nous* remains *nous* in its transformation into soul after the fall and its union with the body, it is joined to body against its nature.

On the other hand, Evagrius knows well enough that "il n'y a rien qui soit en puissance dans l'âme et qui puisse en sortir en acte et subsister séparément; celle-ci, en effet, *est naturellement faite pour être dans les corps.*"[56] Now by that which is "en puissance dans l'âme," Evagrius certainly means the *nous.* He seems to be arguing in effect that *nous* cannot "sortir en acte et subsister séparément" *because* the soul in which it exists "en puissance" is "naturellement

---

[55] EvagPont, *KephGn,* 4.86 (S2; no Greek): "Le *nous* qui possède un corps ne voit pas les incorporels ...." The conclusion reminds us that in the state of final blessedness, *nous* will be without body at all: "et, quand il sera sans corps, il ne verra pas les corps."

[56] *Ibid.,* 1.47 (S2; no Greek); italics mine.

faite pour être dans les corps."[57] Yet, how "naturellement," if soul includes *nous* and *nous* is joined to a body only *against* its nature? Clearly because the *nous* which soul comprehends is not *"nous* nu" but fallen *nous, nous* which even before its union with the body had in its negligence acted against its nature, *nous* which now is joined to body so that by means of its contemplation of the visible world through that body, it may reattain its pure and natural state. It is only as including fallen *nous* that soul is "naturellement faite pour être dans les corps."

And what about Leontius? To be sure, Leontius never mentions Evagrius' intellects by name, for reasons which we have just noticed. However, there is no slightest doubt that Leontius believes that soul and body are of utterly different natures[58] and that, as we have already said, soul and body are united not by any natural inclination of one for the other, but by a divine decree.[59] For Leontius as for Evagrius, it is not by nature that soul is conjoined to body. On the other hand, Leontius strongly suggests that soul is at least necessarily associated with body. To be sure, he never says, as Evagrius does, that soul is "naturellement faite" for the body, but he does indeed assert the virtual equivalent of the formula when he argues that neither the Word in Jesus Christ nor the soul in man is ever "seen apart from" the body.[60] In short, though the soul is of a different

[57] I note that, if this interpretation of the sentence is correct, it renders the sentence an almost formal denial of any ἔκστασις; for, if *nous* cannot "sortir" from the soul "en acte," yet cannot see God unless freed from its visible body, how can it ever be found in an ἔκστασις?

[58] Beside the passage from *SolArgSev* cited *infra*, note 59, see Leontius' vigorous affirmations in the last part of *CNE* 1.3, PG, 86, 1281B 7 ff., and especially B 10–C 7. But then, the paradigm soul : body = Word : flesh would be impossible for so earnest a Chalcedonian as Leontius if he did not believe that soul and body are two different natures.

[59] LeontByz, *SolArgSev*, PG, 86, 1940A 10–B 12 and especially B 3–12, discussed *supra*, p. 54 f.

[60] Explicitly in LeontByz, *CNE* 1.2, PG, 86, 1280D 7–1281A 4, reflected in 1281C 15–D 4, in which Leontius notes that as the Word alone is not the whole and complete Jesus Christ, but only the Word in his flesh, so also the soul is not whole and complete man unless the body be taken with it. These remarks clearly expound *CNE* 1.1, PG, 86, 1277D 4–6: "ἐνυπόστατον signifies that that is not accidental which has its being in another and is not seen in itself"—that is, is seen only in and with another being. See 1277D 11–1280A 3. Here ἐνυπόστατον, I suggest, is to be predicated *both* of soul *and* of body, *both* of the Word *and* of his flesh. Later (1280A 13–B 10), Leontius says the second definition of hypostasis offered there pertains to "beings

nature from the body, it is always, associated with a body—just as for Evagrius. The very least that may be said is that Leontius' argument perfectly covers the psychology of Evagrius.

b. *The union of soul and body: providence and judgement*

Nous, then, is united to body both according to and against its nature. We now go a step further. This same essential ambiguity in the relations of *nous*-soul to body is the occasion for Evagrius' peculiar development of the divine providence and the divine judgement. Evagrius' intellect, we have learned, has of itself nothing to do with visible realities. On the other hand, Evagrius is more than once at pains to emphasize that the body is a good, indeed, that it is the indispensable means by which the soul may reascend to the pure vision of God.[61] The question then arises: if it is not by nature that *nous*-soul is united to body, how did *nous*-soul obtain such a good? Evagrius' answer: fallen *nous* obtained its body not by reason of its nature but by the providence and judgement of God. For Evagrius, as for Leontius after him, man comes into being by a divine decree. How that may be we must now examine.

It is plain that Evagrius' doctrine of providence and judgement constitute the major divisions of what we have termed his *second creation*: that is, the creation of the visible world. The *locus classicus* here is surely *KephGn*, 6.75, which briefly describes the whole course of the fall, the second creation, and the gradual restoration of the intellects to their original glory. "La science première qui est dans les *logikoi* est celle de la Trinité sainte," he begins. "Ensuite il y a eu la mouvement de la liberté"—that is, the fall—"*la providence secourable et le non-délaissement, et ensuite, le jugement* et, de nouveau"—and here he introduces the succession of worlds which will follow the first—"le mouvement de la liberté, la providence, le jugement,

---

composed of different natures but having the unity (A 15 κοινωνίαν) of [their] being [both] simultaneously *and in one another*"; so that "the nature and ousia of the other [being] is *not seen in and of itself* (καθ' ἑαυτήν) *but only with the [nature] which is compounded and united [with it]*." This assertion applies to the union of soul with body too.

[61] See EvagPont, *KephGn*, 4.60, 4.62, 4.76, 4.83, and 4.85, all cited *supra*.

et cela jusqu'à la Trinité sainte." The paradoxical conclusion, meant to emphasize the succession of worlds: "Ainsi un jugement est interposé entre le mouvement de la liberté"—that is, in an earlier world—"et la providence de Dieu"—that is, God's grace in creating the subsequent world.[62]

This sentence reveals that God's providence and judgement are inseparably linked, but are nonetheless not identical. They are linked because both obviously have to do with the creation of bodies for fallen intellects;[63] yet in that creation they have different functions. For Evagrius providence creates the world of bodies and unites each fallen intellect to one of them, in order that it may thereby reascend to God: "Double est la providence de Dieu; une partie, on dit qu'elle garde la *sustasis* des corps et des incorporels, et l'autre, qu'elle pousse les *logikoi* de la malice et de l'ignorance vers la vertu et la science."[64] On the other hand, God's judgement assigns to each fallen *nous* a body appropriate to the virtue or sin which it has demonstrated in the previous dispensation: "Le jugement de Dieu est la genèse du monde, auquel il donne un corps selon le degré de chacun des *logikoi*."[65] Hence it is that providence is prior in order to judgement.[66] So also it is that Evagrius can say that "la providence de Dieu accompagne la liberté de la volonté"— that is, that *réceptivité* of *nous* in which the fall occurred—"mais son jugement considère l'ordre des *logikoi*"—that is, the degree of their virtue or sin.[67]

The similarity of Evagrius' *divine providence* to the *divine decree* by which soul is joined to body by Leontius is unmistakable. But more. We recall that it was also by a *divine decree* that Leontius

[62] *Ibid.*, 6.75 (S2; no Greek); italics mine.

[63] The conjunction of providence and judgement is further established by the fact that there is a single contemplation of the *logoi* of both. See *ibid.*, 1.27, 5.4, 5.7, and 5.16, all in S2.

[64] *Ibid.*, 6.59 (S2; no Greek). Evagrius emphasizes the first point in 6.75, quoted *supra*, by identifying providence with "le non-délaissement." On the second point, see also 6.76 and 6.88.

[65] *Ibid.*, 3.38 (S2; no Greek); cf. 3.47 (S2; no Greek). See also 2.59.

[66] *Ibid.*, 5.24 (S2; no Greek): "Les *logoi* qui concernent le jugement sont seconds, à ce qu'on dit, par rapport aux *logoi* qui concernent le mouvement et la providence." Note also the order of providence and judgement offered by 6.75, quoted *supra*.

[67] *Ibid.*, 6.43 (S2; no Greek).

joined the *four elements* in order to compose body. Now, this same decree, I suggest, finds its exact counterpart in Evagrius' doctrine of the *divine judgement*. The elements of that doctrine already before us enable us to expatiate without preface.

Evagrius' divine judgement, he tells us, is "la genèse du monde, auquel il donne un corps selon le degré de chacun des *logikoi*."[68] We ask now: in what does a *good* body differ from an *evil* body?[69] Evagrius' answer is unambiguous. The quality of a body varies with the relative proportion of the four elements which compose it. To be sure, he admits, this answer will not be obvious to everyone: "Qui connaîtra la *sustasis* du monde et l'activité des éléments? Qui comprendra la composition de cet *organon*"—that is, the body—"de notre âme?" etc.[70] Nonetheless, the principle stands: "Il y a en commun ceci que tous les mondes sont constitués de quatre éléments, mais en particulier ceci que chacun d'eux a une variation de qualité,"[71] that is, in the proportion of elements in the whole. Of this world, therefore, Evagrius tells us that "il y a chez les anges prédominance de *nous* et de feu, chez les hommes (prédominance) d'*epithumia* et de terre, et chez les démons (prédominance) de *thumos* et d'air"[72]—as plain an association of each power or part of the soul with the predominance of a single element as one could wish.[73] Indeed, even the difference between spiritual knowledge and spiritual ignorance is to be associated with a difference in combinations of elements; for "le char de la science, (ce sont) le feu et l'air; mais le char de l'ignorance, l'air et l'eau."[74] Again, what is true for this

---

[68] *Ibid.*, 3.38 (S2; no Greek), quoted *supra*.

[69] The distinction between "corps bons" or "excellents" and "corps mauvais" is very nearly a commonplace in *KephGn*. See, e.g., *ibid.*, 3.51 (S2; no Greek).

[70] *Ibid.*, 1.67 (S2; no Greek).

[71] *Ibid.*, 3.23 (S2; no Greek).

[72] *Ibid.*, 1.68 (S2; no Greek). 4.37 (S2; no Greek) mentions "les démons et tous les *logikoi* qui possèdent des corps d'air."

[73] It is probably in the light of *loc. cit.*, 1.68, that we are to interpret 2.68 (S2; no Greek): "On dit que sont en haut ceux qui possèdent des corps légers, et en bas (ceux qui possèdent des corps) lourds; et au-dessus des premiers ceux qui sont plus légers qu'eux; mais au-dessous des seconds ceux qui sont plus lourds qu'eux." However, 6.26 (S2; no Greek) adds the qualification that "ce n'est pas le feu lui-même qui est dans nos corps, mais c'est sa qualité qui a été mise en eux," etc. On the distinction we have no time now to digress.

[74] *Ibid.*, 2.51 (S1 and S2; no Greek).

world will be true for the next world too, though Evagrius clearly hopes for an improvement; for "dans le monde à venir les corps d'ignorance"—probably identical with "le char de l'ignorance, l'air et l'eau," just mentioned—"seront dépassés, et dans celui qui le suivra le changement recevra une augmentation de feu et d'air. ..."[75] At the last judgement, of course—called *last* by Evagrius not because it stands at the end of the world, but because it is last in a series of judgements—there will be an end to worlds and bodies; but at the same time there will be an end, too, to the spiritual differences which the differences among worlds and bodies reflect; for at the end there will remain only "l'égalité de la science selon l'égalité des substances."[76]

There can be no question, then, that the quality of a world or of a body varies with the relative proportion of the elements which compose it. However, if the quality of the body of each soul is determined by the divine judgement, it follows that the function of the judgement of God is not only to blend the four elements which compose every body, but also to blend them *in the proportions proper to the body* which is itself proper to each *nous*. So to our conclusion. Since we have already learned from Leontius that it is by a divine decree that God joins the elements to compose bodies, is it unreasonable to suppose that the divine decree mentioned by Leontius is identical not only with Evagrius' providence, but also with Evagrius' divine judgement? And is it not the strongest confirmation of the agreement of the two theologians that Leontius describes the four elements as "existing autonomously and capable of being in and of themselves"?[77] For this formula precisely describes the status of Evagrius' elements also, which not only remain what they are throughout all the changes proper to the body in any given world, but also persist throughout the recurring destruction of old worlds

---

[75] *Ibid.*, 3.9 (S2; no Greek). Here, of course, "le monde à venir" is the next in the succession of worlds, not the end of all worlds.

[76] *Ibid.*, 2.17 (S1 and S2), probably quoted in the fourteenth anathema of the *Canones adversus Origenem* attributed to the Council of Constantinople of 553: in FDiekamp, *OrigStreit*, p. 95, ll. 20–22, the words just quoted are in Greek: ταυτότης ... τῆς γνώσεως, καθάπερ καὶ τῶν ὑποστάσεων.

[77] LeontByz, *CNE* 1.7, PG, 86, 1304B 11-12: τῶν αὐθυποστάτων καὶ καθ' ἑαυτὰ εἶναι δυναμένων...

and the creation of new. In relation to any given body or any given world, then, the four elements may very appropriately be said to "exist autonomously and to be capable of existing in and of themselves."[78] It is then perhaps not merely coincidence that Evagrius and Leontius are at pains to reduce the body or each of its elements to the same two components: form and matter.[79] Here too Leontius' argument perfectly covers the psychology of Evagrius.

c. *The union of soul and body: the psychologies of Evagrius and Leontius*

(1) Evagrius

We have said above that for Evagrius soul is fallen *nous*. This definition must now be clarified. It does not mean that soul is a *nous* which has ceased to be *nous*, as if soul were essentially something other than *nous*. Rather, soul is a certain state of *nous*. Soul is distinguished from *nous* as such only because soul is *nous* in its fall, that is, *nous* in a state contrary to what *nous* essentially is, contrary to what *nous* ought to be. The distinction between *nous* as such and soul is the distinction between *nous* as it ought to be and *nous* as it ought not to be but yet is. Nonetheless, *nous* which is what it ought not to be is still *nous*.

With the definition of soul as fallen *nous* Evagrius associates a second, quite different definition of soul: soul is *nous* bound to a body. A passage in his "grande lettre à Mélanie" clearly distinguishes the two definitions: "L'intellect est tombé de son rang

---

[78] I note in passing that it is surely in this sense that we are to understand the position attacked in the sixth anathema of the *Canones adversus Origenem* (553) (FDiekamp, *OrigStreit*, p. 92, ll. 27-32): [εἴ τις λέγει] ὅτι ὁ κόσμος πρεσβύτερα τῆς ὑπάρξεως αὐτοῦ στοιχεῖα ἔχων ἐνυπόστατα, ξηρόν, ὑγρόν, θερμόν, ψυχρόν, καὶ τὴν ἰδέαν, πρὸς ἣν ἀπετυπώθη, οὕτως γέγονε ... ἀνάθεμα ἔστω. It is not said by the Origenists that the elements are *uncreated*, but only that they are ontologically prior to the worlds which they compose and indeed temporally prior to all but the first world.

[79] See EvagPont, *KephGn*, 5.62 (S2; no Greek): " ... celui qui résout la nature des corps la fait consister absolument en matière et en forme." Compare Leontius' analysis of body in *CNE* 1.6, PG, 86, 1296D 5-9, and especially D 9.

premier et fut appelé âme ... et il est descendu de nouveau et il fut appelé corps."[80]

The distinction between *nous* fallen and *nous* bound to a body ought not be pressed, for with the single exception of the *nous* Jesus Christ there is no *nous* which is not *both* fallen *and* bound to body.[81] The more serious problem is to establish for Evagrius a definition of soul which can comprehend both predicates of *nous*. In short, the question is: does its fall exert an effect upon *nous* somehow in congruence with its later union with the body; and if so, what is that effect? The answer to the first question, I think, is *yes*; and the effect required, I believe, is that, for Evagrius, *nous* after its fall obtains by God's providence *two other faculties* besides itself, that is, just those faculties of the soul which govern the body. These two faculties, of course, are τὸ θυμοειδές or θυμός, and τὸ ἐπιθυμητικόν or ἐπιθυμία. With this we may revise our definition of soul: soul is *nous* which after its fall has obtained from God two new faculties besides itself, by means of which it possesses its body when God, as it were, later gives it. As soul, then, *nous* has three faculties: itself (*nous*), its *thumos*, and its *epithumia*[82]—facul-

---

[80] WFrankenberg, *EuagPont*, p. 618, ll. 1–3 (Syriac), and p. 619, ll. 2–4 (Frankenberg's retroversion in Greek). I quote the translation of AGuillaumont, *KephGn*, p. 108, note 124.

[81] Nonetheless, I emphasize with AGuillaumont, *KephGn*, p. 108, note 124, that Evagrius clearly distinguishes the two definitions. As Guillaumont says of the passage in Evagrius' letter to Melania quoted *supra*, "il ne saurait faire de doute que pour lui le passage de l'âme au corps est tout différent de celui de l'intellect à l'âme: il y intervient, en effet, un création, la création du corps, tandis qu'il n'y a pas de création propre pour l'âme, celle-ci n'étant autre que l'intellect déchu. En d'autres termes, la relation de l'âme au corps n'est pas de même nature que celle de l'intellect à l'âme." I supplement Guillaumont's remarks with the observation that Evagrius' distinction between soul as fallen *nous* and soul as *nous* bound to body seems to be reflected in his distinction between *malice* (κακία) and *ignorance* (ἄγνοια): *malice* is the aberration peculiar to the soul as fallen *nous*, and *ignorance* the sin proper to the soul as principle of the body. On the one hand, then, Evagrius can attribute *malice* to the faculties of the soul (EvagPont, *KephGn*, 3.59 [S2; no Greek]) or simply to "la nature raisonnable" (3.75 [S2; no Greek]). On the other hand, though "l'ignorance ... n'est pas naturellement faite pour être dans une nature corporelle" (1.76 [S2; no Greek]) and so is properly predicated only of soul, *ignorance* seems to be predicated of soul *as principle of the body*; for 3.68 (S2; no Greek) associates "la destruction des corps" with "la diminution de l'ignorance," as also 3.9 (S2; no Greek).

[82] These three faculties of the soul are listed in EvagPont, *KephGn*, 1.53, 1.68, 1.84, *et passim*. See also *CapPrac*, 6, 58, and 61, PG, 40, 1224A 10–14, 1233D 10–1236A 2, and 1236A 13–B 4, respectively. *Nous, epithumia*, and

ties which Evagrius regularly calls "parts"[83] or "powers" of the soul.[84]

It remains to confirm our reconstruction of his definition of soul from Evagrius himself. We put it to two tests.

First, if the soul is soul even before its union with the body, that is, if it consists of *nous*, *epithumia*, and *thumos*, then it follows that not only *nous* but also soul as such and in all its faculties is of a different order of being from the body. This is just what Evagrius believes. Granted that he says that the soul is "naturellement faite pour être dans le corps."[85] As we have heard, this is not

---

thumos are the words used by Guillaumont to translate the Syriac. *Nous* also appears as "la partie intelligente" (*KephGn*, 1.25; 5.34; 6.51), *epithumia* as "la partie concupiscible" (4.32; 4.72; 6.41; 6.84), and *thumos* as "la partie *thumiké*" (4.73; 6.41) or "la partie colérique de l'âme" (6.84). The original Greek of the Syriac translated *nous*, *epithumia*, and *thumos* was surely νοῦς, ἐπιθυμία, and θυμός, as in, e. g., the Greek originals of 1.53 and 5.27 in IHausherr, "NouvFrag," *OrChrPer*, V (1939), 230 and 231, respectively, with which compare *CapPrac*, 6, PG, 40, 1224A 10–14. The original Greek of the other terms must have been τὸ λογιστικόν (EvagPont, *KephGn*, 6.51; IHausherr, *op. cit.*, 232 [E 20]), τὸ ἐπιθυμητικόν, and τὸ θυμικόν (e.g., *CapPrac*, 58 and 61, PG, 40, 1233D 10–1236A 2 and 1236A 13–B 4, respectively)—substantive adjectives presupposing the noun μέρος as in the formula τὸ ἐπιθυμητικὸν αὐτῆς [τῆς ψυχῆς] μέρος in *CapPrac*, 58, PG, 40, 1233D 10f.

[83] For *KephGn*, see the passages quoted *supra*, note 82.

[84] The Greek original of the Syriac of S2 which Guillaumont translates as "puissance" (EvagPont, *KephGn*, 2.9, 3.59, 6.51, and 6.85) must have been δύναμις, as in the original of 6.51 in IHausherr, *op. cit.*, 232 (E 20), and in *CapPrac*, 45, 51, and 99, PG, 40, 1232D 9f., 1233B 3, and 1245C 14–D 1, respectively.

[85] EvagPont, *KephGn*, 1.47 (S2; no Greek): "Il n'y a rien qui soit en puissance dans l'âme et qui puisse en sortir en acte et subsister séparément; celle-ci, en effet, est naturellement faite pour être dans les corps." I note in passing that if the Greek original of the Syriac translated by Guillaumont as "naturellement faite" was πέφυκε or πεφυκυῖα, the original sense of the phrase was not "naturally made to be in a body" but "of such a nature as to be in a body." Guillaumont's translation—and perhaps his Syriac original also—assumes that its union with the body is the true potentiality of the soul, a proposition, alas, which flatly contradicts 1.45 (S2; no Greek): "Il n'y a rien parmi les incorporels qui soit en puissance dans le corps; incorporelle, en effet, est notre âme." My emendation will rather have it that its union with the body is only a *possibility* of the soul. To be sure, that possibility is a possibility inherent in the nature of the soul; but then, the nature of the soul is that of a *fallen* being, no longer able to enjoy the vision of God. Therefore, to describe a possibility inherent in the nature of the soul is by no means to describe the true potentiality of the soul, that is, that activity for which *nous* was originally made. In short, Evagrius, just as Augustine in the West, resolutely refuses to identify potentiality with nature, at least in this aeon—the chief criticism of late classical philosophy by the advocates of a doctrine of original sin.

to say that he believes that the soul is *naturally united* to a body; and the arguments already suggested as proof of the point readily find confirmation elsewhere. So in *KephGn*, 1.48, Evagrius flatly asserts that "tout ce qui est attaché aux corps accompagne aussi ceux par lesquels ils sont engendrés, mais *rien de cela n'est attaché à l'âme.*"[86] So also the souls of the virtuous remain untarnished by their association with the body: "De même qu'un miroir reste sans être taché par les images qui y sont regardées, de même l'âme impassible (reste sans être tachée) par les choses qui sont sur terre."[87] There is no reason to believe that what Evagrius calls *soul* here is not *nous* possessing *thumos* and *epithumia*; whence it follows that *nous* obtains its *thumos* and *epithumia* not by reason of its union with a body but, as it were, before or apart from that union.[88] In *CapPrac*, 99, he removes all doubt: the *nous*, he says, *"even apart from the body* struggles with the demons over *all the powers of the soul.*"[89]

A second test. If the *thumos* and *epithumia* of the soul together constitute as it were a later addition to its *nous*, then we may reasonably expect Evagrius to distinguish the *nous* of the soul from that later addition, that is, from *thumos* and *epithumia*. In fact, such a distinction is a commonplace for Evagrius. He makes it most sharply perhaps in *KephGn*, 6.51: "If the rational part is the most honorable of all of the powers of the soul, and this [part] alone is endowed with [its] quality by wisdom, then the foremost of all the virtues will be wisdom; for this [wisdom] our wise instructor called 'the spirit of adoption'."[90] Here as elsewhere "the rational part of

---

[86] *Ibid.*, 1.48 (S2; no Greek).

[87] *Ibid.*, 5.64 (S2; no Greek).

[88] Here we may profitably recall—as Antoine Guillaumont has graciously reminded me in a letter of 15 May 1967—that, although the *nous* does not obtain its *thumos* and *epithumia* solely by reason of its union to body, neither does it obtain them only by reason of the fall; for then they would be evil, not good. Evagrius seems to hold that *nous* obtains *thumos* and *epithumia* by a providential act of God intervening after the fall but before the providential union of soul to body.

[89] EvagPont, *CapPrac*, 99, PG, 40, 1245C 14–D 1: [τὸν νοῦν] ... καὶ δίχα τούτου τοῦ σώματος καὶ ὑπὲρ πασῶν τῶν τῆς ψυχῆς δυνάμεων τοῖς δαίμοσι μάχεσθαι.

[90] EvagPont, *KephGn*, 6.51; IHausherr, *op. cit.*, 232 (E 20): εἰ πασῶν τῶν τῆς ψυχῆς δυνάμεων τὸ λογιστικὸν μέρος ἐστὶ τιμιώτατον, τοῦτο δὲ μόνον τῇ σοφίᾳ ποιοῦται, προτέρα ἂν εἴη πασῶν τῶν ἀρετῶν ἡ σοφία· ταύτην γὰρ καὶ

the soul" is the *nous*, and the other powers to which it is compared
are the *thumos* and *epithumia*. The same distinction of *nous* and an
even greater emphasis upon its superiority appear in *KephGn*, 6.85:
"Si toutes les puissances que nous et les bêtes avons en commun
appartiennent à la nature corporelle, il est évident donc que le
thumos et l'*epithumia* ne semblent pas avoir été créés avec la nature
raisonnable avant le mouvement."[91] A more formal assertion that
the *thumos* and *epithumia* of the soul are merely additions to fallen
nous can hardly be imagined. Of equal interest is the identification of
thumos and *epithumia* with the animal soul and "la nature corporelle"
in general. Here, of course, Evagrius treats soul primarily as the
principle of the body. From this follow two further attributes of the
pair *thumos* and *epithumia*. First, Evagrius identifies them as the
seat of the senses: "The body of the soul is the likeness of a house,
and the senses resemble the windows, through which, when it bends,
the *nous* sees the sensible beings (outside)."[92] It is probably because
the *thumos* and *epithumia* administer the senses that Evagrius
regularly contrasts them to *nous* as "the passible part of the soul";
saying, for example, that "le *nous* ne s'unit pas à la science, avant
qu'il n'ait unie la partie passible de son âme à ses propres vertus."[93]
Elsewhere, he calls it "the irrational part of the soul"[94] or "la

---

υἱοθεσίας πνεῦμα ὁ σοφὸς ἡμῶν διδάσκαλος εἴρηκεν. The Greek original of S2
here seems to have shown only two significant variants. The first: ποιοῦται,
s'unit (S2; Greek ἑνοῦται ?). The second: ἀρετῶν ἡ] σοφία, *la science* (S2; Greek
γνῶσις ?). In favor of the reading σοφία in the second set of variants is the
observation of Hausherr, *loc. cit.*, that Evagrius' master here is Gregory
of Nazianzus, who does indeed—as Hausherr establishes—identify "the
spirit of wisdom" with "the spirit of adoption."

[91] EvagPont, *KephGn*, 6.85 (S2; no Greek).

[92] *Ibid.*, 4.68; IHausherr, *op. cit.*, 231: οἴκου μὲν εἰκόνα σώζει τὸ σῶμα τὸ
τῆς ψυχῆς, αἱ δὲ αἰσθήσεις θυρίδων ἐπέχουσι λόγον, δι' ὧν παρακύπτων ὁ νοῦς
βλέπει τὰ αἰσθητά. A similar distinction between *nous* and the other powers
of the soul as "les puissances de ses organes de sens," in EvagPont, *KephGn*,
4.85 (S2; no Greek).

[93] EvagPont, *KephGn*, 5.66 (S2; no Greek). Evagrius distinguishes the
nous or rational part of the soul from the passible part of the soul in
KephGn, 1.25 and 6.55, and in *CapPrac*, 46 and 56, PG, 40, 1233A 1–3 and
1233C 13–D 4, respectively. The two sentences from *CapPrac* establish that
the corresponding Greek is τὸ λογιστικὸν μέρος τῆς ψυχῆς. Evagrius mentions
"la partie passible [de l'âme]" by itself in *KephGn*, 3.18, 5.5, 5.31, and 6.53.

[94] EvagPont, *CapPrac*, 38, PG, 40, 1232B 3–7: ... τοῦ ἀλόγου μέρους τῆς
ψυχῆς ....

puissance passible" of the soul[95]—the latter of especial interest because we have already met with *passible* or *affective powers* of the soul in Leontius' *CNE* 1.3.[96]

With this, I think, our hypothesis is confirmed: for Evagrius, soul is *nous* which after its fall has obtained two faculties beside itself, *thumos* and *epithumia*, by means of which it, as it were, later possesses and administers its body. Now the question is: can we find traces of this doctrine of the soul in Leontius of Byzantium?

(2) Leontius

We notice at once that Leontius, too, divides the soul into *nous*, *thumos*, and *epithumia*,[97] and that he, too, calls them powers or parts of the soul—even raising the question which of the two is the more proper term.[98] However, all this is so nearly commonplace in late antiquity that it can hardly establish that Leontius depends upon Evagrius; only that he traverses the same orbit.

Fortunately, Leontius' psychology offers us more concrete evidence of his dependence upon Evagrius.

(a) *The functions of the faculties of the soul.* First, Leontius, like Evagrius, holds that of all the faculties of the soul, *nous* alone is the agent of the activity truly proper to soul, that is, the vision of God. For Evagrius, of course, the point is self-evident. In the beginning, when *nous* was what it ought to be, it was without *thumos* or *epithumia*, and at the end, it seems, it will be without them once again. Even now, after its fall to soul, *nous* is "the most honorable of all the powers of the soul"[99] and is called "tête de l'âme."[100] Not,

---

[95] EvagPont, *KephGn*, 3.14 and 3.16 (S2; no Greek), both of which 3.18 (S2; no Greek) plainly identifies with "la *partie* passible" of the soul (my emphasis).

[96] LeontByz, *CNE* 1.3, PG, 86, 1284C 10 ff., and especially D 1 f., discussed *supra*, p. 56 ff.

[97] E.g., *ibid.*, PG, 86, 1285A 9–14, and *CNE* 1.6 in 1296C 10 f. However, Leontius never calls *nous* νοῦς, but either τὸ λογιστικόν, as in the first passage cited, or τὸ ἡγεμονικόν, as in the second passage.

[98] LeontByz, *CNE*, 1.6, PG, 86, 1296D 2–5. It is worth noting that the scholiast of G takes the trouble of resolving the problem. See notes 83, 84, *supra*.

[99] EvagPont, *KephGn*, 6.51; IHausherr, *op. cit.*, 232, quoted *supra*, p. 109.

[100] EvagPont, *KephGn*, 5.45 (S2; no Greek).

to be sure, that *nous* can attain its end without the help of the
thumos and *epithumia*, for "le *nous* ne s'unit pas à la science, avant
qu'il n'ait uni la partie passible de son âme"—that is, *thumos* and
epithumia— "à ses propres vertus."[101] On the other hand, it is only
so far as the *nous* transcends the passible part of the soul that it
can be supposed to have attained its end: "It is then that the
nous apprehends intellectual [beings] when it is no longer endowed
with its quality"—or "made what it is"—"by considerations
[advanced by] the passible part of the soul."[102] In short, the soul is
what it ought to be when *thumos* and *epithumia* have finally brought
nous to the vision of God.

Now how does it stand with Leontius? We have already had
occasion to consider the passage in which he gives his answer. The
soul, he tells us, "may suffer divine [affections?] according to [the
will of?] God, [yet suffers them] in no way by reason of the body—
for how [could it], since [the body] often strives against [the soul?
God?]—but [rather] by reason of itself and its own nature. The
appetitive faculty strains passionately toward God; the spirited
faculty braces itself firmly and steadily supports the appetitive
faculty; [and] the cognitive faculty receives unshaded [its] immaterial reflections and is integrally illumined. Indeed, it was well said
by a certain divinely wise man from those [gone] before us"—
none other than Evagrius of Pontus— " '[that there is] one desire
[which is] good and eternal, the [desire] which strives for the true
gnosis.' "[103] The resemblance to Evagrius' doctrine is clear: all powers of the soul strain towards the vision of God, but it is *nous* alone
which actually attains it; for, as we have observed earlier, to
"receive unshaded [its] immaterial reflections and to be integrally

---

[101] *Ibid.*, 5.66 (S2; no Greek). See also 4.72, quoted *supra*. Thus 4.79
(S2; no Greek) tells us that the "*thumos* affermit le *nous*," while 4.72
(S2; no Greek) says that "la mortification de la partie concupiscible ... se
fait pour la science de Dieu."

[102] *Ibid.*, 6.55; IHausherr, *op. cit.*, 232: ὁ νοῦς τὸ τηνικαῦτα ἐπιβάλλει τοῖς
νοητοῖς, ὁπηνίκα ἂν μηκέτι ποιῶται τοῖς ἀπὸ τοῦ παθητικοῦ μέρους τῆς ψυχῆς
λογισμοῖς. See also *CapPrac*, 38, PG, 40, 1232B 3–7.

[103] LeontByz, *CNE* 1.3, PG, 86, 1285A 6–B 1. For passages of similar
tenor in EvagPont, see *KephGn*, 4.73 (S2; no Greek), and *CapPrac*, 61,
PG, 40, 1236A 13–B 4. Nevertheless, the content of these passages, though
by no means incompatible with Leontius' words, is different enough to establish that Leontius is following Evagrius only at a distance.

illumined" can be nothing less than to enjoy the ultimate blessedness.

(b) *The two sources of the affections*. The passage just cited will serve as introduction to a second similarity in the psychologies of Leontius and Evagrius: the distinction between two kinds of affections or πάθη in the soul, one properly *psychic* and the other *somatic*. Evagrius' position here is clear. We have just established that Evagrius' soul possesses its affective part, the *thumos* and *epithumia*, as it were even before and apart from its union with the body. We shall expect, then, to find that affective part not without affections proper to it, but we shall not expect them to be quite the same as the affections of the soul as principle of the body. Indeed, Evagrius is obligingly explicit: "The affections of the soul," he tells us, "take their origins from [other] men; but the [affections] of the body from the body;"[104] and elsewhere tells his monks that "the [demons] presiding over the psychic affections persevere until death, but those [presiding over] the somatic affections give way more quickly."[105]

Now precisely the same distinction constitutes the backbone of Leontius' defense against the Nestorians in *CNE* 1.3. The Word, he insists, neither himself suffers nor is circumscribed in his union with the flesh, because he is impassible and uncircumscribed by nature. Indeed, not even the soul suffers simply by reason of its union with the flesh. To be sure, the soul, unlike the Word, is passible, but just as the natural impassibility of the Word is not altered by his union with the flesh, so also the affections proper to the soul as such are and remain what they are even apart from the flesh. "The soul of man," he argues, "does not suffer these [affections] simply by reason of its being in a body, but because it is its nature to suffer even apart from a body."[106] Shortly after he adds: "the soul suffers in an absolute sense, as receiving affective

---

[104] EvagPont, *CapPrac*, 24, PG, 40, 1228C 2–4: τὰ μὲν τῆς ψυχῆς πάθη, ἐκ τῶν ἀνθρώπων ἔχει τὰς ἀφορμάς· τὰ δὲ τοῦ σώματος, ἐκ τοῦ σώματος.

[105] *Ibid.*, 25, PG, 40, 1228C 6–8: οἱ μὲν [δαίμονες] τῶν ψυχικῶν προεστῶτες παθῶν ἄχρι θανάτου προσκαρτεροῦσιν· οἱ δὲ τῶν σωματικῶν, θᾶττον ὑποχωροῦσι.

[106] LeontByz, *CNE* 1.3, PG, 86, 1284C 10–13.

powers conformed to what is good for it; though it suffers somatic affections too [that is,] from its mixture with the body to which it is bound and [from] the properties of the places in which it dwells; for though it is by its nature that it suffers in an absolute sense, it is susceptible of such [somatic] affection[s] too."[107] In short, Leontius distinguishes between psychic and somatic affections just as Evagrius does.

(c) *The affective powers of the soul.* A third similarity of the psychologies of Evagrius and Leontius is that both describe those elements of the soul which suffer the affections proper to the soul as παθητικά—*affective* or *passible.* For Evagrius, we need no more than refer to the evidence adduced immediately above that he regularly describes the *thumos* and *epithumia* of the soul as its "partie passible," its "irrational part," or its "puissance passible." As for Leontius, we have long since heard from him that the soul "does not suffer [affections] because it possesses them in its essence as receiving them from God, but [rather] it suffers [them] *as having [in itself] affective powers* (παθητικὰς δυνάμεις), which it takes with it even when it departs from the body .... The soul suffers in an absolute sense *as receiving affective powers* (παθητικὰς ... δυνάμεις) conformed to what is good for it."[108] Still another likeness in the two psychologies.

Here an objection may be raised. It is true, it may be objected, that both Evagrius and Leontius describe those elements of the soul which suffer the affections proper to the soul as *affective* or *passible powers.* Nonetheless, Evagrius and Leontius differ on which of the powers of the soul are affective. For Evagrius, only the *thumos* and *epithumia* of the soul are its affective powers; while for Leontius *all three* powers of the soul are affective powers, i.e., not only the *thumos* and *epithumia* but also the *nous.* Have we not argued above that for Leontius all three powers are comprised by the second component of the soul, its incorporeal quality, in which,

---

[107] *Ibid.* Again, the distinction between psychic and somatic affections is explicitly assumed by Leontius in his charge 33 against Theodore of Mopsuestia, in *CNE* 3, PG, 86, 1373C 1–4.

[108] *CNE* 1.3, PG, 86, 1284D 1 f., 11–13. See our discussion of the passage in Chapter Two, 56 ff.

we have suggested, the affective powers are determined to be good or evil? In short, the likeness of Evagrius and Leontius here is more apparent than real.

We reply: not the likeness but the discrepancy is more apparent than real. Granted indeed that Leontius seems to number the *nous* among the affective powers, for his account of the way in which the rational part of the soul appropriates its "immaterial reflections"[109] is itself part of a description of the way in which the soul *suffers* or apprehends τὰ θεῖα.[110] Granted, too, that Evagrius distinguishes sharply between the mode in which the *thumos* and *epithumia* apprehend visible reality and the mode in which the *nous* apprehends invisible reality. Nonetheless, in the very sentence preceding the sentence of *KephGn* in which he emphasizes the difference most vigorously,[111] Evagrius admits that "de même que chacun des arts a besoin d'un sens aiguisé qui convienne à sa matière, de même aussi le *nous* a besoin d'un sens spirituel, pour distinguer les choses spirituelles";[112] whence it follows, if a sense perceives its proper objects by an affection, that for Evagrius, too, *nous* unites to its object by an affection, that is, by a spiritual affection. It may well be, then, that Leontius calls τὰ θεῖα *affections* in this wider sense, and so in no way differs from Evagrius. At all events, it is quite incredible that Leontius should believe that the rational faculty of the soul apprehends its objects in the same mode as that in which the *thumos* and *epithumia* apprehend theirs. In short, the objection falls and the likeness stands.

(d) *Rational ousia and incorporeal quality.* The mention of the incorporeal quality of Leontius' soul reminds us of the first division of his analysis of the soul, that is, the division of soul into rational ousia and incorporeal quality,[113] and prompts us to ask whether this division, too, is a reflection of Evagrius. Again the answer is

---

[109] *Ibid.*, 1285A 12–14.
[110] *Ibid.*, 1285A 6ff.: πάσχει ... τὰ θεῖα, etc.
[111] EvagPont, *KephGn*, 1.34 (S1 and S2; no Greek): "Le sens est naturellement fait pour sentir par lui-même les choses sensibles; mais le *nous* en tout temps se dresse et attend (de voir) quelle contemplation spirituelle se donnera elle-même à lui en vision."
[112] *Ibid.*, 1.33 (S2; no Greek).
[113] LeontByz, *CNE* 1.6, PG, 86, 1296C 10.

yes. Specifically, Leontius' distinction between the rational ousia of the soul and its incorporeal quality corresponds remarkably well to Evagrius' definition of *nous* as "la substance susceptible d'une opposition,"[114] a being possessing a certain "réceptivité"[115] or susceptibility on the one hand of a likeness to God,[116] and on the other hand, of utter corruption.[117] As a being always remaining itself throughout its changes, Evagrius' *nous* might well be described as *rational ousia*; while as a being which nevertheless enters into genuinely distinct and different states of being, it will always be capable of description as a being of such-and-such a kind, and so possess *quality*—quality which must be qualified as incorporeal, because *nous* itself, after all, is incorporeal.[118]

[114] EvagPont, *KephGn*, 5.62 (S2; no Greek), the original Greek of which probably read, if EvagPont *sub* BasMag, *ep* 8.9 (SBasile, *Lettres*, I, p. 33, ll. 11–13) may be taken as a model: [ὑπόστασις] τῶν ἐναντίων δεκτική. Compare *KephGn*, 1.4 (S2; no Greek) and 1.64.

[115] *Ibid.*, 1.49, 6.73 (S2 both; no Greek).

[116] *Ibid.*, 6.73 (S2; no Greek).

[117] *Ibid.*, 1.55 (S2; no Greek).

[118] I cast my description of the similarity of Evagrius' analysis of *nous* to Leontius' analysis of the soul in just these terms in order to anticipate the objection that Evagrius himself could never speak of an *incorporeal quality* because, for him, "les qualités sont dans les corps" (*KephGn*, 1.2 [S1 and S2; the Greek in JMuyldermans, *Evagriana*, 56, is not available to me]; with which compare 2.47 [S2; no Greek] and 3.31 [S2; no Greek]); and that indeed, in 3.31 (S2; no Greek), he clearly assumes that *nous* as such cannot possess qualities.

Now, it cannot be denied that here, at least, Leontius does not hold closely to Evagrius' own terminology. I emphasize, however, that to say that Evagrius' *nous* and soul are without *quality* is not to say that they do not exist in different, admittedly incorporeal *states*. Is it then a betrayal of Evagrius' sense, or indeed proof of his utter independence of Evagrius here, that Leontius calls these states *qualities*? Especially since he at once qualifies the term with the adjective *incorporeal*, just as Evagrius himself would have had to do under similar circumstances; for, after all, not the least of Evagrius' reasons for refusing to attribute qualities to *nous* and soul is that they are incorporeal.

The importance of the adjective *incorporeal* to Leontius' sense can be established in another way. We consider a second quality of qualities. In *KephGn*, 2.18 (S2; no Greek), Evagrius says that "... la nature des corps est cachée par les qualités qui restent en eux *et les font sans cesse passer de l'un à l'autre* ...." Here another likeness to Leontius, who says, anent the unions of beings whose unions serve him as examples of the union of Word and flesh, that "none of the [beings thus] united undergo change or confusion, [because] neither one of the [beings] united has affective qualities (παθητικὰς ... ποιότητας)" (*CNE* 1.7, PG, 86, 1305A 4–6). For both Evagrius and Leontius, then, it is in and by their qualities that beings change—change, that is, not from state to state, but from one thing into a different thing.

Of course the most important of these changes of Evagrius' *nous* is its original fall from the vision of God, and so a further recommendation of our hypothesis: it enables us to tell the tale of the fall of Evagrius' *nous* in the language of Leontius' analysis of the soul. Our preface is a *caveat*: we must resist the temptation to identify the rational ousia of Leontius' soul with Evagrius' *nous*, and the incorporeal quality of Leontius' soul with Evagrius' passible part of the soul; for, if we assume, as we shall, that it was by reason of a change in its incorporeal quality that *"nous* nu" fell in the first place, then *"nous* nu" must have possessed not only rational ousia but also incorporeal quality, and with the incorporeal quality a passible or affective element. On, then, to the tale itself.

In the beginning, the *nous* was with God, the monad, together with all its brother *noes*, with whom it composed the henad, the company of intellects united to one another through their union with God in the vision of God. The *nous* was united with God not by necessity, but by an act of will; that is, beside its rational nature, the *nous* possessed a certain "réceptivité," a freedom to choose God or not to choose God; in Leontius' terms, an *incorporeal quality*; for if we ask what kind of thing the *nous* is, the answer is, *its quality*, and its quality is the consequence of its choice for or against God. By an incomprehensible "négligence" *nous* fell, that is, entered

---

Yet, in *CNE* 1.6, Leontius uses the very same word, *quality*, to describe an element of a being, soul, which he elsewhere insists can suffer no "change or confusion" at all.

A contradiction? Hardly; for in *CNE* 1.6, as we have noticed, he qualifies the quality in question not as *affective* but as *incorporeal*; thereby suggesting that the quality in question is not such a quality as he will mention in *CNE* 1 7; that is, in Evagrius' formula, not such a quality as "makes things constantly pass from one [thing] to another." On these grounds, too, we are justified in holding that Leontius' qualification of quality as *incorporeal* in *CNE* 1.6 renders his argument there wholly consonant with that of Evagrius.

Finally, here is perhaps the point to ask: is not Evagrius' distinction between the change of *states* in an incorporeal being and the change of *qualities* in a corporeal being—a change which plainly produces an utterly new being—exactly congruent to Leontius' distinction between the two modes of motion in *CNE* 1.2; that is, the distinction between the motion of "all the rational ousiai, [which are] susceptible of increase and decrease according to [their] virtue" (PG, 86, 1284A 4–6) and the motion of "things which come into being and pass away" (*ibid.*, 1284A 4)?

upon what Evagrius calls "le mouvement de la liberté."[119] With this fall, as we have suggested, its incorporeal quality changed: as a kind of emanation of the incorporeal quality of the *nous*, there appeared *thumos* and *epithumia*. With their appearance, *nous* has become soul. The *propria* of what we now may call these two faculties or powers of the soul are themselves two: first, that they are by definition incapable of the vision of God—as to be sure *nous* obtained them only because it pleased to turn away from God; and second, that they are by nature fit to rule a body. For both of these reasons Evagrius calls them the *passible part* of the soul. There follows then the creation of bodies by divine decree. The same decree joins each fallen *nous* to a body appropriate to it. This body the soul is by nature able to govern; but of itself and apart from the divine decree, the nature of the soul would not have been able to unite soul to a body. So matters stand at the creation of the visible world.

How shall we describe the soul now? We draw a diagram.

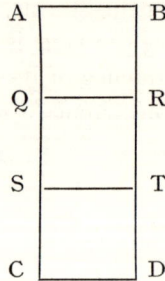

```
A ┌──────┐ B

Q ├──────┤ R

S ├──────┤ T

C └──────┘ D
```

In the fall, *nous* (ASTB) has become a soul (ACDB). This soul consists of three powers or faculties: the original *nous* with its rational ousia (AQRB) and incorporeal quality (QSTR), and two faculties as it were emanated from the incorporeal quality, the *thumos* and *epithumia*; emanations by Evagrius identified as the passible part of the soul (SCDT), but by Leontius lumped together

---

[119] For "réceptivité," "négligence," and "le mouvement de la liberté," see EvagPont, *KephGn*, 6.75 (S2; no Greek), quoted *supra*, p. 91 f., in our description of Evagrius' doctrine of the fall.

with the incorporeal quality of the *nous* (QSTR) and called the incorporeal quality of the *soul* (QCDR). Such the soul of Evagrius and Leontius.

We ask now: if it is possible so perfectly to correlate Evagrius' tale of the fall of the *nous* to Leontius' analysis of the soul, is it not at least highly probable that the latter is in fact the interpretation of the former?

With this, an end. The evidence just adduced is more than enough, I think, to show that Leontius borrows his anthropology from Evagrius. The soul of Leontius' anthropology is none other than the fallen *nous* of the cosmology of Evagrius. The major premise of the syllogism with which we began has been proved, so that we now may assert: *since* the soul of Leontius' anthropology is the *nous* of the cosmology of Evagrius, and *since* one of Evagrius' *noes* is Jesus Christ, *therefore* we may suppose it at least highly probable that one of the souls described by Leontius' anthropology is Jesus Christ: that is, the one unfallen *nous* joined to a body for the salvation of his brothers.

Now, can we confirm this conclusion from Leontius' own writings?

2. The Confirmation

We shall find the confirmation we seek in Leontius' discussions of what he calls λογικαί οὐσίαι, that is, rational ousiai. We begin by recalling the evidence—we have already mentioned all the critical passages—and then go on to analyze it.

a. *The evidence*

Leontius discusses rational ousiai or natures in three passages in *CNE* I.

(1) *CNE* I.7

As we have noticed in our chapter analyzing *CNE* I.7, Leontius' criticism there of the union κατ' ἀξίαν includes a long digression on the rational ousiai, here called rational creation or rational nature. The occasion is Leontius' peculiar argument that the union κατ' ἀξίαν implies a mixing and confusion of God and man; for, he argues, if the ἀξία of a being is proper to its nature, then to suppose a union κατ' ἀξίαν in Jesus Christ is to suppose a single nature in him, i.e., a confusion of Word and flesh into a *tertium quid*.[120] Then, quite abruptly, he turns to a new objection:

> However, if they wish to join the rest of the saints beside Christ to some other one of the Trinity [than the Word], be it in the power of their impiety [to do so]; for [the saints] are called both 'gods,' and 'sons of God,' and 'holy spirits'; for 'he who is united to the Lord is one spirit [with him]'. Yet, why is it that of the whole rational and blessed creation, both among angels as well as among men, full as it is of the grace of the [Holy] Spirit, which makes [them] gods and sons, [why is it that] he alone who took his appearance from the Virgin is both called God and son of God in the Scriptures (and rightly so) and is worshipped by the whole rational nature? For these godless people must understand that even though the better portion of the variegated dispensation [of the creation] belongs rather to [those beings] nobler and more excellent than to [those] inferior [to them], nevertheless the grace of God's activity over all and the gift of dignity [and honor] are common to all.[121]

(2) *CNE* 1.2

Earlier, in *CNE* 1.2, we have found the same rational ousiai in a different context. Here Leontius must answer the charge of his Nestorian that the paradigm *Word : flesh = soul : body* does not hold: the Word, says the Nestorian, exists before his flesh, but the soul does not exist before its body. Leontius replies that the definition of a being defines it only in its present state, not in its subsequent states. Why? "Otherwise," says Leontius, "none of the

---

[120] LeontByz, *CNE* 1.7, PG, 86, 1300C 7–D 10.
[121] *Ibid.*, 1301A 1–15. For the Greek of the critical passages, see our translation of these lines in the chapter on *CNE* 1.7, *supra*, p. 26. Antoine Guillaumont reminds me that A 6–8 πάσης τῆς λογικῆς ... χάριτος πληρωθείσης may be read as a genitive absolute.

[class of] things which come into being <and pass away> would be susceptible of a definition of its being what it is, since none [of them] persist; for things which come into being and pass away, all change into all others. For that matter, all the rational ousiai, which are susceptible of increase and decrease according to [their] virtue and are seen now in one state, now in another, [they] also are [always] seen in motion; for to remain in the same state is not a property of the created nature—[that is,] if 'but you are the same' is properly said of God alone."[122]

(3) CNE 1.6

Finally, of course, there is Leontius' brief notice of rational ousia in the analysis of the soul, discussed just above: the first division of the analysis is the division of soul into rational ousia and incorporeal quality.[123]

b. The analysis

In examining these passages, we ask first: just what are the rational ousiai of which they speak?

Of the third passage there is little doubt: here the rational ousia is one of the two parts of the soul discovered in the first division of the analysis of soul. Closer investigation has established that this rational ousia belongs not to all three faculties of the soul—as does its counterpart, the incorporeal quality of the soul—but only to the highest faculty of the soul. This highest faculty Leontius himself calls τὸ λογιστικόν or τὸ ἡγεμονικόν, but there is no doubt that it is the exact equivalent of Evagrius' nous: e.g., its peculiar and proper function is identical with that of nous, that is, the vision of God. The rational ousia of Leontius' soul is therefore a part of that "nous nu" which existed long before the body of its soul and indeed long before the soul itself, for soul, as we have seen, is simply fallen nous. So much then for the third passage cited.

---

[122] CNE 1.2, PG, 86, 1284A 1–10, discussed in the chapter on CNE 1.7, supra, p. 52 f.
[123] CNE 1.6, PG, 86, 1296C 8–10.

Now what of the others? Let us begin with the obvious. The rational ousiai of our first and second passages are not *as such* what the rational ousia of the last passage is: that is, they are not *as such* parts of souls or even parts of the highest faculty of souls, the *nous*. If the passage cited from *CNE* 1.6 be taken as Leontius' proper and established definition of rational ousia, we must suppose that in *CNE* 1.2 and 1.7 he offers us each of the terms rational ousia, rational creation, and rational nature as *pars pro toto*: e.g., the rational ousiai here are simply beings distinguished by the possession of rational ousia and therefore called rational.

The next question is: what are these beings? In *CNE* 1.7 Leontius is obligingly explicit: the rational creation or nature includes Jesus Christ, angels, and men. With this, we begin to make headway. In the system of Evagrius and Leontius, all of these beings are essentially *noes* or intellects. The only question is which of their several states describes them here. We begin with the first division. Intellects are either "*noes* nus" or incarnate *noes*. Now, Leontius' rational ousiai are not "*noes* nus," for angels and men, though rational ousiai, are not "*noes* nus," nor do "*noes* nus" have such a movement as *CNE* 1.2 attributes to the rational ousiai. If *noes*, but not "*noes* nus," then *incarnate noes*: the first division. Can we press on? For there are at least three classes of *incarnate noes*: Jesus Christ, angels, and souls, that is, human souls. Here, however, it is plain that Leontius breaks off the division, for his rational ousiai number all three: Jesus Christ, angels, and men are all rational ousiai. In short, Leontius' rational ousiai, the components of his rational creation or rational nature, are simply *incarnate noes*.[124] We note: *noes incarnate* and not *fallen*; for Jesus Christ is numbered among rational ousiai, but he is not a fallen *nous*.

The consequences of our argument are clear. We have established earlier that Leontius' soul is Evagrius' fallen *nous* or, as we will have it here, Evagrius' incarnate *nous*; and now we learn that Leon-

---

[124] From this conclusion it follows, by the way, that Leontius' use of *rational ousia* in *CNE* 1.6 to describe a part of the *soul* is slightly improper: he assumes correctly enough that *soul* is incarnate *nous*, but does not specify, as he ought, that not every incarnate *nous* is soul, i.e., that not every incarnate *nous* is such a *nous* as possesses a human, but not an angelic, body.

tius describes these same incarnate *noes*, both angelic and human, as rational ousiai. The climax: *Leontius numbers Jesus Christ, too, among the rational ousiai*, thus in effect describing him just as Evagrius had described him; that is, as *one of the incarnate noes*. With this, the whole passage just quoted from *CNE* 1.7 becomes clear. The ἀξία of Jesus Christ in which the saints participate is the dignity not of the Word of God but of Evagrius' henad, the cosmos of pure intellects.[125] As a *nous*, Jesus Christ is indeed one of the saints, is indeed numbered among angels and men. To be sure, he is the most noble and excellent of all, but only because he has persisted in the vision of God; it is by reason of this union with God that he alone is called god and son of God and is worshipped by the rest of the intellects. Nonetheless, he is at bottom only what each of us is: a *nous*. Though Jesus is pre-eminent among us, Leontius does not hesitate to remind us that "the grace of God's activity over all and the gift of dignity [and honor] are *common* to all." Will not each of us become in the end what Jesus Christ is now?

With this, I think, what we have called the high probability that Leontius' Jesus Christ is the *nous* Jesus Christ of Evagrius of Pontus stands confirmed.

III. CONCLUSION

In the two chapters before this, we have described what we have termed Leontius' *formal Christology*, and in this chapter we have tried to establish the proper *matter* for that form, that is, to identify the Jesus Christ described by the formal Christology. Our conclusion is that Leontius' Jesus Christ—the matter of his formal Christology—is none other than the *nous* Jesus Christ of the Christology of Evagrius of Pontus. There remains only one test of our analyses: to

---

[125] This is why Leontius implicitly rejects the argument of Cyril of Alexandria that ἀξία cannot unite. For Leontius it is precisely the ἀξία of a being which designates its nature, and its nature is that which *unites* it to its ὁμοούσιοι. Leontius rejects the union κατ' ἀξίαν for other reasons than Cyril's: if he who possesses the ἀξία of the Son is of one essence with the Son, and if as *nous* Jesus Christ is not of one essence with the Son, then Jesus Christ cannot posses the ἀξία of the Son, that is, cannot be united to the Son κατ' ἀξίαν.

fill the forms described earlier with the matter discovered just now. If the matter fills the forms, we shall have still another proof of the thesis. We have two forms to fill: Leontius' analysis of being in *CNE* 1.7 and his description of the unions καθ' ὑπόστασιν and κατ' οὐσίαν in *CNE* 1.4.

A. *The Place of the* Nous *Jesus Christ in Leontius' Analysis of Being*

The first question is: can we locate the *nous* Jesus Christ in Leontius' analysis of being? If not, we have erred either in our identification of Leontius' Jesus as a *nous* or in our account of Leontius' analysis. We begin by noting a critical peculiarity of Evagrius' *nous*, then identify that peculiarity with a peculiarity of one of Leontius' orders of being.

First, then, Evagrius' *nous*. In its original state, Evagrius' *nous* was united to God; and, after its fall, God's providence united it to a body. From these observations we may derive an important general characteristic of *nous* in all its states: it never stands alone. It is always bound to a being of a different nature: before the fall to God, according to its nature, and after the fall to its body, against its nature. In other words, *nous* is always united to one or more other beings of a different nature.

This conclusion may be enlightened from another side by Evagrius' doctrine of contemplation. *Nous*, we have just suggested, is always united to another being of a different nature. This union, or rather the nature of the being to which *nous* is united, plainly reflects the spiritual state of the *nous* either before its fall or after its fall, i.e., at one of the judgements preceding one of the creations following the fall: in its good and pristine state, *nous* is united to God; in its subsequent and sinful state, to the body. We now carry Evagrius' argument a step further. Just as a *nous* must always be in union with another being of a different nature, so must it also possess a *mode of contemplation* of other beings. To this mode of contemplation corresponds a certain *object of contemplation*. This is so first of all of the *nous* in its natural and proper state, its union with God. Evagrius emphasizes that "lorsque la nature raisonnable" —that is, *nous*—"recevra la contemplation qui la concerne"—that is, is natural and proper to it—"alors aussi toute la puissance du *nous* sera saine."[126] And what is "la contemplation qui la concerne?" "Le *nous* nu est celui qui, par la contemplation qui le concerne, est uni à la science de la Trinité."[127] Because the *nous* adopts the appropriate *mode* of contemplation, it receives the Trinity as its *object* of contemplation and thereby is rendered healthy and whole. On the other hand, the *nous* necessarily possesses a contemplation in its fallen state also, for it is only by the contemplation of visible reality that it can reattain to the knowledge of God. Here, however, the *nous* stands before a choice of modes of contemplation and so also a choice of objects of contemplation. To be sure, its choice is not unlimited; because the *nous* is bound to a body, it must always begin with the contemplation of the visible creation and cannot hope, at least in this particular world, to attain that mode or object of contemplation proper only to incorporeal beings. Nonetheless, it has a choice. First, it must decide whether or not to follow the way of Jesus Christ, that is, whether to love the visible creation for the sake of the creation itself or whether to love it for the sake of him who made it in order that the creation might reveal him. If the *nous* chooses the way of Jesus Christ, it may, as we have seen, attain various stages of perfection, in each of which there is a mode of contemplation proper to the stage of perfection and an object of contemplation proper to the mode of contemplation. These latter choices of the *nous*, of course, represent what Leontius calls, in *CNE* 1.2, its "increase and decrease according to [its] virtue,"[128] its motion, which we know from Evagrius began with its fall and will end only with its restoration to the vision of God. Indeed, not even Jesus Christ himself is exempt from these choices, though he takes them upon himself willingly and not by necessity.[129] However, the details of the doctrine of contemplation do not concern us here. Here we notice only that within the limits imposed upon it by the being to which it is united by God's

---

[126] EvagPont, *KephGn*, 2.15 (S2; no Greek).
[127] *Ibid.*, 3.6 (S2; no Greek).
[128] LeontByz, *CNE* 1.2, PG, 86, 1284A 5 f.
[129] *CNE* 2, dialogue, PG, 86, 1349A 1 ff. and especially C 5–D 2.

judgement, the mode of contemplation of a *nous* reflects the nature of the object of its contemplation just as the nature of the being to which it is united reflects the spiritual state of the *nous* either before the fall or at the most recent judgement. Every *nous* stands in two relations. First, it is always united to a being of another nature by what Leontius calls its essential relations; and second, it always contemplates a being of another nature, whether the being which it contemplates is identical with the being to which it is united or whether the being which it contemplates is revealed to it by the being to which it is united.

Back now to the question: Can we find place for such a *nous* in Leontius' analysis of being? Indeed we can. For Leontius, we know, all beings which have their *mode of nature* or their relation of union and distinction as *composite* (that is, all beings of class B) are as such and necessarily found also in their *mode of union*. Can we not now locate Evagrius' *noes* among Leontius' beings of class B? For, as we have just said, the *noes* by their very definition must be in union either with God or with one of the visible creation; so that, in Leontius' terms, they are always found both in their *mode of nature*—i.e., as what they are by nature, *noes*—and in their *mode of union*.[130] To be sure, only the *nous* Jesus Christ has

[130] This identification of Leontius' beings which have their essential relations as *composite* with Evagrius' *noes* reminds us of a further parallel. Leontius, we know, distinguishes the Trinity from its creatures as beings having their essential relations as *simple*—the Trinity—from beings having them as *composite*—beings whom we now propose to identify with Evagrius' *noes*. Evagrius, on the other hand, distinguishes God from his creatures as a being which exists by reason of his essence (the Trinity) from beings which do not (the *noes*). Now, are not the two definitions of God identical? Not only that the formulae of both Evagrius and Leontius contrast God to the *noes* rather than to the visible creation; but, more important, because Evagrius' *being which exists by reason of his essence* is identical with Leontius' *beings which have their essential relations as simple*. We note of Evagrius that he, just as Leontius, uses the word *simple* of the Trinity; e.g., EvagPont *sub* BasMag, *ep* 8.2, in SBasile, *Lettres*, I, 24, l. 22 f.: ὁ δὲ Θεὸς ἁπλοῦς καὶ ἀσύνθετος παρὰ πᾶσιν ὁμολογεῖται, and *passim*. I do not imply, of course, that Evagrius had developed the definition of God's simplicity as far as Leontius later did, that is, as far as the definition of the Trinity as beings having their *essential relations* as simple. As for Leontius, we have already found compelling reasons to believe that his definition of beings of class I—that is, beings having their essential relations as simple—implies that they possess their existence as identical with their essence, just as Evagrius argued.

always been united to the *same* being of a different nature; for, in the fall, the other intellects fell from that being—God, of course—and obtained instead union with bodies; but nonetheless all intellects have always been united to *some* being of different nature; and so they qualify perfectly as beings of class B. In short, the *noes* of Evagrius have a clear and distinct place in Leontius' analysis of being. The matter fills the form.

B. *A Retranslation of the Christology of Leontius of Byzantium into the Christology of Evagrius of Pontus*

The second and last form into which we must pour the *nous* Jesus Christ of Evagrius of Pontus is Leontius' description of the unions of Word and flesh both καθ' ὑπόστασιν and κατ' οὐσίαν. Here we dispense with formal proof, and referring the reader to our account of *CNE* 1.4 (Chapter Three), simply retell the tale of the incarnation of Evagrius' *nous* Jesus Christ in the terms of Leontius' two unions. The reader may judge for himself whether the translation is possible.

Let us begin our reconstruction just before the incarnation. Just before the incarnation the universe of Evagrius and Leontius comprehends God on the one hand, and on the other hand the visible creation. God, as always, is the Trinity: Father, Son, and Holy Spirit, united as ousiai and distinguished as hypostases. To the Son or Word is united the single one of a world of intellects which has not fallen from the vision of God to become soul and thereupon to obtain a body in the visible world created for it. The union of this last *nous* to the Word is of course a union καθ' ὑπόστασιν,[131] for, if it is as hypostasis that the Word is *distinguished* from the Father and the Holy Spirit in his mode of nature, it will be as hypostasis that the Word is *united* to *nous* in his mode of union. Word and *nous* will then be distinguished as ousiai, here because they are ἑτεροούσιοι, beings of different natures. But more. Because the *nous* later named Jesus is united to the Word as hypostasis and

---

[131] See p. 77, note 25, on PG, 86, 1289A 8, πρὸς ἑαυτόν, in our analysis of the syzygies of *CNE* 1.4, in which we suggested that the *nous* Jesus is united to the Word as hypostasis.

distinguished from him as ousia, the same *nous* is united to the Father as ousia and distinguished from him as hypostasis. The union of the *nous* with the Father κατ' οὐσίαν does not imply that the *nous*, as the Son, is ὁμοούσιος with the Father. Rather, the union of *nous* with the Father through the Son is called κατ' οὐσίαν as being, as it were, the opposite of the union καθ' ὑπόστασιν of the *nous* to the Son. We may say that it is through its union with the Son that the *nous* is united to the Father and so is called a *god*. The specific difference between the *nous* and God is that the three hypostases of God exist by reason of their very essence, while the *nous* does not. The existence of the *nous* is not at all identical with its essence. Indeed, it is only in its union with the Word as hypostasis or existence and its consequent union with the Father as ousia or essence that *nous* finds its existence in accord with its essence; for the Father and the Son with which its essence and existence have their respective unions are themselves ὁμοούσιοι and inseparable, and therefore as it were unite the essence of *nous* with its existence in and by the unity of God. This simultaneous union of the *nous* Jesus with Father and Son is of course his vision of God, that unity of Jesus Christ with the Father so emphasized in the New Testament.

And how does it stand with the brothers of the *nous* Jesus? They are not united to God at all. Not that they will find the identity of their existence with their essence anywhere else than in God, but that they have turned away from him by virtue of that liberty which they possess just because the existence of intellects is not identical with their essence. Now fallen to be souls, they contemplate the visible world by means of the bodies to which God, through the *nous* Jesus, has joined them. Since they have been given the world as an object of contemplation in place of the Word from whom they have fallen, it is only proper that each is united to the body in which it contemplates the world in just the same way as it was formerly united to the Word, that is, by a union καθ' ὑπόστασιν; a mode of union necessary also because, as an incorporeal soul, fallen *nous* differs from its body as ousia. Whence it follows, of course, since bodies are ὁμοούσια, that the *nous* united to any given body *as hypostasis* is united to all other bodies *as ousia*; not, again, because it is ὁμοούσιος with them, but because its union

with the ὁμοούσια of its body must be in the determination
opposite to its union with that body itself. In this, of course, we
recognize that union of soul and body which Leontius holds to be
the paradigm of the union of Word with flesh.

Now, the incarnation. In the incarnation, the single *nous* not fallen from God but united to the Father as ousia by reason of his
union to the Son as hypostasis is now, as were his brothers before
him, made soul and joined to a body, being born of the Virgin
Mary as Jesus of Nazareth. He is joined to his body, of course, not
because he has sinned, but because it is through his body that God
himself intends to approach men; and, therefore, even in his union
with his flesh the *nous* Jesus remains united to God. *Flesh*, we must
say, because in his incarnation the *nous* Jesus does not *assume* a
soul and with it a body, but himself *becomes* a soul and *assumes*
a body. How could he assume a soul, for every soul other than
Jesus is a fallen *nous*? Besides, how could one *nous*, Jesus, assume
another *nous*, even a fallen *nous*?

The terms of the incarnation, then, are three: *God* and *flesh* united
in the *nous* Jesus. Here, of course, God includes both Father and
Son, for, because the *nous* Jesus is united to the Son as hypostasis,
he is also united to the Father as ousia; and on the other hand, flesh
includes both the body assumed by the *nous* Jesus and all other
bodies also, for, because the *nous* Jesus is united to the one as
hypostasis, he is joined to the others as ousia. This definition of
flesh, of course, allows Leontius to insist that the human nature
assumed by the Word is *both* nature conceived as individual being
and nature conceived as species.[132]

This analysis of Leontius' *Heilsgeschichte* reveals why he must
insist that the union of God, Jesus Christ, and flesh demands unions
both καθ' ὑπόστασιν and κατ' οὐσίαν: for it is καθ' ὑπόστασιν
that Word is united to flesh, and κατ' οὐσίαν that the *nous* Jesus
Christ is united to the ὁμοούσιοι of Word and flesh, that is, to God
the Father and to other bodies. We look at these unions more closely.

---

[132] LeontByz, *SolArgSev*, PG, 86, 1916D 4 ff. The Monophysite asks:
Φύσιν ὁ Λόγος ἀναλαβὼν ἀνθρωπίνην, τὴν ἐν τῷ εἴδει θεωρουμένην ἢ τὴν ἐν ἀτόμῳ
ἀνέλαβεν; (1916D 4–1917A 2); and later: Τὴν τίνα οὖν ἀνέλαβε φύσιν [ὁ λόγος];
(1917B 9); to which Leontius replies: Ναί. ἀλλὰ τὴν αὐτὴν οὖσαν τῷ εἴδει
(1917B 10).

First, the union καθ' ὑπόστασιν. We begin by recalling that, *before* the incarnation, neither God nor the visible world belonged to the essential relations of the other. They had, so to speak, broken relations. It is not even possible to say that, before the incarnation, God and flesh differed *as ousiai*; for, if to say so implies that each belonged to the essential relations of the other, it follows that, even before the incarnation, God and flesh were *united as hypostases*; which is not so. It is only in the incarnation that essential relations between God and flesh are established; only in the incarnation, that is, in the incarnate *nous* Jesus, that one can describe even the difference of Word and flesh as ousiai.[133]

Then what is the relation of the Word to the flesh of the *nous* Jesus?

In the *nous* Jesus, both Word and body in their modes of union yet preserve their modes of nature, so that they cannot be compounded in one another to form a *tertium quid*. Because each preserves its mode of union, it preserves its essential relations with other beings of the same nature: Word is joined to Father and Holy Spirit as ousia and distinguished from each as hypostasis; and the body of Jesus is distinguished from other bodies in the same way. However, to say that in their modes of nature the Word and the body of Jesus are both hypostases is not to imply that Jesus Christ is in two hypostases or even that he is composed *from* two hypostases—as Leontius of Jerusalem charges by implication.[134] How so? The single *nous* joined to the Word joins Word to flesh—and so himself becomes Jesus Christ—not in their modes of nature, but in their modes of union. Now, in the modes of *union* of Word and flesh, the order of the essential relations of Word and flesh is just the opposite of their order in the modes of *nature*. If in its mode

---

[133] See, e.g., *ibid.*, 1936D 1 ff. and especially 1937C 1–3: οὐ γὰρ προεπινοεῖται [ἡ διαίρεσις] τῶν πραγμάτων ἐν οἷς αὐτὴ θεωρεῖται, ἀλλ' οὐδὲ αὐτῆς τῆς ἐνώσεως· ἀλλ' ὅτε τὰ πράγματα <γέγονε> καὶ μετὰ τὴν τούτων ἔνωσιν ....

[134] As we shall notice *infra*, p. 139 ff., LeontJer, *AdvNest*, 2.13, PG, 86, 1560A 5 ff., is a direct reply to LeontByz, *CNE* 1.1, PG, 86, 1278C 14–1280A 3. Now, the title of *AdvNest*, 2 (PG, 86, 1525[-1526]B 10 f.) tells us that it is directed against those who assert *two* hypostases in Jesus Christ. How did Leontius of Jerusalem come to believe that Leontius of Byzantium held this opinion? Almost certainly from the latter's description, in *CNE* 1.7, of Word and flesh in their modes of nature, in which each is distinguished from its ὁμοούσιοι as hypostasis.

of nature Jesus' body is united to other bodies as ousia and distinguished from them as hypostasis, then in its mode of union to the Word in Jesus it will be united to the Word as hypostasis and distinguished from him as ousia—as becomes a body—and the Word will be united to and distinguished from the body in the same way. In their modes of union, then, Word and flesh are not united as two *hypostases* in one hypostasis, but as two *ousiai* in one hypostasis. This is the union καθ' ὑπόστασιν, the union of the body of Jesus with the *Word*.

Next, the union κατ' οὐσίαν, the union of the *nous* Jesus to the ὁμοούσιοι of the Word and flesh. In Jesus, the Word is joined to his body as hypostasis. Now, both the Word and his body have ὁμοούσιοι: the Word has the Father and the Holy Spirit, and the body has all other bodies. The relation of the *nous* Jesus to the Father and the Holy Spirit on the one hand and to these other bodies on the other? The *nous* Jesus, in whom Word and flesh are united, is related to their ὁμοούσιοι in a relation opposite to the relation in which Word and flesh are united in him. Therefore, since in him Word and flesh are united as hypostases and distinguished as ousiai, he himself is united to their ὁμοούσιοι as ousia and distinguished from them as hypostasis. This is Leontius' union κατ' οὐσίαν — the union of the *nous* Jesus to God the Father and to bodies other than his own. We note: this union κατ' οὐσίαν is identical on the one hand with the union κατ' οὐσίαν with the Father and the Holy Spirit which the *nous* later named Jesus enjoyed even before the incarnation, and identical on the other hand with the union κατ' οὐσίαν which each fallen and incarnate *nous* now enjoys with bodies other than its own. In the incarnation, the *nous* Jesus Christ obtains unions κατ' οὐσίαν with both the Father and these other bodies.

The point, then, may be taken as established: Leontius' analysis of the union of Word and flesh in Jesus Christ perfectly corresponds to the union of Evagrius' *nous* Jesus to Word and flesh. Once more, the matter prescribed fills the form. And with this we rest our case: the Jesus Christ of Leontius of Byzantium is surely none other than the *nous* Jesus Christ of Evagrius of Pontus.

CHAPTER FIVE

ENHYPOSTASIZED NATURES

With Leontius' definitions of ousia and hypostasis well in hand, we are now able to answer clearly a question which has occupied all his commentators from his own day to this. In *CNE* 1.1 Leontius speaks of τὸ ἐνυπόστατον, "what is enhypostasized," and by this clearly means a φύσις ἐνυπόστατος, an "enhypostasized nature." Now, just what is an enhypostasized nature? Are both natures of Jesus Christ enhypostasized or only one, that is, the human nature alone as existing *in the hypostasis* of the Word of God?[1]

I. Introduction: The Scholarly Literature

The judgement of modern scholars is nearly unanimous: Leontius posits an enhypostasized nature in order to explain the union of the two natures of Jesus Christ in one hypostasis, and, more exactly, to account for the subsistence of his human nature *in the hypostasis of the Word*. We may let Friedrich Loofs introduce the majority. "Die menschliche Natur in Christo," he says, "ist nicht ἀνυπόστατος, nicht selbst ὑπόστασις, sondern ἐνυπόστατος ([*CNE* 1.1, MPG, 86], 1277D ff. [i.e., 1277C 14–1280A 5]), d. h. sie hat ihr ὑποστῆναι ἐν τῷ λόγῳ ([*SolArgSev* in] 1944 C [4])."[2] To be sure, Leontius was not always clear on the point: e.g., Loofs notes Leontius' use of a torch as paradigm of the incarnation but observes: "Welcher der

---

[1] I note in passing that I am not asking who first employed the formula *enhypostasized nature*, but what Leontius means by it. It has long been established that Leontius is not the first to use it. On the state of the question, see Siegfried Helmer, *Der Neuchalkedonismus. Geschichte, Berechtigung und Bedeutung eines dogmengeschichtlichen Begriffes*, Inaugural Dissertation, printed reproduction (Bonn, 1962), 35.

[2] FLoofs, *LeontByz*, 65. N.B.: the formula ὑποστῆναι ἐν τῷ λόγῳ belongs *in loc.* to Leontius' adversaries.

beiden Teile des Zusammengesetzten das ἐνυπόστατον ist, welcher in seine Hypostase auch die φύσις des andern aufnimmt, sagt der Verfasser hier nicht."[3] Nonetheless, says Loofs, his occasional ambiguities cannot blind us to the larger truth: Leontius reproduces here the Christology of Cyril of Alexandria.[4] With all but the last point of Loofs' analysis, Johann Peter Junglas agrees: "Nach Leontius ist in Christus deshalb nur eine Hypostase, weil die ganze menschliche Usie oder Physis mit all ihren Eigentümlichkeiten und Tätigkeiten ins Bereich der göttlichen Hypostase des Logos hinein-gezogen wurde, so dass alles Menschliche ἴδιον des Logos geworden ist"[5]—only that Leontius' open attacks upon propositions considered *de fide* by Cyril forbid us to see in Leontius a disciple of Cyril.[6] In 1926, in his excellent article on Leontius in the *Diction-naire de Théologie catholique*, Venance Grumel came to the same conclusions, but not, we notice, without a certain hesitation. For, after the keenest analysis of Leontius' position in the whole litera-ture, he was constrained to admit that "en tout ceci, rien n'ap-paraît encore de la prépondérance ontologique du Verbe dans la constitution de l'unique hypostase du Christ, car ce qu'on vient de dire de l'humanité du Sauveur peut s'appliquer aussi, *mutatis mu-tandis*, au Verbe lui-même: il n'y a que cette différence que le Verbe présubsistait à l'union, circonstance étrangère, selon Léonce, à la nature de l'union hypostatique."[7] Alas, Grumel could not find it in his heart to believe that our hero meant what he was saying, and so insisted forthwith: "Il ne faudrait pas cependant en conclure que notre auteur établit une égalité parfaite entre les deux compo-sants de l'hypostase du Christ. A la vérité, Léonce insiste avec force sur la réalité, l'intégrité des deux natures et leur distinction, mais il n'oublie pas que la subsistance commune aux deux parties du Christ, c'est la subsistance du Verbe .... Il n'y a pas eu seulement con-cours de deux natures, mais prise de possession hypostatique de l'une par l'autre ...."[8] More recently, Charles Moeller has raised

---

[3] *Ibid.*, 67.
[4] *Ibid.*, 65.
[5] JPJunglas, *LeontByz*, 150.
[6] E.g., *ibid.*, 137, 146–148.
[7] VGrumel, "LéonceByz," *DTC*, IX, 412.
[8] *Ibid.*

the same doubts,[9] but rejoins the majority when he confesses of a passage in *SolArgSev* that "on a l'impression que les propriétés concrètes de la nature humaine de Jésus se combinent avec les propriétés concrètes de l'hypostase du Verbe au sein de la Trinité."[10] Indeed, to the best of my knowledge, it is Marcel Richard alone who will have it otherwise; not because he says so explicitly, but because he believes (against the majority, by the way) that for Leontius, *all* natures are enhypostasized;[11] whence we must conclude, for lack of a clearer statement, that he believes *a fortiori* that *both* natures of Leontius' Christ are enhypostasized.

II. Leontius' Answer: Two Enhypostasized Natures

A. *The Argument of Leontius of Byzantium*

Now what is the truth of the matter?

1. Are All Natures Enhypostasized?

Let us take up first the suggestion of Marcel Richard that, for Leontius, *all* natures are enhypostasized. Indeed, Leontius of Jerusalem believed so;[12] but how is it with Leontius of Byzantium?

We begin by asking: just what is an *enhypostasized* ousia or nature? What does the adjective ἐνυπόστατος mean for Leontius? Leontius himself gives us an answer in the *locus classicus* of *CNE* I.1: οὐ ταὐτόν, ὦ οὗτοι, ὑπόστασις καὶ ἐνυπόστατον, ὥσπερ ἕτερον οὐσία καὶ ἐνούσιον· ἡ μὲν γὰρ ὑπόστασις τὸν τινὰ δηλοῖ, τὸ δὲ ἐνυπόστατον τὴν οὐσίαν· καὶ ἡ μὲν ὑπόστασις πρόσωπον ἀφορίζει τοῖς χαρακτηριστικοῖς ἰδιώμασι, τὸ δὲ ἐνυπόστατον τὸ μὴ εἶναι αὐτὸ συμβεβηκὸς δηλοῖ, ὃ ἐν ἑτέρῳ ἔχει τὸ εἶναι, καὶ οὐκ ἐν ἑαυτῷ θεωρεῖται.[13]

---

[9] CMoeller, "Chalcédonisme et néo-chalcédonisme," *KonzChalk*, I, p. 701, note 17; compare p. 705, note 29, and p. 717, note 86.
[10] *Ibid.*, 701.
[11] MRichard, "Léonce et Pamphile," *RevScPhilTheol*, 27 (1938), 32 f.
[12] E.g., LeontJer, *AdvNest*, 2.13, PG, 86, 1561C 3 f., to be discussed *infra*.
[13] PG, 86, 1277C 14–D 6.

Now what does Leontius mean by *this*? We call our description of his analysis of being to our rescue.

We ask first: Of what does Leontius predicate the term *enhypostasized* here? In fact, he predicates it first, of *ousia* and, second, of "that which has its existence in another and is not seen in itself," that is, almost certainly, a being—one of the beings to be discussed in *CNE* 1.7.[14] Is Leontius inconsistent? Not at all. For Leontius, ousia is one of the determinations of the relations *of a being*; so that, if τὸ ἐνυπόστατον is predicated of an ousia, it must be predicated also of the *being* of that ousia.

Leontius' analysis of being next bids us ask: a being in which of its modes? Its mode of nature or its mode of union? The answer is evident. A being which has its existence in another and is not seen in itself can only be a being in its *mode of union*.

With this the way is clear. *Enhypostasized*, we know, is a predicate proper to ousia or nature, and we now may add: to the nature of a being in its *mode of union*; that is, such a nature or ousia as *distinguishes* its *being* from the ἑτεροούσια to which its hypostasis unites it. But what of the word itself? Why does Leontius choose ἐνυπόστατος? Usually, of course, the word designates what *exists*, as opposed to what does *not* exist; but this seems not to be Leontius' use of it. Nonetheless, when we consider the relations of ousia and hypostasis in a being, we understand why Leontius chose the word. The stem, -ὑπόστατος, clearly points to the mate of ousia, that is, hypostasis, which the prefix ἐν- somehow describes; but how? We have here a being in its mode of union, which is therefore united to beings of another nature as hypostasis. Its hypostasis, then, is an hypostasis by virtue of which its being is *with* and *in* another being; and so the mate of such an hypostasis, that is, its nature or ousia, may be called an *enhypostasized* nature. By the way, the equivalent predicate for the hypostasis of a being in its mode of nature is ἐνούσιος as ὥσπερ ἕτερον οὐσία καὶ ἐνούσιον (D 1) suggests. The hypostasis of a being in its mode of nature is the hypostasis of a being united to other beings as ousia, so that its ousia is an ousia which unites, an ousia

---

[14] *Ibid.*, 1301D 5: πάντα τὰ ὄντα, etc.

by virtue of which its being is *with* and *in* another being; and so the mate of such an ousia, that is, its hypostasis, may be called an ἐνούσιος hypostasis. And so the definition of Leontius' ἐνυπόσ-τατος: *the predicate of the ousia of a being which in its mode of union is united as hypostasis to beings of another nature.*

Now back to the question. Are *all* natures enhypostasized for Leontius? That is, is every instance of that determination of the essential relations of beings called *ousia* a determination of a being in its *mode of union*? The answer is, obviously, no. *Ousia* determines the essential relations of beings not only in their modes of union but also in their modes of nature. The ousia of a being in its mode of nature cannot be called enhypostasized, for its mate, its hypostasis, does not unite its being *to*, does not, as it were, bring it to existence *in* other beings, but rather distinguishes it from them. Richard is wrong. For Leontius, not *all* but only *some* natures are enhypostasized.

2. Is Only the Human Nature of Jesus Christ Enhypostasized?

So much then for Richard; what of the others? Is the consensus right in supposing that only the human nature of Leontius' Christ is enhypostasized? By no means! Let us take the short way to our answer. We have just established that the nature or ousia of any being in its mode of union is an *enhypostasized* nature. Now the Word and flesh united in the *nous* Jesus Christ are by definition beings in their mode of union. Therefore, in their union in Jesus Christ, in which Word and flesh remain distinguished as natures, *the natures of Word and flesh are both enhypostasized natures.*

Here it may be objected that Leontius is defining the formula *one* hypostasis in two natures, but that our interpretation of him seems to demand that he say *two* hypostases—just as his Nestorian will have it. The answer to the objection demands another question: how does Leontius define the *oneness* of Jesus Christ's hypostasis?

We begin with what it is not: the *one* hypostasis of Jesus Christ cannot be either the hypostasis of the Word or the hypostasis of the flesh. Why? Not least of all because, that granted, the other of the beings united in Jesus Christ would be deprived of its hypostasis. Yet were, e.g., the flesh so deprived, it would either not have united with the Word at all—for is it not *as hypostasis* that the flesh is united to the Word?—or it would have been mixed and mingled with the Word so as to lose its very being, and with it not only its hypostasis but also its ousia; for Leontius believes, we remember, that ousia and hypostasis are *simultaneous* determinations of the essential relations of a being. In short, even in their union, the determination *hypostasis* persists in *both* beings; and thus far the objection stands.

Where then *does* the oneness of hypostasis lie? For Leontius, I think, there is no question: the *oneness* of hypostasis in Jesus Christ reflects the *oneness* of the determination of the essential relations of both Word and flesh to *one* and the same being, the *nous* Jesus Christ. Both Word and flesh are united to the *one nous* Jesus Christ in the *one* determination, that is, as hypostasis.

In short, as *determination* of the essential relations of its being, the hypostasis of each being must persist even in its unions; for does not the being of each persist? On the other hand, because Word and flesh have the *same* determination (that is, hypostasis) to the *same* being, the *nous* Jesus Christ, their hypostases are not unreasonably called one. Therefore the objection does not hold: the persistence of the hypostases of both Word and flesh as determinations—and so also the persistence of the natures of both Word and flesh as *enhypostasized* natures—does not necessarily prevent Leontius from asserting that Jesus Christ is *one hypostasis*.

All honor to Grumel, then! Had he but stuck to his guns! For our more exact analysis of Leontius' Christology establishes that Grumel's original understanding of Leontius' argument was very little short of the mark. Leontius is not a Cyrillian. He did not believe in the preponderance of the divine nature of Christ over the human nature. He did not suppose that the nature of Christ's manhood attained hypostasis only in the hypostasis of God the Word— by no means! To the contrary, Leontius is an Origenist, for whom Jesus Christ is the single unfallen *nous* of the intellectual creation; who by the will of God took flesh of the Virgin Mary and was made man *without losing that union with God in which he had per-*

sisted from the beginning. In Jesus Christ, God and flesh are united not *to one another*, but each to the *nous* Jesus Christ, and only *in him* to one another. Jesus is just as much God as man, but no more; just as much man as God, but no more. God and man are *components* of Jesus Christ, and *as such*, equals. Leontius cannot say that Jesus Christ *is* God,[15] for he believes that *both* natures of Christ are enhypostasized.

[15] Thus far—but no further—we may confirm the suspicion of, e.g. FLoofs, *LeontByz*, 71 f., that Leontius' union of God and man in Jesus Christ is very little less a ἕνωσις σχετική than the union proposed by Leontius' *bête noire*, Theodore of Mopsuestia. Plainly, the Neochalcedonians were not without reason in lumping Origenists and Antiochians together as those who deny that Jesus Christ is one of the Trinity. See, e.g., CyrScyth, *VSabae*, p. 127, ll. 19–24 (Cyril on the Nestorians): ἕτεροι δύο μοναχοὶ τῆς Νεστορίου ... αἱρέσεως ὑπέρμαχοι ... οὐδὲ ἕνα εἶναι τῆς ἁγίας καὶ ὁμοουσίου τριάδος ἐπρέσβευον Χριστὸν τὸν ἀληθινὸν θεόν; with which compare *VCyriaci*, p. 230, l. 3 f. (Cyriacus on the Origenists): λέγουσι μὴ εἶναι ἕνα τῆς τριάδος τὸν Χριστόν. (Note that Cyril lumps the two parties together on other occasions also. During his visit to Justinian in 531, Sabas asks the Emperor to condemn Origenists and Nestorians together with the Arians of the West [*VSabae*, p. 175, l. 19-p. 176, l. 20—although here Sabas' pairing of Origenism with Nestorianism rests more upon a quirk of fate than upon an analysis of theological concepts]. Again, Cyril represents the abbot Gelasius of the Grand Laura of Sabas as admonishing his monks, before his departure for Constantinople, to avoid the heresy of Theodore of Mopsuestia, since Sabas had condemned him with Origen [*VSabae*, p. 194, ll. 19–22]. Again, Cyril regularly reminds us that the Fifth Ecumenical Council [Constantinople, 553] condemned *both* Nestorians *and* Origenists [*VEuthymii*, p. 83, ll. 7–10; *VSabae*, p. 179, ll. 3–7; p. 199, ll. 1–6]. Finally, in the close of his *Life of Iohannes Hesychastes*, Cyril speaks of the Saint's struggles against the doctrines of both the Origenists and the advocates of Theodore of Mopsuestia [CyrScyth, p. 221, ll. 18–21]). Nonetheless, the σχέσις of the union proposed by Theodore is very different from that of Leontius' union, not least of all because Theodore did not believe that Jesus Christ was a pre-existent and eternal *nous*, a point in which even a Neochalcedonian would find the comparison very favorable to Theodore. Leontius' reply? After all, he might say, the οὐσιώδεις σχέσεις or *essential relations* by which he, Leontius, binds Word to flesh implies their *essential union* too, a ἕνωσις οὐσιώδης in which Leontius can honestly predicate a *communicatio idiomatum* and so also that genuine transformation of the human nature demanded by the tradition of Cyril of Alexandria. For Theodore, on the other hand, a union of beings in their *essential* relations is unthinkable. Why? Because, as it seems, Theodore insists that to predicate a rational soul of Jesus Christ—a point in which he and the Origenists are heartily at one—necessarily implies his hypostatic distinction, and that not only from every other human soul, but also from the Word of God to which the soul of Jesus Christ was united. We recall that Leontius is at pains to avoid this pitfall: for him, the man assumed by God in Jesus Christ is distinguished by *hypostasis* only from other men, not from the Word; to whom indeed the flesh is *united* as hypostasis.

B. *The Report of Leontius of Jerusalem*

To Leontius' own evidence that he holds both of the natures of Jesus Christ as enhypostasized, we add the testimony of no less an authority than one of Leontius' own contemporaries, Leontius of Jerusalem.

It has so far passed unnoticed that Leontius of Jerusalem, *Adversus Nestorianos*, book two, the thirteenth paragraph,[16] paraphrases and answers the first part of the second argument of Leontius of Byzantium in *CNE* 1.1,[17] that is, the passage in which our Leontius argues that what is not ἀνυπόστατον need not therefore be itself hypostasis, but may be ἐνυπόστατον. Now, in *AdvNest*, 2, Leontius of Jerusalem is attacking those who assert that there are to be seen in the Word incarnate not *one* hypostasis only, but *two*.[18] In the thirteenth paragraph, he finds occasion to introduce certain Dyophysites who agree "that in fact there is no nature without hypostasis," but do not thereby imply two hypostases in Jesus Christ; "for," these Dyophysites say,

> we too say that *the natures* [of Jesus Christ] are ἐνυπόστατοι. Nonetheless, [it does] not [follow that] if a thing is ἐνυπόστατον, it is also hypostasis, as [also] of course [it does] not [follow that] if a thing is ἐνούσιον, it is also ousia; for, after all, we say that the hypostases of the holy Trinity are three and that these [three] are ἐνούσιοι, yet do not say [that there are] beside the three hypostases three ousiai also, even though we recognize that each of the hypostases is ἐνούσιος. If indeed it is possible, we say, to predicate three ἐνούσιοι hypostases in a single ousia, then *surely it is also possible to predicate two* ἐνυπόστατοι *natures in one hypostasis*.[19]

Can there be any doubt that Leontius of Jerusalem is replying here to the arguments of Leontius of Byzantium? Hardly.

First, Leontius of Byzantium might very well be numbered among those who assert two hypostases in Jesus Christ. Does he not admit

---

[16] LeontJer, *AdvNest*, 2.13, PG, 86, 1560A 5–1565A 8.
[17] LeontByz, *CNE* 1.1, PG, 86, 1278 C 14–1280A 3.
[18] The title of LeontJer, *AdvNest*, 2, PG, 86, 1525[–1526] B10 f.: δευτέρας ἀσεβείας αὐτῶν ἔλεγχος λεγόντων δύο καὶ οὐ μίαν τὴν ὑπόστασιν ἐκ τῆς κατὰ τὴν σάρκωσιν τοῦ λόγου οἰκονομίας ὁρᾶσθαι.
[19] *Ibid.*, 2.13, PG, 86, 1560A 8–B 3.

that both the Word and flesh of Jesus Christ are hypostases—the Word, of course, in relation to the Father and the Holy Spirit, and the flesh in relation to other flesh?[20] Granted that Leontius' critic here has taken no account of his doctrine of the essential relations of being; but then neither have his modern critics.

Second, the assertion ascribed to his adversary by Leontius of Jerusalem—"that in fact there is no nature without hypostasis"[21] —corresponds exactly to the insistence of Leontius of Byzantium in CNE 1.1 that ὁ τοίνυν λέγων, οὐκ ἔστιν φύσις ἀνυπόστατος, ἀληθὲς ... λέγει.[22]

Third, the distinction of the opponent of Leontius of Jerusalem between [φύσις] ἐνυπόστατος and hypostasis—ἀλλ' οὐκ εἴ τι ἐνυπόστατον, τοῦτο καὶ ὑπόστασις, as Leontius of Jerusalem phrases it[23] —is precisely the argument of Leontius of Byzantium: οὐ ταὐτόν, ὦ οὗτοι, ὑπόστασις καὶ ἐνυπόστατον ....[24] The report of Leontius of Jerusalem is all the more significant here because it is this argument that he attacks. Will Leontius of Byzantium distinguish between natures existing as hypostases and natures existing as *enhypostasized* natures, that is, not ἐν ἑαυτῷ but ἐν ἑτέρῳ?[25] For Leontius of Jerusalem, *every* nature, if it exists at all, must be ἐνυπόστατος, for ἐνυπόστατος simply means *existing*: ... ἐπεὶ μέν εἰσιν αἱ φύσεις, ἀναγκαῖον αὐτὰς καὶ ὑφεστηκέναι καὶ ἐνυποστάτους εἶναι...[26]—whether the nature exists ἰδίᾳ[27] or not.

Finally, the argument attributed by Leontius of Jerusalem to his adversary, that hypostasis is different from enhypostasized nature just as ousia is different from ἐνούσιον,[28] is precisely the argument

[20] E.g., in LeontByz, CNE 1.4, PG, 86, 1289A 3–11 and especially 5 f.— remembering always that A 5 *post* πρὸς *add.* τὸν πατέρα διὰ τὴν θεότητα μετὰ τῆς ἀνθρωπότητος· καὶ ὑπόστασις ὢν ὅλως (*sed* ὅλος O) πρὸς VOG.

[21] LeontJer, *AdvNest*, 2.13, PG, 86, 1560A 8: ... ὅτι ὄντως φύσις οὐκ ἔστιν ἀνυπόστατος....

[22] LeontByz, CNE 1.1, PG, 86, 1277D 11 f. Compare 1280A 1–3: ἀνυπόστατος μὲν οὖν φύσις, τουτέστιν οὐσία, οὐκ ἂν εἴη ποτέ.

[23] LeontJer, *AdvNest*, 2.13, PG, 86, 1560A 9 f.

[24] LeontByz, CNE 1.1, PG, 86, 1277C 14.

[25] *Ibid.*, 1277D 4–6.

[26] LeontJer, *AdvNest*, 2.13, PG, 86, 1561C 3 f.

[27] The word preferred by Leontius of Jerusalem. See *ibid.*, 1561B 14, C 5, C 6, *passim*.

[28] *Ibid.*, 2.13, PG, 86, 1560A 9–11: ἀλλ' οὐκ εἴ τι ἐνυπόστατον, τοῦτο καὶ ὑπόστασις, ὥσπερ ἀμέλει οὐκ εἴ τι ἐνούσιον, τοῦτο καὶ οὐσία, etc.

of Leontius of Byzantium: οὐ ταὐτόν, ὦ οὗτοι, ὑπόστασις καὶ ἐνυπόστατον, ὥσπερ ἕτερον οὐσία καὶ ἐνούσιον.[29] Indeed, Leontius of Jerusalem's expansion upon the point is as admirable a commentary as we could wish. And does not Leontius of Byzantium thereupon establish a parallel between the relation of enhypostasized nature to hypostasis and the relation of ποιότητες, qualities, to the ousia to which they belong?—arguing that just as enhypostasized nature is not hypostasis because it is always seen in another being, so also "no [quality] is [itself] ousia ... but [is rather] what is always seen περὶ τὴν οὐσίαν, as color in a body and as knowledge in a soul."[30] No surprise then that Leontius of Jerusalem presents his adversary as arguing that ἐγχρωμάτιστον λέγοντες σῶμα, οὐ ταυτὸν ἴσμεν τῷ χρώματι τὸ σῶμα· οὐκ εἴ τι γὰρ ἐγχρωμάτιστον, τοῦτο ἤδη καὶ χρῶμα, etc.[31]

And when we consider at the end that every single one of these arguments of Leontius of Byzantium occurs in a single chapter of a single book[32]—and a rather short one at that—there can remain no doubt of it: the adversary of Leontius of Jerusalem in this thirteenth chapter of *Adversus Nestorianos* is none other than Leontius of Byzantium. We are even able to cap the climax: Leontius of Jerusalem acidly remarks of his opponents here that "by reason of these [arguments], they say that they themselves are from [among] the cherubim."[33] The words clearly direct us to the

[29] LeontByz, *CNE* I.I, PG, 86, 1277C 14–D 1.

[30] *Ibid.*, 1277D 8–11. I note in passing that MRichard, "Léonce et Pamphile," *RevScPhilTheol*, 27 (1938), 29 f., interprets 1277D 1–11 as asserting "la jonction à l'accident des ποιότητες οὐσιώδεις καὶ ἐπουσιώδεις et l'opposition de cet ensemble à la substance ...." He is wrong. 1277D 6 τοιαῦται does not refer to D 5 συμβεβηκός but to D 4 τὸ ... ἐνυπόστατον, as FLoofs, *LeontByz*, 65, reads. Leontius intends to establish, not that qualities are accidents, but that ἐνυπόστατα are *not* accidents, even though the definition of accident may properly be applied to them. On the other hand, Loofs is certainly wrong in supposing that Leontius says that qualities *are* ἐνυπόστατα, for then enhypostasized natures will be seen in and around *ousia* or *nature*, just as qualities; whereas Leontius clearly means us to understand that ἐνυπόστατα are seen in and around *hypostasis*. Plainly Leontius intends the parallel ἐνυπόστατον: *hypostasis* = *quality* : *ousia* only of the *relations* of the elements of each pair.

[31] LeontJer, *AdvNest*, 2.13, PG, 86, 1560B 8–10, which exactly reproduces the argument of LeontByz, *CNE* I.I, PG, 86, 1277D 13–1280A 1.

[32] *CNE* I.I, of course.

[33] LeontJer, *AdvNest*, 2.13, PG, 86, 1560C 2 f.: διὰ τούτων ἀπὸ χερουβὶμ ἑαυτοὺς ὀνομάζοντες.

definition of the Christian life as the angelic life, a commonplace
in patristic times. More specifically, Leontius of Jerusalem is
accusing his adversaries of a perversion of that definition: they
claim not only to be living the angelic life, but even somehow to be
immediately associated with the highest orders of the angels; that
is, they claim to be "from [among] the cherubim." Plainly enough,
such an assertion seems blasphemous to Leontius of Jerusalem;
but in Origenist circles it would be quite understandable. For the
Origenists all rational beings, both men and angels, belong to a
single *genus*: all are fallen *noes*. Angels differ from men only in
having as it were fallen less far; God grants them a higher rank
than men and devils only in order that they may guide men and
devils to salvation. It is easy enough, then, to suppose that at least
some of the Origenists looked upon the saints and teachers of the
church (and perhaps themselves!) as intellects of an order higher
than that of ordinary men; intellects not properly human, but
angelic, descended among us in order to reveal God's will with
more perfect clarity and authority. Or it may be that these saints
and teachers seemed so certainly to have merited promotion to
angelic rank in the next aeon that their disciples (or they themselves!) claimed the name of angel for them even in this world. In
any case, the words of Leontius of Jerusalem apply to no one more
perfectly than to a disciple of Evagrius.[34]

[34] The clear identity of the thought of the adversary of Leontius of
Jerusalem in *AdvNest*, 2.13, with the thought of Leontius of Byzantium in
CNE 1.1 must not tempt us to suppose that the source of Leontius of
Jerusalem is *CNE* 1.1 itself. Leontius of Jerusalem plainly knows more of
the argument of Leontius of Byzantium than *CNE* 1.1 itself could have
taught him; e.g., the full sense of the contrast of ἐνυπόστατον to ἐνούσιον
and the argument that *both* natures of Jesus Christ are enhypostasized. We
ought not be surprised at this. Does not Leontius of Byzantium himself say
that *CNE* reduces to writing the arguments of his public lectures (*CNE
prol*, PG, 86, 1268B 2–7)? Is it not highly probable that he or other
members of his party had composed other brief accounts of his doctrine,
short treatises like *CapTrig*? Either could have served Leontius of Jerusalem
as source. However, the report of Leontius of Jerusalem is by no means
useless for the literary history of the times; e.g., we learn from it that the
doctrines of Leontius of Byzantium had at least some slight circulation in the
period in which *AdvNest* was written, that is, *ca.* 536–544. (On the date of
composition of *AdvNest*, see the *Literaturbericht* in S. Helmer, *Der Neuchalkedonismus*, 203 f.) I note, however, that the report of *AdvNest* tells us nothing more of the places to which the Origenist Christology had spread than
we learn from, e.g., the life of Leontius of Byzantium: we ought hardly be

On then to the conclusion. The significance of our identification of the adversary of Leontius of Jerusalem as Leontius of Byzantium is this: that Leontius of Jerusalem twice attributes to his opponents the assertion that *both* natures of Jesus Christ are enhypostasized; for they assert, Leontius of Jerusalem reports, " 'we, too, say that the natures [of Jesus Christ] are ἐνυπόστατοι' "[35] and again that " 'if indeed it is possible ... to predicate three ἐνούσιοι hypostases in a single ousia, then surely it is also possible to predicate two enhypostasized natures in one hypostasis.' "[36] Therefore the evidence of Leontius' own contemporary joins with the necessities of his argument to establish that, for him, *both the Word and the flesh in Jesus Christ are enhypostasized natures.*

III. Epilogue

We stand at the end of the argument of the first part of this essay. Time now to take stock. Where we have been, we know; but where are we now, and where do we go from here?

Where we are, it seems, is nowhere near where our predecessors on this path had left us. We have proved two theses. The first: that for Leontius ousia and hypostasis are not links in the chain of being, much less beings themselves, but rather are simultaneous determinations of the essential relations of beings. Of this definition, it is fair to say, only the faintest traces appear in the earlier literature. The second thesis: that the Jesus Christ of Leontius is the *nous* Jesus Christ of the Origenist Evagrius of Pontus. For this thesis the ground had been well laid: it had long been suspected that the theologian Leontius was one man with the Origenist monk Leontius of Cyril of Scythopolis' *Vita Sabae*. Nonetheless, our argument here has upset at least three assumptions of the previous consensus.

---

surprised that a monk of Jerusalem was acquainted with the Christology of a monk of the New Laura near Tekoa.

[35] LeontJer, *AdvNest*, 2.13, PG, 1560A 8 f.: ἐνυποστάτους γὰρ φαμεν τὰς οὐσίας καὶ ἡμεῖς....

[36] *Ibid.*, 1560A 15–B 3: εἰ τοίνυν ἔστι λέγειν ... τρεῖς ὑποστάσεις ἐνουσίους ἐν μιᾷ οὐσίᾳ, ἐνδέχεται δηλονότι καὶ φύσεις λέγειν ἐνυποστάτους δύο ἐν μιᾷ ὑποστάσει.

First of all, it was generally agreed that the work of our theologian Leontius showed no trace of Origenism. The consequence was that the identification of the Origenist monk Leontius with the theologian Leontius seemed to demand either that we discount the charges of Cyril of Scythopolis or that we suppose the theologian Leontius a charlatan. We know better now. Leontius' Christology is now proved thoroughly Origenist. Paradoxically, Leontius thereby is made an honest man. His doctrine is heretical, to be sure; but it is his very own. However we may judge the uses to which he put it, we can no longer suppose that he planted and watered it merely to screen acts of violence and vengeance. Leontius meant what he said; and what he said demonstrated a perspicuity in matters theological so much superior to the acumen in matters historical of some of his recent critics that it is not perhaps altogether unfair to ask whether they are not themselves in some degree liable to the judgement which they have pronounced. Cyril of Scythopolis, too, proves honest. We need no longer harbor suspicions that Leontius' side of the story of the Origenistic controversy in Palestine might wipe Cyril's account from the board. Just as Cyril said, Leontius was an Origenist heretic.

Here we have done with a second article of the consensus: that Leontius was, or at very least claimed to be, a disciple of Cyril of Alexandria, that he believed with Cyril that the one person or hypostasis of Jesus Christ is the second person of the Trinity, God the Son. Nothing further from the truth. Leontius was an Origenist, not a Cyrillian. His Jesus Christ was not the Word incarnate but an incorporeal *nous*, united to God from all eternity in the vision of God, who by the grace of God took a body while yet united to God in order that he might reveal the sense and purpose of the visible creation which God had made to save us. It is indeed the tradition of Cyril and the decrees of the Council of Chalcedon which Leontius pretends to expound; but in fact he casts both tradition and decrees into the shape of the spirituality of Evagrius of Pontus.

Here also the consensus has seen with only one eye: it has tacitly assumed that the spirituality of such a man as the monk Leontius of the New Laura could have made little headway in the loftier air of the debates on the person and natures of Jesus Christ. Spirituality has been supposed incapable of dogma. Indeed, the marriage of spirituality and dogma in Maximus the Confessor has recently been heralded as something new in its times.[37] Here, too, we know better now. In Leontius and his work we see the translation of what we may call the spirituality of the Origenist movement into the language of the christological controversies. We add that the Origenist spirituality on which he drew now seems to have possessed a metaphysics at once more profound and more articulate than we had thought.

So much then for the consensus. An *Ehrensrettung* here for Leontius? Is he once again what Angelo Mai called him a century ago, *princeps theologorum suae aetatis* ? Hardly, for he was a heretic. In fact, we have done little more than to restore him to the ranks of men of integrity and to prove him a theologian of uncommon depth and competence.

Now what lies ahead? Have our discoveries here set new tasks for students of the history of Christian thought? I offer three suggestions.

First, the history of Origenism must be revised. Previous studies on Evagrius of Pontus and Maximus the Confessor have almost ignored the role of Origenism and Origenists in the dogmatic controversies of the high patristic period. With Antoine Guillaumont's study of the Christology of Evagrius of Pontus, this essay has established, I hope, that the Origenist party possessed both a theology capable of the highest sophistication and theologians willing and able to develop it. Hereafter we must watch for its traces as closely as we watch for the traces of the schools of Antioch and Alexandria. Was it Evagrius' teaching that Jesus Christ is a *nous* that moved Apollinaris to deny *nous* to Jesus Christ? Is it significant that certain of the first generation of Monophysites

---

[37] So Hans Urs von Balthasar, *Kosmische Liturgie. Das Weltbild Maximus' des Bekenners*, 2nd rev. ed. (Einsiedeln, 1961), 41–47 ("Scholastik und Mystik"). For the theologians of the sixth century the author has little use: "Der Dualismus zwischen Scholastik und Mystik, Schultheologie und Mönchsspiritualität, war im 6. Jahrhundert vollkommen" (p. 41 f.). In express contrast stand the works of Maximus: "sie distinguieren nur, um das Mysterium im ganzen heller aufleuchten zu lassen, sie arbeiten immerfort im Dienst einer Spiritualität" (p. 43). Our analysis of Leontius' thought suggests that all such comparisons may be unjust, or at least requires that an exception be made for Leontius.

(e.g., Philoxenus of Mabboug) had felt the influence of Evagrius? Is it possible that Maximus the Confessor derived his concepts of ἐνέργεια and will from the Origenist analysis of *nous*?

Second, the history of the concepts *ousia* and *hypostasis* must be completely rewritten. Nothing in the present literature has prepared us for what we have found in Leontius. Above all: what are Leontius' sources? Evagrius and the Origenist tradition? The school of Antioch, with which the Origenist tradition has so many affinities? Proclus and the Neoplatonists? Pseudo-Dionysius the Areopagite?

Finally, the clearer definition of the accomplishment of Leontius of Byzantium offers a better norm of comparison for the study of his influence than we have had before. Perhaps the most intriguing question here is raised by our recovery of Leontius' peculiar definition of *enhypostasized nature*. It has long been known that Leontius was not the first to use the formula; but it has generally been agreed that his use of the formula was Orthodox. Now we know that he used the formula to expound a Christology flatly heretical. Indeed, we can only suppose that he meant his definition of enhypostasized nature as a formal critique of the Orthodox definition; i. e., that definition earlier advanced by John the Grammarian and later adopted by the tradition. We may ask then: Does Leontius' peculiar definition survive in later theologians? Does it come to influence the Orthodox definition?

However—and with this we close—the tale of Leontius and his secret heresy will interest students of Byzantine history too; for, in restoring its sense to his Christology, we have also begun the reconstruction of the program of the Origenist party in the christological controversies. That party, we know, was especially influential in Constantinople in the reign of Justinian; indeed, after about A. D. 536, the Emperor's chief theological advisor was an Origenist. Now there is no reason to doubt that Leontius of Byzantium was as it were the official theologian of this party, and so we pass on to the second part of our essay: a study of the life of Leontius during the years 513–536—years spent in Constantinople in those constant debates with his theological adversaries which begot his theological treatises; years devoted to the establishment of an Origenist party in the very seat of the imperial power.

CHAPTER SIX

LEONTIUS' LIFE

In this chapter we shall have to do chiefly with that period in the life of Leontius in which we suppose he brought his Christology to maturity, that is, the first five years of his public life—five years spent in Constantinople, the years 531-*ca.* 536. However, in order to set this period in perspective, we begin with two prefaces, one on the sources for Leontius' life and one on the outline of his life itself.

I. TWO PREFACES

A. *The Sources for Leontius' Life*

In the study of Leontius, the name of the game is: *which Leontius?* The student of the history of Christian doctrine asks whether Leontius the author of *CNE*, *CapTrig*, and *SolArgSev* is identical with the Leontius of Jerusalem who wrote *Contra Monophysitas* and *Adversus Nestorianos*—and answers *no*. The biographer of Leontius asks whether our theologian Leontius is identical with the Origenist monk Leontius of Cyril of Scythopolis' *Vita Sabae*.[1] The course of the scholarly controversy ought not detain us here.[2] Enough to note the only serious objection to the identifica-

---

[1] On Cyril of Scythopolis and his work, see our notes to our description of *Evagriana* in Leontius in Chapter Four, p. 84 f., *supra*.

[2] The debate over the identification of the two Leontii is almost as old as the *editio princeps* of the *corpus Leontianum* in Turrianus' Latin, but the modern literature begins with Friedrich Loofs' defense of the identification in his *LeontByz* (1888), 274–297 ("Leontius von Byzanz, der Origenist der *Vita Sabae*"). After Loofs, WRügamer, *LeontByz* (1894), 56–63, was the first to challenge the identification; he found influential support in ESchwartz, *KyrSkyth* (1939), p. 388 [–389], note 2. However, most other students of the problem have accepted the identification: the current consensus in its favor may be said to have been established in 1947 by MRichard, "Léonce …

tion: that the monk Leontius of the *Vita Sabae* was a fanatical Origenist, while the works of the theologian Leontius (*CNE, Cap Trig, SolArgSev*) showed, as it seemed, only the faintest traces of Origenism. How then could the two be one? Unless, of course, the theologian Leontius was, as they say, only putting us on.[3] Now, however, we are better advised. We know now that the Christology of the theologian Leontius is Origenist to the core. With this the chief obstacle to the identification vanishes. From now on the *Vita Sabae* must be accepted as a source for the life of our theologian Leontius, indeed as the major source.

However, the *Vita Sabae* is not our only source. From Leontius himself we have in *CNE* 3 a short account of his youthful flirtation with the doctrines of the school of Antioch and his subsequent salvation in Palestine by wise and pious men whom we can now quite certainly identify as Origenists.[4] Alas, of his later life he tells us as good as nothing.

There are two sources for Leontius' life, then: his own report of his youth and the *Vita Sabae* of Cyril of Scythopolis. All other documents claiming to be sources must be measured by these. Now we ask: what is the outline of the life they portray?

B. *The Outline of Leontius' Life*

As our two sources represent it, the life of Leontius falls into two periods: his youth and his public career. Our source for the first is his own report in *CNE* 3; for the second, Cyril of Scythopolis' *Vita Sabae*, here reinforced by wisps of indirect evidence from Leontius' *corpus*. For the present we set the first period aside; important as it must have been for the development of his thought, it is too poorly documented to serve our immediate purpose, that is, to describe the immediate occasion of his Christology. We turn instead to his public career.

---

origéniste?" *RevEtByz*, V (1947), 31–66, who defends the identification, but only at the price—as we have noticed above—of calling the Christology of *CNE* 1 a mere facade. See also p. 1, note 1.

[3] MRichard, "Léonce ... origéniste?" *RevEtByz*, V (1947), 55, is of this opinion.

[4] LeontByz, *CNE* 3 *prol*, PG, 86, 1357C 3–1360B 5.

If the account of Cyril of Scythopolis is to be trusted, Leontius' public career may be divided into three parts: his coming up to Constantinople with Sabas in 531 and his stay there until after the Council of 536; his return to Palestine and the New Laura *ca.* 536 and his residence there until about 540, a time in which he was among the leaders in the campaign of the Origenists to seize control of the monasteries; and finally, his return to Constantinople *ca.* 540 and his stay there until his death there in—as I think—543, a journey probably undertaken in order to defend the Origenist cause against charges forwarded to the Emperor Justinian by its adversaries in Palestine.

Now, of these three periods it is certainly the first which had the most influence on the production of Leontius' *corpus*, not only because it is in these years, 531-*ca.* 536, that Leontius seems first to have entered public life, but also because these are the years of the great truce between Orthodox and Monophysites and the public disputations between them in Constantinople, in which Leontius surely took part. Even if the *corpus* itself was published only after 540—the exact date remains unknown—its doctrine certainly dates from the earlier period. In any case, the evidence for Leontius' participation in the encounter of Orthodox with Monophysite in this time deserves reassessment; and so we turn to the years 531–536.

II. CONSTANTINOPLE 531—*circa* 536
THE CAMPAIGN AGAINST THE MONOPHYSITES

When Cyril of Scythopolis first mentions Leontius, it is to report that in the summer of 531 Sabas, who had taken Leontius on a mission to Constantinople, had separated from him because he had discovered that Leontius inclined to the opinions of Origen.[5] For Cyril, Leontius' journey to Constantinople marks the beginning of his public career. More specifically, it marks the beginning of the first period of his public career, his involvement in that particular stage of the controversy between Orthodox and Monophysites which began when Justinian relaxed his persecution of the Monophysites

[5] CyrScyth, *VSabae*, p. 176, ll. 10-20.

about 531. The controversy ends with the expulsion of the Monophysites by the Council of 536, which, as we shall see, Leontius
attended as observer and petitioner; and shortly later we find
Leontius back in Palestine, vigorously engaged in a new controversy
which will occupy him, it seems, to his death. We shall deal here
with the first of these two phases of Leontius' career.

The scene is Constantinople, the time, the years between Sabas'
arrival in Constantinople in the summer of 531 and the Council of
Constantinople which adjourned 4 June 536. What do we know of
Leontius in these years? We look for the answer in two steps. First,
we shall examine the testimony of Cyril of Scythopolis in his *Vita
Sabae*. Second, we deal with two important questions of detail:
whether Leontius was present at the colloquy of 532 between
Orthodox and Monophysites; and again, whether he was the Leontius observer and petitioner of the Council of 536 already mentioned.

A. *The Account of Cyril of Scythopolis*

1. The Summer of 531: The Debates with the Monophysites and Leontius' Separation from Sabas

As we have noticed above, when Cyril begins his account of
Leontius' public career, Leontius is already under a cloud. Cyril is
explaining why Sabas had petitioned the Emperor Justinian to
condemn the heresies of Arius, Nestorius, and Origen. Why just
these three? Cyril explains in detail.

> The heresy of Arius, because the Goths, Visigoths, Vandals,
> and Gepides, who were Arians, then ruled the whole West, and
> he [Sabas] knew of course by the Spirit that the Emperor was
> soon to overcome them. He named the heresy of Nestorius,
> because he had discovered that in their debates with the Mono-
> physites in the Royal Stoa certain of the monks who had
> come up with him [to Constantinople] held by Theodore of
> Mopsuestia. Finally, he included the pernicious heresy of Origen
> in the condemnation of the other two because one of the monks
> with him [there], a native of Byzantium, Leontius by name and

one of the [monks] admitted with Nonnus to the New Laura after the death of the abbot Agapetus, held to the doctrines of Origen. Though he pretended to support the Council of Chalcedon, he was known really to believe the opinions of Origen. When our father Sabas heard this and remembered the words of the blessed Agapetus, he used [great] severity and ejected both him and those of the opinions of Theodore from his company, and thereupon recommended to the Emperor the condemnation of the heresies of both.[6]

Soon after, we hear that in September of the same year (531) Sabas sailed back to Palestine, leaving Leontius and the disciples of Theodore of Mopsuestia in Constantinople.[7]

What can we learn of Leontius from this account?

In Cyril's account, Sabas' mission in Constantinople seems to have had no connection whatever with affairs ecclesiastical or dogmatic: he was sent simply to ask the Emperor to remand the taxes of those parts of Palestine ravaged in the recent (529) uprising of the Samaritans.[8] However, in the very year of the mission (531), Justinian had proclaimed a sort of amnesty to the Monophysite bishops and monks expelled from their seats by Justin I on his accession in 518, and Constantinople was full of Monophysites come to the capital to plead their cause in the discussions which the amnesty seems to have been meant to promote.[8a] Now it was surely in just these discussions that certain monks of Sabas' company revealed their proclivities to Theodore of Mopsuestia and so brought down on themselves the wrath of Sabas; and we may suppose besides that Leontius, who suffered the same fate, had joined in the same conversations.

---

[6] *Ibid.*, p. 176, ll. 3-20. *Monophysites* translates ἀποσχιστῶν (l. 9); literally *schismatics*, but in Cyril a *terminus technicus* for Monophysites. "The words of the blessed Agapetus" (l. 17) were spoken about 514, when he threw Nonnus and his followers out of the New Laura: "they promote the doctrines of Origen to the destruction of the fellowship, and I would rather leave the place than bring them into the fellowship entrusted to me" (*ibid.*, p. 125, ll. 10-13).

[7] *Ibid.*, p. 179, ll. 8-12.

[8] *Ibid.*, p. 171, l. 26-p. 173, l. 11; see also E Stein, *BasEmp*, II (Paris, 1949), 287 f., 373 f.

[8a] On Justinian's relaxation of the persecution of the Monophysites, E Stein, *BasEmp*, II, 377 ff., and especially p. 377, note 1.

That Leontius was present at some such disputations, he himself indicates clearly. The Royal Stoa of Cyril's account—ἡ βασιλικὴ στοά, but commonly called simply ἡ βασιλική—was if not itself the site, at very least near the site of the university at Constantinople, and so a place in which courses of instruction seem to have been held.[9] Now, in the very first words of the prologue to *CNE*, Leontius tells us that "certain men beloved of God and deeply concerned with the divine teachings, after hearing with approval the public discourses which I have often held (τὰς εἰς τὸ κοινὸν διαλέξεις, ἃς συχνῶς πεποιήμεθα), have encouraged me to give them in writing an outline of the questions and answers [so] often discussed (τῶν πολλάκις εἰρημένων ἐπαπορήσεων καὶ λύσεων ὑποτυπώσεις τινάς)."[10] Leontius himself says, then, that at least his *CNE* had as its occasion precisely the sort of discussion which Cyril reports was held in the Royal Stoa during Sabas' stay in Constantinople. May we not suppose that the discussions mentioned by Cyril and Leontius are the same and mark the beginning of Leontius' public career?

We may go further. If Leontius did indeed join in the disputations with the Monophysites, it can only have been as an advocate of the formulae of the Council of Chalcedon which he later defends in his writings; and his writings suggest besides that his defense of the Council in the disputations cannot have been altogether without skill. If so, we perhaps have the answer to a question which Cyril of Scythopolis leaves undiscussed. According to

[9] On the βασιλική, see Raymond Janin, *Constantinople byzantine*, Archives de l'Orient chrétien, No. 4A, 2nd ed. (Paris, 1964), 157 f., 162, who cites, among others: Socrates, *Historia ecclesiastica*, III, 1 (ed. Robert Hussey, I [Oxford, 1853], 376; cf. PG, 67, 369A 15–B 7), for the education of Julian there in the middle of the fourth century; Theophanes, *Chronographia* (ed. Carolus de Boor, I [Leipzig, 1883], p. 88, ll. 18–20), who mentions a Εὐσέβιός τις, σχολαστικὸς τῆς βασιλικῆς Κωνσταντινουπόλεως, the first to echo Nestorius' attack on the epithet Θεοτόκος in 429 and presumably a lawyer trained in the βασιλική; and finally, Georgius Cedrenus, *Historiarum compendium* (ed. Immanuel Bekker, I [Bonn, 1838], p. 616, l. 5ff.; cf. PG, 121, 669C 8–12), who reports that the fire of 475 destroyed, among other things, τὴν ... καλουμένην βασιλικήν, ἐν ᾗ ἀπέκειτο βιβλιοθήκη ἔχουσα βίβλους μυριάδας δώδεκα; a testimony which Janin seems to take as evidence that the university was in the βασιλική too. After the fire, both βασιλική and library were promptly rebuilt.

[10] PG, 86, 1268B 1–7.

Cyril, Sabas was no friend to Origenism, and it is only after his death in 532 that Nonnus and his party begin to make serious inroads among Sabas' lauras.[11] Why then did Sabas bring with him to Constantinople a monk closely associated since perhaps 520 with the Origenist Nonnus? Perhaps, of course, because Leontius was a native of Byzantium by birth; but again, what of his Origenism? Had the Origenist monks, as Cyril suggests, been so utterly success-ful in dissimulation?[12] Was Sabas himself, then ninety-two years old,[13] too nearly senile to recognize Leontius for what he was? Or is the opposition to Origenism before Sabas' death rather less em-phatic than it had become in Cyril's times? Can it be that in the days of Sabas the Origenists were tolerated in their spirituality because of their vigorous defense of Orthodoxy on other fronts? That Leontius appears in the summer of 531 as an adversary of the Monophysites strongly suggests so. Alas, he must have spoken too freely, for somehow his Origenism was revealed for what it was, and Sabas left him flat in Constantinople.

2. Constantinople 531–536

In the summer of 531, then, Leontius found himself, as it were, homeless in Constantinople. Cyril of Scythopolis next mentions him only when he tells how the Origenist party began to grow after Sabas' death in 532 removed its most influential adversary.

> About the same time Domitian, the abbot[14] of the monastery of Martyrius, and Theodore called Askidas, then the chief (ἐξάρχων) of the monks of the New Laura, both of whom sufficiently shared in the foul doctrine of Origen, sailed off to Constantinople. On the pretense of defending the Council of Chalcedon and by means of the recommendation of the same Leontius of Byzantium mentioned above, they attached them-

---

[11] Besides the passage translated just above, see CyrScyth, *VSabae*, p. 124, l. 21-p. 125, l. 23 and especially p. 125, l. 22 f., with which com-pare p. 188, l. 7ff. and especially ll. 7–13.

[12] *Ibid.*, p. 125, l. 20ff.

[13] *Ibid.*, p. 171, l. 26ff.; p. 173, ll. 9–11.

[14] As here, I regularly use *abbot* to translate ἡγούμενος, but never to translate ἀββᾶς.

selves to the reverend Eusebius and through him to our most pious Emperor. Because they veiled their evil doctrines in the abundance of their hypocrisy and enjoyed free access to the place, Domitian obtained the jurisdiction of the land of the Galatians and Theodore the seat of Caesarea in Cappadocia. From that time on, the party of Nonnus gained in strength, and zealously and ceaselessly sowed the seeds of Origenism throughout the whole of Palestine.[15]

Just when did Domitian and Theodore meet Leontius in the capital? Sometime before 537 for, as we shall see, by that year Leontius had returned to Palestine.[16] On the other hand we know from another source, the *acta* of the Council of 536, that both Domitian and Theodore attended the Council and so were in Constantinople that year. However, they stand in the *acta* only as monks, not bishops;[17] and so it seems unlikely that Leontius had introduced them to Eusebius much before that date. In short, we may reasonably suppose that it was during their visit to Constantinople for the Council of 536 that Domitian and Theodore fell in with Leontius. If so, the voyage of Domitian and Theodore mentioned by Cyril will be the same as their voyage to the Council of 536,[18] and we may assume besides that Leontius himself was in

[15] CyrScyth, *VSabae*, p. 188, l. 24-p. 189, l. 9. I note that the term ἐξάρχων, which Cyril applies to Theodore, is not necessarily the equivalent of ἡγούμενος; as we shall see, in the *acta* of the Council of 536 Theodore signs only as διάκονος καὶ μοναχὸς τῆς Νέας λαύρας, etc., and not as ἡγούμενος.

[16] CyrScyth, *VSabae*, p. 190, ll. 3-5. When Leontius goes back again to Constantinople about 540, Domitian and Theodore are already bishops (*ibid.*, p. 191, l. 1 ff. and especially ll. 20-25, to the best of my knowledge the earliest mention anywhere of Domitian and Theodore *in office*).

[17] The names of Domitian and Theodore Askidas stand among the Palestinian delegation in the lists of observers of the first four sessions (*ACO*, III [Berlin, 1940], p. 130, ll. 19, 27; p. 158, ll. 23, 33; p. 165, ll. 24, 33; p. 174, ll. 1, 10). The Δομνῖνος of the second, third, and fourth sessions is in fact Δομετιανός. Domitian and Theodore also sign the *libelli monachorum ad Agapetum* (*ibid.*, p. 145, l. 22; p. 146, l. 1 f.), *ad Justinianum* II (p. 36, ll. 30-32; p. 37, l. 3 f.), and *ad Menam* (p. 50, ll. 11-13, 32 f.). Domitian's name stands in either first or (*Ad Justinianum* II and *Ad Menam*) second place; Theodore's name in tenth or (*Ad Justinianum* II) ninth place. Both appear as monks: e.g., Δομετιανὸς πρεσβύτερος καὶ ἀρχιμανδρίτης μονῆς τοῦ μακαρίου Μαρτυρίου (p. 130, l. 18) and Θεόδωρος διάκονος καὶ μοναχὸς τῆς Νέας λαύρας (p. 130, l. 27).

[18] That Cyril of Scythopolis represents Domitian and Theodore on their arrival in Constantinople as pretending to defend the Council of Chalcedon (*VSabae*, p. 188, l. 28-p. 189, l. 1, translated *supra*) only confirms this hypo-

Constantinople in or about that year. He had probably been there since 531.

However, the passage just translated tells us much more. First, we learn from Cyril just how the Origenists of Palestine finally established their influence in the capital itself. Later he will tell more of their tactics for, under the protection of Theodore, the Origenist party was able to carry on its propaganda in Palestine with impunity, even after the first condemnation of Origen in early 543.[19] Second, we obtain a clear indication that the Origenists participated in the public discussion about the formulae of the Council of Chalcedon: specifically, Domitian and Theodore Askidas obtained their influence "on the pretense of defending the Council of Chalcedon." Earlier, as we have seen, Cyril had used precisely the same language about Leontius: "he was known really to believe the opinions of Origen, although he pretended to support the Council of Chalcedon."[20] Just what arguments the Origenists used in the debates of this period Cyril does not say.[21] However, we have other and very much better evidence, for it was certainly in just these years that Leontius conceived at least the first book of his *CNE*. If we add the testimony of *CNE* I to the passing notices of Cyril, we are surely not far wrong in concluding that the peculiar appeal of the Origenists Leontius, Domitian, and Theodore to Eusebius and probably even to Justinian was precisely this: a defense of the formulae of the Council of Chalcedon which possessed some real

thesis: in the face of attacks by the Monophysites, then in the capital in force, the Council of 536 was called to reaffirm the doctrine of the Council of Chalcedon.

[19] By 543 at latest, Theodore has become one of Justinian's most trusted advisors, for in his account of that year Cyril describes him as Θεόδωρος... τοῦ παλατίου κρατῶν (*VSabae*, p. 192, l. 22 f., with which compare p. 197, l. 19 f.). For Theodore's forceful intervention in Palestine in the interest of the Origenists, *ibid.*, p. 191, l. 20 ff.; p. 192, ll. 9–11 (which I understand of Palestine); p. 192, l. 20 ff., and especially p. 193, ll. 15–19; p. 194, l. 28 ff.; p. 197, l. 19 ff.; p. 198, l. 7 ff.

[20] On Domitian and Theodore, *ibid.*, p. 188, l. 28-p. 189, l. 1: ὑπὲρ τῆς ἐν Χαλκηδόνι συνόδου προσποιούμενοι ἀγωνίζεσθαι. On Leontius, *ibid.*, p. 176, l. 15 f.: τῆς γὰρ ἐν Χαλκηδόνι συνόδου προΐστασθαι προσποιούμενος ἐγνώσθη τὰ Ὠριγένους φρονῶν.

[21] For reasons of his own, Cyril does not so much as mention the Council of 536 or the controversy over the Three Chapters. On the latter, see ESchwartz, *KyrSkyth*, 406 ff.

155

hope of answering the criticisms of Severus and his Monophysites
without falling into the snares of Nestorius, in which some of the
earlier Chalcedonians had been caught.

In brief, in the years after 531 the Origenist party of Palestine
wins its way to power as a willing ally of the Emperor in his
campaigns against the Monophysites. In its success Leontius plays
no small part: it is he who makes the contacts at court to which
the party owes the promotion of Domitian and Theodore, and it is he
who molds the Christology of the Origenist Evagrius of Pontus to
the measure of the formulae of the Council of Chalcedon.

B. *The Colloquy of 532 and the Council of 536*

Nevertheless, our account of Leontius' life from 531 to 536 will
not be complete unless we consider two further questions:

First, was Leontius an observer at the colloquy of 532 between
Orthodox and Monophysites?

Second, was Leontius present at the Council of 536 in Constantinople which condemned the Monophysites?

We begin by reproducing the texts that testify to the presence of
a certain Leontius at colloquy and Council, then go on to examine
two earlier interpretations of them: first, the argument of Eduard
Schwartz that the Leontius of colloquy and Council is indeed the
Origenist monk of Cyril of Scythopolis' *Vita Sabae*; and second,
the argument of Marcel Richard to the contrary.

1. The Evidence

a. *Leontius and the colloquy of 532*

In the summer of 531, as we have seen, Justinian relaxed his
persecution of the Monophysites and undertook a campaign to
reconcile them to the christological formulae of the Council of
Chalcedon. His first step seems to have been to propose a colloquy,
and to that end he invited eight Monophysite and six Orthodox

bishops to the capital. After obviously lengthy preliminaries, the two parties met in disputation in 532.[22]

On the colloquy itself we possess a not unsatisfactory report in a Latin translation of a letter of one of the Orthodox bishops participating, Innocentius of Maronia, to a certain Thomas presbyter of Thessalonika.[23] Important as it is, we must pass over Innocentius' account in order to fix upon his notice that each of the delegations was accompanied by certain observers. Among those on the Orthodox side, *dominus vir venerabilis Eusebius presbyter et cimiliarcha sanctissimae maioris ecclesiae ... una cum Leontio viro venerabili monacho et apocrisario patrum in sancta civitate* [i.e., Jerusalem] *constitutorum*.[24]

Our Leontius? There is no evidence in the letter itself for, after the Orthodox bishops and observers are introduced, we hear nothing more of them. Traces of Leontius' thought? Not to be expected here. Hypatius, bishop of Ephesus, spoke for all the Orthodox— *os nostrum factus sicut et beatus Petrus apostolorum*, as Innocentius puts it[25]—and there is no reason to suppose that Hypatius so conformed his arguments to his colleagues' opinions that the one may be described from the other. The only question is: *could* the Origenist monk and theologian Leontius of Byzantium have been *apocrisarius patrum in sancta civitate constitutorum*?

b. *Leontius and the Council at Constantinople in 536*

Whoever the *Leontius apocrisarius* of the colloquy may be, either he or another monk of the same name is reported by the *acta* of the Council of Constantinople in 536 as an observer at the first four sessions, a petitioner at the fifth and last, and a subscriber of each

---

[22] For the date 532, see the careful discussion in EStein, *BasEmp*, II, p. 378, note 1, which may be considered definitive.

[23] InnMar, *DeColl*, in *ACO*, IV, 2 ([Strasbourg], 1914), 167–184.

[24] *Ibid.*, p. 170, ll. 2–7. The Latin *apocrisarius* of Innocentius is an improper transliteration of the Greek ἀποκρισιάριος. Nonetheless, where I refer to the Leontius of the colloquy whom Innocentius calls *apocrisarius*, I use the spelling of the Latin translation of Innocentius' letter. Otherwise I use the more accurate transliteration *apocrisiarius*.

[25] *Ibid.*, l. 27 f.

of three *libelli monachorum* addressed respectively to Agapetus of Rome, Justinian, and the patriarch of Constantinople, Menas.[26] The texts in question:[27]

First, the *acta* report that the Council admitted eighty-seven Orthodox monks to the first session (2 May 536) as observers. Among them: Λεόντιος μοναχὸς καὶ ἡγούμενος καὶ τοποτηρητὴς τῆς ἐρήμου πάσης.[28]

Second, in the same first session, the representatives of the see of Rome read into the record a *Libellus monachorum ad Agapetum* [*papam*], in which ninety-six monks had requested the Pope, since dead but then in Constantinople,[29] to banish the Monophysites Anthimus, Severus, Peter, and Zooras from the capital. Among the signers: Λεόντιος ἐλέει θεοῦ μοναχὸς καὶ ἡγούμενος καὶ τοποτηρητὴς πάσης τῆς ἐρήμου ἀξιώσας ὑπέγραψα.[30]

Third, the *acta* of the second session (6 May 536) list eighty-seven monks present as observers. Among them: Λεοντίου μοναχοῦ καὶ ἡγουμένου καὶ τοποτηρητοῦ τῆς ἐρήμου πάσης.[31]

Fourth, at the third session (10 May 536), among ninety-one monks admitted as observers: Λεόντιος μοναχὸς καὶ ἡγούμενος καὶ τοποτηρητὴς τῆς ἐρήμου πάσης.[32]

Fifth, at the fourth session (21 May 536), among ninety-three monks present: Λεόντιος μοναχὸς καὶ τοποτηρητὴς τῆς ἐρήμου πάσης.[33]

Sixth, the *acta* of the fifth and last session (4 June 536) include no list of observers, but report that the Council admitted as petitioners the monks, now ninety-seven, who had signed a brief *Libellus monachorum ad Justinianum* (that is, *Ad Justinianum* II) asking

[26] Beside the identity of name, both Leontii are monks and representatives of Jerusalem and the desert of Jerusalem. More cannot be said, but, *mirabile dictu*, all scholars have agreed that the Leontii of the colloquy and Council are the same man.

[27] For a similar list, see ESchwartz, *KyrSkyth*, 390.

[28] *ACO*, III, p. 130, l. 24. On the entrance of the monks, p. 128, l. 1 ff. Note that in *ACO*, III, the *acta* of the fifth and last session of the Council stand first (pp. 27–125); the first four sessions follow in order.

[29] Agapetus died probably on 22 April 536, that is, just before the first session of the Council on 2 May.

[30] *Ibid.*, p. 145, l. 34 f.

[31] *Ibid.*, p. 158, l. 29.

[32] *Ibid.*, p. 165, l. 30.

[33] *Ibid.*, p. 174, l. 7.

that the Monophysites be driven from Constantinople. Justinian had forwarded the appeal to the Council. Among the signatures: Λεόντιος ἐλέει Θεοῦ μοναχὸς ποιούμενος τὸν λόγον ὑπὲρ τῶν κατὰ τὴν ἔρημον ἁγίων πατέρων δεηθεὶς ὑπέγραψα.[34]

Finally, to the *libellus* just mentioned, the monks appended a similar but very much longer appeal to the Patriarch Menas: the *Libellus monachorum ad Menam* or *ad synodum*. No less than hundred and thirty monks had signed it. Among them: Λεόντιος ἡγούμενος καὶ μοναχὸς ἰδίου μοναστηρίου καὶ ὑπὲρ τῶν ἐν τῇ ἐρήμῳ καὶ 'Ιορδάνῃ ἁγίων πατέρων ὑπέγραψας ἐπέδωκα.[35]

2. Leontius the Origenist Monk of the *Vita Sabae*:
The Thesis of Eduard Schwartz

Our Leontius?

We may begin with a *caveat*: there is no positive evidence at all to link the Leontius of the colloquy and Council with the Origenist theologian Leontius, author of *CNE* and the other works of the *corpus Leontianum*.[36] As Innocentius and the *acta* report him, *Leontius apocrisarius* has neither face nor mind.

On the other hand, there is very good reason indeed to identify *Leontius apocrisarius* with the Origenist monk of the *Vita Sabae*. So most recently Eduard Schwartz; and since besides no historian has defended the identity of these two Leontii with greater force

[34] *Ibid.*, p. 37, l. 1 f. As ESchwartz, *KyrSkyth*, 390, notes, the Latin translation in GDMansi, *SacConcColl*, VIII (Florence, 1762), 992E 8–11, inserts after *monachus* the words: *et prior proprii monasterii*. Mansi's source seems unknown, but see the apparatus of *ACO* to the text in question and the remarks of Schwartz, *ibid.*, vi f. Compare also the signature next mentioned.

[35] *ACO*, III, p. 50, l. 30. For ἡγούμενος καὶ μοναχός, GDMansi, *op. cit.*, 1019, reads πρεσβύτερος καὶ ἡγούμενος; but the apparatus of *ACO* reports no variant. The *acta*, then, do *not* call Leontius a priest, as FLoofs, *LeontByz*, 272, quite reasonably believed.

[36] The only hints of identification: first, the author Leontius' statement, discussed above, that *CNE* was conceived in the course of disputations with Monophysites, the like of which certainly preceded the colloquy of 532; and second, Cyril of Scythopolis' association of the Origenist monk Leontius with the same Eusebius mentioned by Innocentius as an observer at the Council of 536 together with *Leontius apocrisarius*. For the evidence on the latter, see immediately below.

than he, it is upon his arguments that the following paragraphs expand.[37]

a. *Leontius and Eusebius*

We have already combined the testimony of Cyril of Scythopolis with the signatures of Domitian and Theodore Askidas in the *acta* of 536 to establish that Leontius was in the capital in that year and so could himself have attended the Council. However, the same passage leads us still farther. Cyril tells us that, when Domitian and Theodore arrived in Constantinople, it was Leontius who introduced them to a certain Eusebius, the keeper of the treasure of Hagia Sophia, who in turn recommended them to the Emperor.

The mention of Eusebius hints at an answer to an inevitable question: how might a mere monk have attained the considerable honor of attending the colloquy of 532 and the Council of 536?[38]

[37] The paragraphs following expand upon ESchwartz, *KyrSkyth*, 386–408, so far as he concerns himself with Leontius. A single and notable exception: against Friedrich Loofs and the consensus (including myself), Schwartz denied the identity of the Leontius of the *Vita Sabae* with the author Leontius (*ibid.*, p. 388 [–389], note 2, including a general critique of Loofs' thesis; and so also *idem, Zur Kirchenpolitik Justinians*, Sitzungsber. d. Bayer. Akad. d. Wiss., Philos.-hist. Abt., 1940, Heft 2 [Munich, 1940], p. 54, note 2). In identifying *Leontius apocrisarius* with the Leontius of the *Vita Sabae*, Schwartz follows FLoofs, *LeontByz* (1887), 261–288. After Loofs, WRügamer, *LeontByz* (1894), 56–63, accepted the identification of *Leontius apocrisarius* and the author Leontius, but—for the first time in the modern literature, I believe—denied that this Leontius was also the Leontius of the *Vita Sabae*. V. Ermoni, *De Leontio Byzantino et de eius doctrina christologica* (Paris, 1895), 19–41, follows Loofs in all points; Ermoni does not seem to have known of Rügamer's work. JPJunglas, *LeontByz* (1908), vii, did not treat of the prosopographical problem, "da wir über Loofs hinaus nichts zu sagen wissen." Much later Louis Duchesne, *L'Eglise au VIe siècle* (Paris, 1925), p. 83, note 1, and p. 167, note 1, denied the identification of *Leontius apocrisarius* with the Leontius of Cyril of Scythopolis because "Léonce de Byzance n'était pas higoumène." Nonetheless, VGrumel, "LéonceByz," *DTC*, IX (1926), 400 f., inclines to Loofs' position, as does Silas Rees, "Leontius of Byzantium and his Defence of the Council of Chalcedon," *Harvard Theological Review*, XXIV (1931), 117 f.; *idem*, "The *De Sectis*: A Treatise Attributed to Leontius of Byzantium," *Journal of Theological Studies*, XL (1939), 346 f.; and above all *idem*, "The Life and Personality of Leontius of Byzantium," *Journal of Theological Studies*, XLI (1940), 272–277. So matters stood when Marcel Richard attacked Schwartz's position in 1944 and 1947; of which more *infra*.

[38] On Eusebius, see the notes of ESchwartz, *KyrSkyth*, 263, and AJFestugière, *Moines d'Orient*, III, 2: *Les moines de Palestine. Cyrille de Scythopolis, "Vie de Saint Sabas"* (Paris, 1962), p. 121, note 236.

Perhaps by the influence of Eusebius? At all events, Cyril plainly suggests that Leontius was somehow close to Eusebius. Perhaps they had met when Eusebius, with the Patriarch Epiphanius and the bishop of the colloquy, Hypatius of Ephesus, sent his retainers to greet Sabas and his companions, among them Leontius, on their landing in Constantinople in the summer of 531.[39] Perhaps Leontius' debates with the Monophysites in the Royal Stoa first attracted Eusebius' attention.[40] Perhaps it is not entirely a coincidence that Eusebius too is an observer at the colloquy of 532.[40a] Four years later, it seems, Leontius is close enough to Eusebius to recommend Domitian and Theodore to his patronage.[40b] Again, in a conference in Jerusalem in early 540, when Leontius has returned to Palestine and the New Laura and Eusebius is on his way back from the Council of Gaza, Eusebius grants the appeal of Leontius that the archimandrite of the eremites, Gelasius, make amends for having expelled Nonnus and his fellow-Origenists from the New Laura.[41] Finally, that Cyril unites the names of Leontius and Eusebius even in death suggests their association in life also.[42] In short, even before Domitian and Theodore Askidas attained the gates of power about 537, Leontius' name seems to have carried some slight weight in court circles, and we should not be surprised to find him at the colloquy and the Council. Indeed, if Eduard

[39] CyrScyth, *VSabae*, p. 173, ll. 15–17.

[40] See the description of Leontius' arrival in Constantinople, *supra*, p. 150 f. The evidence: CyrScyth, *VSabae*, p. 176, l. 7 ff. and especially l. 8 f., with which compare LeontByz, *CNE prol* (PG, 86, 1268B 2–7).

[40a] InnMar, *DeColl, ACO*, IV, 2, p. 170, l. 2 f.

[40b] CyrScyth, *VSabae*, p. 188, l. 24 ff. It may be of interest that in the years between the colloquy of 532 and his later meeting with Leontius in 540 Eusebius had much to do with Jerusalem: according to Hugues Vincent and F.-M. Abel, *Jérusalem*, II: *Jérusalem nouvelle* (Paris, 1926), 912, in or about 536 he was busy restoring the finances of the churches there. The mention of Eusebius in the letter of Menas to Peter of Jerusalem after the Council of 536 (*ACO*, III, p. 124, ll. 23–25) probably alludes to this visit.

[41] CyrScyth, *VSabae*, p. 191, l. 1 ff. Gelasius subsequently expelled six anti-Origenist monks from the Grand Laura, whose appeal to Ephraim of Antioch introduced the issue to the Christian public and so may be counted the proper beginning of the campaign against Origenism.

[42] *Ibid.*, p. 192, ll. 20–22. Cyril tells how, when Nonnus and his Origenists heard of Justinian's decree of 543 against Origen, they separated from the Orthodox and abandoned the New Laura; he then adds: καὶ τούτου ἐν Κωνσταντινουπόλει ἀκουσθέντος, ἤδη τοῦ πάπα Εὐσεβίου κοιμηθέντος καὶ Λεοντίου ἀποθανόντος.... Cyril's distinction of κοιμηθέντος from ἀποθανόντος is hardly accidental!

Schwartz is to be believed, it is not unlikely that it was Leontius who saw to it that the Origenist lauras of Palestine were so well represented at the latter.[43]

b. *Leontius and the Palestinian delegation at the Council of 536*

However, the most compelling evidence for the identification of the Leontius of the *Vita Sabae* with the Leontius of the Council lies in the *acta* of the Council itself: the notices of Leontius in the lists of monks present at the first four sessions and Leontius' own signatures to three *libelli monachorum* read into the *acta* of the first and fifth sessions.[44] These notices and signatures make clear that the

[43] ESchwartz, *KyrSkyth*, 394.

[44] Since the *acta* of the Council of Constantinople of 536 are incorporated into the *acta* of the Council of Jerusalem which met to confirm the decisions of the former, the presentation of the *acta* of 536 in the *Collectio Sabbaitica* in *ACO*, III, is more than a little confused. The location of the five *sessiones* in *ACO*, III: first session (2 May), pp. 126–154; second session (6 May), pp. 154–161; third session (10 May), pp. 161–169; fourth session (21 May), pp. 169–189; fifth session (4 June), pp. 27–123. For the seven lists of names in question here, see:

1. *ACO*, III, p. 128, l. 27–p. 130, l. 39 (presence-list of the first session); for the Palestinian delegation, p. 130, ll. 17–34.
2. *Ibid.*, p. 140, l. 1–p. 147, l. 4 (*Libellus monachorum ad Agapetum*, read into the record of the first session at the request of the delegates of the Pope); for the Palestinian delegation, p. 145, l. 22–p. 146, l. 10 and ll. 18–19.
3. *Ibid.*, p. 156, l. 34–p. 159, l. 2 (presence-list of the second session); for the Palestinian delegation, p. 158, ll. 22–39.
4. *Ibid.*, p. 163, l. 30–p. 166, l. 2 (presence-list of the third session); for the Palestinian delegation, p. 165, ll. 24–40.
5. *Ibid.*, p. 172, l. 8–p. 174, l. 22 (presence-list of the fourth session); for the Palestinian delegation, p. 173, l. 43–p. 174, l. 17.
6. *Ibid.*, p. 33, l. 10–p. 38, l. 12 (*Libellus monachorum ad Justinianum* II, read into the acts of the fifth session at the request of the chairman, Theodore); for the Palestinian delegation, p. 36, l. 27–p. 37, l. 26.
7. *Ibid.*, p. 44, l. 16–p. 52, l. 4 (*Libellus monachorum ad Menam*, read into the acts of the fifth session at the request of the Patriarch Menas); for the Palestinian delegation, p. 50, l. 8–p. 51, l. 14.

Finally, I note that the petition just described as the *Libellus monachorum ad Justinianum* II (*ACO*, III, 32–38), which appears in the acts of the fifth session, has a title almost identical with an altogether different petition presented by the same monks to the same Emperor and included in the acts of the first session (*ACO*, III, 131–134). Since we shall have to do with both *libelli* here, I describe the latter (but chronologically prior) petition as *Libellus monachorum ad Justinianum* I and the former, that is, the petition read at the fifth session, as *Libellus monachorum ad Justinianum* II (or simply *Ad Justinianum* I and II, respectively).

Leontius of the Council is not a free agent. He is present at the Council as one of a clearly definable delegation of Palestinian monks. This delegation deserves further study.

First of all, our delegation is one of three major delegations of monks present at the Council: those of Constantinople, Antioch, and the desert of Palestine. There are, besides, three very much smaller delegations. The lists of observers of the first four sessions distinguish the major delegations very clearly: the roster of the Palestinian delegation is regularly introduced after the roster of the delegation from Antioch with the words ἔτι μὴν καὶ τῶν ὑπὸ τοὺς ἁγίους Χριστοῦ τοῦ ἀληθινοῦ Θεοῦ ἡμῶν τόπους[45] and concluded with the formula οἱ πάντες πράττοντες ὑπέρ τε ἑαυτῶν καὶ τῶν οἰκείων μοναστηρίων καὶ πάντων τῶν ἐν τῇ ἐρήμῳ τῆς ἁγίας πόλεως μοναχῶν.[46] The four lists of observers introduce the delegations in a standard order: Constantinople, Antioch (or Syria), the desert of Palestine, and the others. In the three *libelli*, however, the major delegations are not formally distinguished at all, though in fact each signs *en bloc*. In the *libelli*, too, the Palestinians always sign immediately after the Constantinopolitans, while the eleven Syrian monks (or their representative, as in *Ad Justinianum* I and *Ad Menam*) sign last of all.

It is interesting, besides, that what I have called the Palestinian delegation does not in fact include all monks present from Palestine. That the single delegate from Mount Sinai signs separately is not perhaps surprising, but what of the two delegates from the Pedias, that is, it seems, the plain on the ridge just south of Jerusalem?[47] Or what of the delegation from Palestines I, II, and III, a single monk Strategius in the first four sessions, but a full seven in the signatures to *Ad Justinianum* II and *Ad Menam* of the last?[48]

Plainly the Palestinian delegation does not represent all Palestine, much less the whole area of the patriarchate of Jerusalem.

---

[45] *ACO*, III, p. 130, l. 17 *et passim*.

[46] *Ibid.*, l. 33 f. *et passim*, with slight variations.

[47] Only one of the two, a certain John, appears on the lists of observers of the first sessions. However, in the last two *libelli* of the fifth session, he is joined by one Theodore.

[48] *Ibid.*, p. 37, l. 35-p. 38, l. 8; p. 51, ll. 24-37.

The Palestinian delegation of which Leontius is a member is therefore a distinct and definite group of Palestinian monks. We want to know next: just what kind of group, and, above all, whom does the delegation represent?

When we look at the composition of the delegation itself, we notice first that at the first, third, and fourth sessions and in the list of signatures to *Ad Agapetum* (first session) the number of monks in the delegation is fifteen; in the second session a certain John has fallen out, perhaps a casualty of scribal negligence. With one insignificant exception (in *Ad Agapetum*) the order of the names in these five rosters is the same. Leontius always is mentioned, or signs, in seventh place. At the last session the delegation has been reinforced by five monks from five different monasteries, and the order of the signatures shows minor changes. Nonetheless, no name is displaced more than two places from its original position, since four of the five newcomers sign at the very end of the list.

The monks of the delegation represent two κοινόβια—those of Theodosius (three monks at the first four sessions, plus a fourth at the fifth and last) and Martyrius (four monks throughout)—and four lauras—those of Sabas (the Grand Laura: one monk at the first four sessions, two at the last), Firminus (the same), Jacob (here called [μονὴ] τῶν πυργίων τοῦ 'Ιορδάνου: two monks at the first four sessions, three at the last), and, finally, the New Laura (three monks at the first four sessions, four at the last). Leontius, of course, is not included in these figures, because he does not tell us his monastery.[49]

The roster of monasteries makes one thing clear: we are dealing with precisely that group of monastic settlements which is the milieu of the hagiographical cycle of Cyril of Scythopolis. The κοινόβιον of Theodosius was established by the ascetic Theodosius who was, as we shall see, a close friend of Sabas; his biography, we remember, stands fifth in Cyril's cycle and tells us of the founding of the monastery.[50] The Martyrius who established the monastery of that

---

[49] For a similar list, ESchwartz, *KyrSkyth*, 391.
[50] CyrScyth, *VTheodosii*, 235–241; for the founding of his monastery, p. 238, ll. 1–23. See also Schwartz's entry on the monastery in his index, p. 294 f.

name was a disciple of Euthymius, the spiritual master of Sabas; Euthymius' life, of course, stands at the head of Cyril's cycle.[51] The four lauras represented were founded either by Sabas himself (the Grand Laura) or by monks of his circle: Firminus,[52] Jacob,[53] and a group of dissidents for whom Sabas later built the New Laura.[54] The world of Cyril of Scythopolis and the world of the Origenist monk Leontius.

A further step. Why does the Palestinian delegation consist of members of precisely these monasteries? The monastery of Theodosius is represented almost certainly as the monastery of the archimandrite of all of the κοινόβια of Palestine, Sophronius, whose representative at the Council, Hesychius, signs the *Libellus ad Justinianum* in the *acta* of the first session in the name of the whole Palestinian delegation, with explicit appeal to Sophronius' authority.[55] The Grand Laura was surely represented as the monastery of Sabas himself, though it seems not unlikely that Sabas' successors Melitas—who was in office at the time of the Council of 536[56]—Gelasius, George the Origenist, Cassian, and Conon were all *ex officio* archimandrites of all the lauras of Palestine[57] and so might have claimed to be represented in their own right. The claims of the other four μοναστήρια? A certain answer is impossible. However, we know that at least three of the four were centers of Origenism. Of the New Laura, where the tares of the heresy had first taken root, little more need be said than that Nonnus' influence seems to have reigned supreme,[58] and that Theodore Askidas, whom Cyril

[51] CyrScyth, *VEuthymii*, 2–85; for Martyrius' founding of his monastery, p. 50, l. 20 ff. and especially p. 51, ll. 19–21. See also Schwartz's entry in his index, p. 295. On the relations of Euthymius and Sabas, see, e.g., CyrScyth, *VSabae*, p. 90, l. 26 ff.; p. 94, l. 13 ff.

[52] CyrScyth, *VSabae*, p. 99, l. 23 f.

[53] *Ibid.*, l. 20 f.

[54] *Ibid.*, p. 118, l. 21 ff. It must not be forgotten that the first abbot of the New Laura was a trusted disciple of Sabas named John (*ibid.*, p. 123, l. 28 ff., with which compare p. 99, l. 19 f.).

[55] *ACO*, III, p. 133, l. 35-p. 134, l. 2. After Theodosius (CyrScyth, *VSabae*, p. 115, l. 14 ff.), was the abbot of Theodosius' monastery *ex officio* archimandrite of all the κοινόβια of Palestine?

[56] CyrScyth, *VSabae*, p. 187, l. 30 ff., and especially p. 189, ll. 10–14.

[57] In any case, Cyril of Scythopolis seems to hold them responsible for the salvation or perdition of all (e.g., *ibid.*, ll. 3–6).

[58] *Ibid.*, p. 188, l. 7-p. 189, l. 9.

calls τῶν τῆς Νέας λαύρας ἐξάρχων,[59] was one of its representatives to the Council. We remember, besides, when Melitas' successor in the Grand Laura, Gelasius, expels no less than forty Origenists from the Grand Laura in 537, the forty go off to the New Laura,[60] where then, says Cyril, "all the chiefs of the heresy were gathered in one place."[61] As for the monastery of Martyrius and the laura of Firminus, they are just the two establishments, if Cyril is to be believed, to which, after Sabas' death, Origenism first spread.[62] It is no surprise, then, that the abbot of the monastery who attends the Council of 536 and soon after becomes bishop of Ancyra in Galatia, appears in the next decade with Theodore Askidas as head of the Origenist party in Constantinople;[63] and no surprise, either, that the laura of Firminus becomes the stronghold of one of the sects into which the Origenist party divides on the death of Nonnus about 547, that is, the Πρωτόκτιστοι.[64] If we may suppose that the laura of Jacob was infected in the same degree, we can hardly avoid the suspicion that the monastery of Martyrius, the New Laura, and the lauras of Firminus and Jacob were chosen to send representatives to the Council of 536 precisely because they were dominated by Origenists;[65] and that granted, Eduard Schwartz's speculation seems more than reasonable: "wenn die Auswahl der Delegierten aus den Koinobien und Lauren der ἔρημος bei Jerusalem besonders auf Origeniasten gefallen war, so darf man vermuten, dass Leontius sich zum Werkzeug des ganzen, von langer Hand vorbereiteten Manövers hergegeben hatte, um seiner Partei eine gute Position zu schaffen."[66]

[59] *Ibid.*, p. 188, l. 26 f.
[60] *Ibid.*, p. 189, l. 10 ff. and especially p. 190, l. 3 ff.
[61] *Ibid.*, p. 190, l. 7 f.
[62] *Ibid.*, p. 188, ll. 18–22.
[63] *Ibid.*, p. 188, l. 24-p. 189, l. 9.
[64] *Ibid.*, p. 197, l. 4 ff.
[65] We may ask besides: since it was to the Pedias that Nonnus and his disciples withdrew when they were expelled from the New Laura (*ibid.*, p. 125, ll. 2 f., 14 f.), may not the delegation from the Pedias also have been Origenists?
[66] E Schwartz, *KyrSkyth*, 394. To be sure, the Κασιανὸς πρεσβύτερος τῆς λαύρας τοῦ μακαρίου Σάββα of the Palestinian delegation is almost certainly identical with the anti-Origenist Cassian whose accession to the ἡγεμονία of the Grand Laura in 547 marks the turning of the tide against Origenism among the monasteries of Palestine (CyrScyth, *VSabae*, p. 196, ll. 3–18; *VCyriaci*, p. 231, ll. 11–19): Cyril expressly describes him as καὶ πρεσβύτερον τῆς Μεγίστης λαύρας γεγονότα (*VSabae*, p. 196, l. 12). At the Council of

The conclusion seems inescapable. So far as the manuscript tradition of the *acta* of 536 may be trusted, its testimony establishes beyond reasonable doubt that the Leontius of the *acta* is identical with Leontius the Origenist monk of the *Vita Sabae* and so also with the theologian Leontius.

3. Leontius ἡγούμενος? The Thesis of Marcel Richard

In fact, of course, the identification of *Leontius apocrisarius* with the Leontius of the *Vita Sabae* is not entirely self-evident. The Leontius of colloquy and Council represents himself as a person of some weight in ecclesiastical circles: *apocrisarius patrum in sancta civitate constitutorum* at the colloquy—Marcel Richard will have it that he was in fact the *apocrisiarius* of the patriarch of Jerusalem[67]— and at the Council of 536 ἡγούμενος (indeed, ἡγούμενος καὶ μοναχὸς ἰδίου μοναστηρίου) and τοποτηρητὴς πάσης τῆς ἐρήμου. Now, though Cyril of Scythopolis is more than willing to have us believe that Leontius had that substantial influence in ecclesiastical circles proper to the *bêtes noires* of hagiography, he offers no slightest hint that Leontius ever possessed these particular dignities, and the same must be said of the manuscript tradition of the theologian Leontius.[68] Strange, then, as Richard notes, that so soon after his arrival

---

536, however, Cassian represents the anti-Origenist Grand Laura; and, as I have just suggested, the Grand Laura itself was represented probably because it had been the laura of Sabas. Surely it was not represented because it was a stronghold of Origenism!

[67] MRichard, "LéonceJér et LéonceByz," *MélScRel*, I (1944), p. 82, note 174 f., reiterated in "Léonce ... origéniste?" *RevEtByz*, V (1947), 64. The argument: since the patriarch of Constantinople is represented at the colloquy by his *syncelli* and the patriarch of Antioch by three *venerabiles presbyteri et oeconomi atque apocrisarii* (InnMar, *DeColl*, in *ACO*, IV, 2, p. 170, ll. 1 6), *Leontius apocrisarius* must represent "le patriarche de Jérusalem plus encore que les moines de la sainte cité" (MRichard, "LéonceJér et LéonceByz," *MélScRel*, I [1944], 82) — "sinon," he adds (*ibid.*, note 175), "seul des trois patriarches orientaux celui de Jérusalem n'aurait pas été représenté, tandis que ses moines l'étaient."

[68] Leontius' titles in the three manuscripts at the root of the tradition:

V (tenth century), p. 165 (*AdvFraudes*, title): τοῦ αὐτοῦ ὁσίου λεοντίου πρὸς τοὺς, etc. It will be remembered that the title of Leontius' works in V, p. 1, has been obliterated.

O (tenth century), fol. 1ʳ (*CNE prol*, title): τοῦ μακαρίου λεοντίου τοῦ ἐρημίτου πρόλογος, etc.

in Constantinople he should attain such prominence; and all the
more strange because he attains it so soon after the holy Sabas had
ejected him from his laura. Finally, the most serious objection of all,
which we may let Richard pose for himself:

> D'autre part, malgré certaines apparences contraires, Léonce de
> Byzance semble bien être resté tout à fait en marge de la
> camerilla théologique dont aimait à s'entourer l'empereur. On a
> voulu faire de lui le conseiller le plus écouté de Justinien. C'est
> une grosse erreur. Il était sans doute en très bons termes
> avec un membre influent de cette camerilla, le Papas Eusèbe,
> trésorier de Sainte Sophie et c'est grâce à cette amitié qu'il
> a pu y introduire ses amis Domitien et Théodore; mais lui-
> même était de caractère trop indépendant pour y faire bonne
> figure. A partir des conférences de 532, l'empereur et son
> entourage se sont lancés résolument dans la voie du néo-
> chalcédonisme et se sont efforcés d'absorber la quasi-totalité
> de la doctrine cyrillienne. Léonce est resté absolument étranger
> à cette nouvelle politique. Il est demeuré, presque seul, fidèle
> jusqu'au bout au chalcédonisme le plus strict et pour cela fait
> figure assez étrange au milieu des théologiens de son temps. En
> somme il aurait fait un protégé de Justinien bien ingrat et un
> curieux défenseur des intérêts des moines du désert.[69]

Ibid., fol. 66ᵛ (*SolArgSev*, title): τοῦ αὐτοῦ μακαρίου λεοντίου μονάξοντος ἐπίλυσις, etc.

Ibid., fol. 106ʳ (*CNE 2*, title): τοῦ αὐτοῦ ἀββᾶ λεοντίου λόγος β', etc.
WRügamer, *LeontByz*, 57, properly notes that ἀββᾶς does not mean *abbot* but something like *father.*

Ibid., fol. 227ᵛ (the last page of the manuscript): τετέλεσται σὺν θεῷ ἡ κατὰ πασῶν αἱρεσέων ἀνατροπὴ καὶ θρίαμβος τοῦ μακαρίου λεοντίου καὶ μεγάλου ἀσκήτου.

G (eleventh century), fol. 328ᵛ (*CNE prol*, title): λεοντίου μοναχοῦ πρόλογος, etc.

Ibid., fol. 330ᵛ (*CNE 1*, title): τοῦ αὐτοῦ λεοντίου ἀσκήτου ἔλεγχος, etc.

[69] MRichard, "Léonce … origéniste?" *RevEtByz*, V (1947), 65. For the whole of Richard's argument that the Leontius of colloquy and Council is not the Leontius of the *Vita Sabae*, see *ibid.*, 64 f., first presented in "Léonce Jer et LéonceByz," *MélScRel*, I (1944), 81–88, where the author goes on to speculate that *Leontius apocrisarius* is identical with Leontius of Jerusalem.

Richard's conclusions—that is, that the theologian Leontius is identical with the Origenist Leontius of the *Vita Sabae* but different from *Leontius apocrisarius*—have made their way only slowly. Berthold Altaner, "Der griechische Theologe Leontius und Leontius der skythische Mönch," *Theologische Quartalschrift*, CXXVII (1947), p. 165 and note 65, knows of Richard's

What is the weight of these objections? We must consider them in detail; and since they depend, we see, upon the testimony of Innocentius that the Leontius of the colloquy of 532 was an *apocrisarius* and the report of the *acta* of the Council of 536 that the Leontius of the Palestinian delegation was an ἡγούμενος, we examine these two titles in turn.

a. *Leontius apocrisarius*

First, the *Leontius apocrisarius patrum in sancta civitate constitutorum* of the colloquy of 532.

(1) The title *apocrisiarius*.

We begin by asking: what is an *apocrisiarius*—as the word is usually spelled—in the reign of Justinian?[70] Broadly speaking, an agent of the head of an ecclesiastical jurisdiction, whether in maintaining order within the jurisdiction itself or in its dealings with other ecclesiastical jurisdictions or the outside world. When the jurisdiction in question is a diocese or patriarchate, an *apocrisiarius* is the legate of the bishop or patriarch to another bishop or to a civil authority: οἱ τῆς ἁγίας Ἀναστάσεως [ἐκκλησίας] ἀποκρισιάριοι whom Cyril of Scythopolis mentions in the *Vita Sabae* are simply the legates of the patriarch of Jerusalem to the Emperor in Con-

---

criticism of Schwartz, but stands by Schwartz *in toto*. So also Robert Devreesse, *Essai sur Théodore de Mopsueste* (Studi e Testi, vol. 141 [Città del Vaticano, 1948]), 244 f.; that is, the Leontius of the *Vita Sabae* is identical with the Leontius of the colloquy and Council, but not with the theologian Leontius, whose *CNE* Devreesse dates 552–553. It is only since Charles Moeller adopted Richard's views in his "Chalcédonisme et néochalcédonisme," *KonzChalk*, I, p. 662, note 67, p. 663, note 72, *et passim*, that they have become quasi-canonical. See also *idem*, "Textes 'monophysites' de Léonce de Jérusalem," *Ephemerides Theologicae Lovanienses*, XXVII (1951), p. 470, note 8.

[70] The Latin *apocrisiarius* is a transliteration of the Greek ἀποκρισιάριος; see note 24. In the *Novellae* of Justinian, the Greek is also translated *responsalis* (*Novella* 79. 1, in *CorpJurCiv*, III, p. 388, l. 27), or *responsarius* (*Novella* 133. 4 f., in *ibid.*, p. 672, ll. 1, 23). In his earlier edition of the *Corpus juris civilis* van Leeuwen (or a previous annotator) seems to consider *apocrisiarius* the equivalent of *adresponsus*; see *Novella* 24. 4, and *Novella* 25. 1, in *Corpus juris civilis*, ed. Simon van Leeuwen, IV (Venice, 1844), p. 204 with note 45, p. 207 with note 16.

stantinople.[71] Such a legate might reside in the place to which he was sent and serve there as the standing representative of his bishop. Often, however, he was only a legate *ad hoc*: the Φίδος [Fidus] τὰς τοῦ πατριάρχου δεξάμενος ἀποκρίσεις—that is, ἀποκρισιάριος—of Cyril's *Vita Euthymii* was simply being sent by the patriarch to the capital with a petition.[72] On the other hand, the ecclesiastical jurisdiction in question might be monastic. Then an *apocrisiarius* might be, as it were, the inspector general of an ἔξαρχος having authority over a number of monasteries,[73] or one of the stewards of the abbot of his own monastery: *qui eorum [monasteriorum] rebus et eorum occupentur utilitatibus*, as one of the *Novellae* puts it.[74] However, the same *Novella* implies that the *responsarius* is also one of the few monks allowed to leave the monastery,[75] and from two other *Novellae* we learn that it is his duty to represent the monks in their relations with the world outside, e.g., in lawsuits[76]—passages in which the *apocrisiarius* clearly acts not only as steward of his community but also as its legate. When Cyril of Scythopolis tells us that Euthymius' anonymous spiritual master made Abraamius the ἀποκρισιάριος of the monastery in Constantinople of which he had himself been made abbot, we may suppose that Abraamius' duties were something like these; in short, he was the steward of the monastery and the authorized representative of its members in all matters of

---

[71] CyrScyth, *VSabae*, p. 192, l. 23 f. Louis Duchesne, *Eglises séparées* (Paris, 1896), 185, says of the papal legate in Constantinople that "c'est auprès de l'empereur qu'il était accrédité, et non auprès du patriarche," and the passage here cited implies the same of the legates of the patriarch of Jerusalem.

[72] CyrScyth, *VEuthymii*, p. 63, l. 4, adduced by A J Festugière, *Moines d'Orient*, III, 2, p. 123, note 290; with which see *ibid.*, III, 1: "*Vie de Saint Euthyme*" (Paris, 1962), p. 117, note 138.

[73] E.g., *Novella* 133. 4, in *CorpJurCiv*, III, p. 671 f. and especially p. 671, l. 29 ff.

[74] *Novella* 133. 5, *ibid.*, p. 672, l. 24 f. This chapter requires the appointment of such *responsarii* in each *monasterium sub abbate constitutum*, even in nunneries. *Novella* 123. 36 requires that the *responsarius*—for I suppose that the same man is in question—be a deacon or presbyter (*ibid.*, p. 620, l. 4 ff.).

[75] *Novella* 133. 5, *ibid.*, p. 673, l. 5 f., with which compare *Novella* 123. 42, *ibid.*, p. 623, ll. 10–12.

[76] *Novella* 79. 1, *ibid.*, p. 388, ll. 26–28; *Novella* 123. 42, *ibid.*, p. 623, ll. 12–14.

law.⁷⁷ Such ἀποκρισιάριοι may represent their communities at councils too: in the *acta* of the Council of 536, each of five monks in the delegation from Antioch is regularly described as ἀποκρισιάριος —that is, simply legate—of his own monastery (four) or church (one);⁷⁸ and a certain Θεωνᾶς πρεσβύτερος τοῦ Σινᾶ ὄρους καὶ ἀποκρισιάριος τοῦ τε ὄρους καὶ τῆς ἐκκλησίας Φαρὰν καὶ λαύρας Ῥαιθοῦ ὑπὲρ πάντων τῶν ἐκεῖσε μοναχῶν seems to have represented an even broader constituency.⁷⁹ Again, in the lists of monks observing the second and fourth sessions, we see in the Palestinian delegation the name Ἡσυχίου πρεσβυτέρου καὶ ἀποκρισιαρίου μονῆς τοῦ μακαρίου Θεοδοσίου⁸⁰—and if ἀρχιμανδρίτης replaces ἀποκρισιάριος in otherwise identical notices in the lists for the first and third sessions it can only be by reason of scribal error.⁸¹ As if to confirm his claim to the title, Hesychius signs the *Libellus monachorum ad Justinianum* I of the first session for the whole Palestinian delegation; and though he does not use the word ἀποκρισιάριος here, he openly claims its substance, for he signs: Ἡσύχιος ἐλέει θεοῦ πρεσβύτερος καὶ μοναχὸς μονῆς τοῦ μακαρίου ἀββᾶ Θεοδοσίου τὸν τόπον ἐπέχων Σωφρονίου πρεσβυτέρου καὶ ἀρχιμανδρίτου τῆς αὐτῆς μονῆς καὶ πρώτου πάσης τῆς ἐρήμου Ἱεροσολύμων....⁸² Plainly the ἀποκρισιάριοι of the *acta* of 536 are

---

⁷⁷ CyrScyth, *Vita Abraamii*, in ESchwartz, *KyrSkyth*, p. 244, ll. 1–7.
⁷⁸ *ACO*, III, 130 (list of observers at the first session); 146 f. (*Libellus monachorum ad Agapetum*); 158 (second session); 165 (third session); 173 f. (fourth session). Among these five is the apparent chief of the delegation, Παῦλος μοναχὸς καὶ ἀποκρισιάριος μονῆς τῆς Μάρωνος (p. 130), who signs the *Libellus monachorum ad Justinianum* II (p. 38) and the *Libellus monachorum ad Menam* (p. 52) for all the monks of Syria II, still calling himself ἀποκρισιάριος μονῆς τοῦ μακαρίου Μάρωνος, etc.
⁷⁹ For the description here, *ibid.*, 130 (first session). The name of the same man stands in the same lists as the name of the Παῦλος μοναχός mentioned *supra*, note 78: see *ibid.*, 130, 146, 158, 165, 174, 37, 51.
⁸⁰ *Ibid.*, p. 158, l. 24; p. 174, l. 2.
⁸¹ A scribal error because the archimandrite of the monastery of Theodosius in 536 is not Hesychius but Sophronius. So anyhow Hesychius' own signature to the *Libellus monachorum ad Justinianum* I, to be quoted immediately below; and so also CyrScyth, *VSabae*, who testifies that Sophronius succeeded to the post on Theodosius's death in 527 (p. 171, l. 26 ff.) and was still living about 540 (p. 190, l. 12 ff.). Since we know that Hesychius was not ἀρχιμανδρίτης but was indeed ἀποκρισιάριος, it is inevitable to assume that at a later date the former and more common term was accidentally substituted for the latter and less common.
⁸² *ACO*, III, p. 133, ll. 35–37.

legates, and legates representing not only each his own community, but, in the case of Hesychius, an archimandrite with authority over many communities.[83]

(2) Leontius *apocrisarius* and Leontius the Origenist monk

Then what of *Leontius apocrisarius*? In calling him *apocrisarius patrum in sancta civitate constitutorum*, Innocentius of Maronia plainly takes the Leontius of the colloquy not for a simple steward but for a legate, and specifically, of course, the legate of the monks of Jerusalem. If Innocentius is right, we may presume that Leontius had been appointed to the post by one or both of the two archimandrites of the area, that is, Sophronius, archimandrite of the monasteries, or Sabas, archimandrite of the lauras, just as the monk Hesychius seems to have been appointed *apocrisiarius* by the same Sophronius in 536 in order that he might represent him at the Council. We may suppose besides that the Leontius of the colloquy is a legate *ad hoc*; for, to the best of my knowledge, there is no evidence that the archimandrites of the desert of Jerusalem maintained a resident legate in Constantinople, at least at this time. Such is the picture of *Leontius apocrisarius* as we may reconstruct it from Innocentius' notice.

Now, can *Leontius apocrisarius* have been Leontius the Origenist monk? *Prima facie*, the answer is *no*; at least, that is, if we assume,

---

[83] *N. B.*: Hesychius is the legate of the archimandrite Sophronius and not of the patriarch of Jerusalem, Peter. In the presence-lists of the Council of 536, the legate of Peter is a certain deacon Sabinus: *ACO*, III, p. 127, l. 33 f. (first session); p. 156, l. 9 f. (second session); p. 163, l. 7 f. (third session); p. 171, l. 24 f. (fourth session); p. 29, l. 10 f. (fifth session). *Pace* A J Festugière, *Moines d'Orient*, III, 2, p. 122, note 288, that Sophronius had succeeded Theodosius not only as abbot of his monastery but also as archimandrite of all the κοινόβια of the desert is not absolutely certain from the evidence of Cyril of Scythopolis alone; for in CyrScyth, *VSabae*, p. 171, l. 29–p. 172, l. 1, the ἡγεμονία may be that of the monastery of Theodosius alone, as clearly in CyrScyth, *Vita Theodosii* (ESchwartz, *KyrSkyth*, p. 240, l. 1 f.): τὴν μέντοι ἡγεμονίαν τῆς τοῦ ἀββᾶ Θεοδοσίου μονῆς διεδέξατο Σωφρόνιός τις..., and *VSabae* (*ibid.*, p. 190, l. 14 f.): τόν τε τῆς μονῆς ἡγούμενον Σωφρόνιον τὸν ἀοίδιμον.... Nonetheless, Hesychius' signature here pretty well proves that Sophronius is archimandrite of all the κοινόβια and not only of his own. Interesting that Hesychius represents only Sophronius, the archimandrite of the monasteries, and not also Melitas, Sabas' successor as archimandrite of the lauras (*ibid.*, p. 189, l. 10).

as we have, that Leontius was made *apocrisiarius* by the archi-mandrites of the desert or by the patriarch of Jerusalem. How so? We may begin by asking: *when* could the Origenist monk Leontius have been appointed *apocrisiarius*? The answer seems clear. Since Cyril of Scythopolis seems to imply that Leontius came to Con-stantinople only as one of Sabas' subordinates,[84] we suppose that Leontius was not then *apocrisiarius*; in short, that if he ever be-came *apocrisiarius* at all, it was only after his arrival in Constan-tinople and his break with Sabas. Here the difficulty appears. Can it be that an Origenist would be chosen to represent the archiman-drites of the desert, or, as Marcel Richard will have it, the patriarch himself?[85] Can it be that an Origenist would be chosen, who had been expelled from the company of the archimandrite of the lauras, the venerable Sabas himself, and that within the year? We under-stand how Leontius might have been appointed *apocrisiarius before* his departure for Constantinople, that is, before he had revealed his sympathies with Origenism;[86] but afterwards, no.

[84] *ACO*, III, p. 176, l. 11 f., describes Leontius only as τὶς τῶν μετ'αὐτοῦ [i.e., Σάβα] μοναχῶν.

[85] Whether Leontius is *apocrisarius*, as Innocentius testifies, of the *patrum sancta civitate constitutorum*, or, as Richard insists, of the patriarch of Jerusalem, is a question of little importance here: neither party would have been likely to choose an Origenist as their representative. In the meantime, we may, I think, stand on Innocentius' express statement that Leontius was *apocrisarius* of the monks, that is, of their archimandrites. First, be-cause the colloquy was only a colloquy, not a council; and no serious at-tempt can have been made to assure the universal representation proper to a council: e.g., the representatives of the patriarch of Constantinople—if indeed Eusebius did not rather represent the Emperor—and of the patriarch of Antioch were themselves, like Leontius, only observers. (The Orthodox bishops participating seem to have been the Emperor's men.) Second, the colloquy was itself, or at least presupposed, a colloquy of theologians, and it would be no surprise to find among the observers a representative of so distinguished a community of theologians as the monastic settlements around Jerusalem.

[86] CyrScyth, *VSabae*, p. 176, ll. 11–15, clearly implies that Leontius' true position had not been known to Sabas before their journey to the capital: εὑρέθη...Λεόντιος...τῶν 'Ωριγένους δογμάτων ἀντιλαμβανόμενος. This agrees exactly with Cyril's earlier assertion that after their readmission to the New Laura about 520, Nonnus and his disciples, including Leontius, kept their opinions to themselves (*ibid.*, p. 124, ll. 20–22); except that we hardly need believe that they did so out of fear of Sabas (*ibid.*, l. 20 f.). More probably their opinions were simply ignored. To be sure, Sabas' circle includes the likes of Agapetus, the abbot of the New Laura (*ca.* 514–*ca.* 520) who first expelled Nonnus and his crew from the New Laura about 514 (*ibid.*, p. 124, l. 21 ff.). Nonetheless, Origenism does not seem to be a burning issue in

Marcel Richard, we know, answers these questions simply and directly: *Leontius apocrisarius* cannot possibly have been the Origenist monk Leontius. For those who disagree with him, the question still stands: how could the Origenist Leontius have become an *apocrisiarius*? Two solutions have been offered.

First, the solution of Eduard Schwartz. As we have noticed, Cyril of Scythopolis seems to imply that in the summer of 531 Leontius was no more than a *protégé* of Sabas; that is, that he was not, or not yet, an *apocrisiarius*. This Schwartz candidly accepts as fact. How then did Leontius become *apocrisiarius*? "Es bleibt kaum eine andere Vermutung übrig, als dass es der Kaiser selbst getan hat."[87] The sponsor of Leontius' career from 532 to 536 is none other than Justinian.

Earlier, however, Friedrich Loofs had proposed a more radical answer: "531 im April reist [Leontius] mit Sabas nach Constantinopel, *vielleicht in der Absicht und auf die Aufforderung hin, an dem geplanten Religionsgespräch teilzunehmen.*"[88] In a note he adds:

> Ich sage nicht mehr, weil mit Sicherheit nicht geurteilt werden kann, muss aber wenigstens hier darauf hinweisen, dass die Bezeichnung des Leontius in den Akten der Collatio "apocrisiarius patrum in sancta civitate constitutorum" ... und die Einholung des Sabas und Leontius durch Hypatius von Ephesus, den Vorsitzenden der *collatio cum Severianis*, und durch den Presbyter Euseb, einen ihrer Theilnehmer ... sehr dafür

---

Palestine before Sabas' death in 532, or perhaps even much before its new, bold influence (*ibid.*, p. 188, l. 7 ff.) prompted the abbot Gelasius to attack it openly about 537 (*ibid.*, p. 189, l. 10 ff.). In any case, Cyril—even Cyril!—does not lend Sabas so emphatic a distaste for Origen as he finds in Agapetus; we notice that, when the Patriarch John summons Sabas and Agapetus to discuss Agapetus' expulsion of Nonnus from the New Laura, it is Agapetus who speaks, although Sabas is archimandrite (*ibid.*, p. 125, l. 4 ff.). Some seventeen years later, when Sabas cuts off Leontius, his decision is prompted, says Cyril, by his recollection of Agapetus' words to John. Not, we notice, by his own and proper sense of the matter.

In short, before the summer of 531, Leontius' Origenism remained hidden, if only because no one felt it worth his time to ferret it out.

[87] ESchwartz, *KyrSkyth*, 391; the same speculation explains the title τοποτηρητής which the *acta* attribute to the Leontius of the Council of 536.

[88] FLoofs, *LeontByz*, 300. (Italics mine). In Loofs' text "Jerusalem" stands in place of "Constantinopel," an obvious error.

spricht, dass der Bericht des Cyrillus Scythopolitanus über diese Reise des Sabas und Leontius das Wichtigste tendenziös verschweigt.[89]

Kurz und gut, what Cyril seems to imply is not the truth, or at least the whole truth: Leontius comes to the capital in 531 in Sabas' company, but not as his *protégé*, for he has himself been sent as a legate *ad hoc* of the monks of Palestine to join in the theological discussions expected to attend the forthcoming colloquy with the Monophysites. Loofs might have added: and perhaps the same may be said of his confreres of the persuasion of Theodore of Mopsuestia. Leontius' Origenism? Still unsuspected. No matter that he later quarreled with Sabas. They quarreled not in Palestine but in Constantinople, the city of the Emperor; and an Emperor and a court who were soon to promote the Origenists Domitian and Theodore Askidas to the episcopacy were not likely to refuse the credentials of a competent and congenial theologian because he had fallen out with an aging ascetic, however revered.

How shall we assess these answers to our question? *Pace* Richard, the evidence of the *acta* of the Council of 536 strongly supports the identification proposed; and we have no reason to believe that the Leontius of the Council is not also the Leontius of the colloquy. The objection that no Origenist could have become *apocrisiarius* is resolved by either of two reasonable speculations. Which is more reasonable? Let it be granted Schwartz that Justinian could very well indeed have made Leontius an *apocrisiarius*. Nevertheless, Loofs' proposal seems to do less violence to the probabilities, indeed would be the virtually mandatory interpretation of the evidence were it not for the peculiar testimony of Cyril. That testimony, however, is not a denial but only a significant silence. We may ask of it: is Cyril's silence about Leontius here such a significant silence as not infrequently veils the activities of Cyril's adversaries elsewhere?[90] We are, besides, all the more willing to press his account because he says almost nothing about the controversy with the Monophysites between 531 and 536.

[89] *Ibid.*, note.
[90] E.g., of the purpose of the voyage of Domitian and Theodore Askidas to Constantinople and the Council of 536, Cyril says hardly a word; only that they "sailed off" (CyrScyth, *VSabae*, p. 188, l. 24 ff.).

We need go no farther for the moment: there is, it seems, no compelling reason why the Origenist monk Leontius could not have been the *apocrisarius patrum in sancta civitate constitutorum* of the colloquy of 532.

b. *The Leontius of the Council of 536*

What of the Leontius of the Council of 536? Like *Leontius apocrisarius*, he is one of the monks of the desert of Palestine: we have already noticed that he is reported in the *acta* of the Council and signs the *libelli monachorum* as one of a distinct and definite group of monks from just those monastic settlements established there by Euthymius, Sabas, and their disciples. Evidence in itself almost enough to identify the Leontius of the colloquy and Council with the Origenist monk Leontius of Cyril of Scythopolis' *Vita Sabae*. Alas, there are difficulties, and to these we turn now.

(1) Leontius and the delegation of monks from Palestine

However, our examination of the disputed passages in the *acta* of 536 will be much the more clear for a prefatory note: the *acta* show not only that the Leontius of the Council is a member of the Palestinian delegation, but also that within the delegation he enjoys no special prominence whatever. To be sure, his signature is quite distinctive, as we shall see. Nonetheless, in 536 Leontius never claims the title *apocrisiarius*, unless perhaps he intends the term τοποτηρητής as its equivalent. When a representative of the group signs for the whole, that representative is not Leontius, but, as we have seen, Hesychius, who signs in the name of his archimandrite Sophronius.[91] Leontius' name does not even stand at or near the head of the list of his delegation: e.g., of fifteen monks in the delegation at the first four sessions of the Council, he is regularly mentioned seventh. That Leontius signs the *Libellus monachorum ad Justinianum* II of the fifth session as one ποιούμενος τὸν λόγον

---

[91] *Libellus monachorum ad Justinianum* I (first session), *ACO*, III, p. 133, l. 35-p. 134, l. 2.

ὑπὲρ τῶν κατὰ τὴν ἔρημον ἁγίων πατέρων,[92] and the *Ad Menam*
ὑπὲρ πάντων τῶν ἐν τῇ ἐρήμῳ καὶ 'Ιορδάνῃ ἁγίων πατέρων[93] is
hardly enough to lend him peculiar authority: almost identical
phrases commonly adorn the signatures of all of the other members
of his delegation.[94] The conclusion is obvious: if the Leontius of
the Council is identical with the *Leontius apocrisarius* of the colloquy, he has somehow fallen out of favor, at least in Palestine; for
in 536 he is *apocrisiarius* of neither patriarch nor archimandrite,
but only one of a delegation of fifteen or twenty monks.

(2) Leontius ἡγούμενος?

(a) *The problem.* However, if the Leontius of the Council is not
an *apocrisiarius*, he is not therefore a nobody. First, in the *acta* he
is always described, and in the *Ad Agapetum* signs himself, as
τοποτηρητὴς τῆς ἐρήμου πάσης. Second, in the same documents, he
stands also as μοναχὸς καὶ ἡγούμενος; and in the *Ad Menam*, he
signs himself as μοναχὸς καὶ ἡγούμενος ἰδίου μοναστηρίου—a description perhaps reflected in the *prior proprii monasterii* in the Latin
version (and only the Latin version!) of his signature to the *Ad
Justinianum* II.[95] The difficulty? Nowhere do our sources call Leon-

---

[92] *ACO*, III, p. 37, l. 1 f.
[93] *Ibid.*, p. 50, l. 30 f.
[94] In the *Ad Justinianum* II, Hesychius, the first member of the delegation
to sign, signs as ποιούμενος τὸν λόγον ὑπὲρ πάσης τῆς ὑπὸ τὴν ἁγίαν πόλιν ἐρήμου (*ACO*, III, p. 36, l. 28 f.), and his signature serves as model for the five
signatures following. The seventh to sign, one Traianus, omits the clause
ποιούμενος τὸν λόγον; but Leontius, in eighth place, takes it up again. The
ninth to sign, Theodore Askidas, drops it, and the next eleven signers follow
him. (N. B.: in the fifth session, the delegation had increased in number
from fifteen to twenty.) Nonetheless, *every* signature includes an ὑπέρ clause
much like that of Hesychius. In *Ad Menam*, Hesychius sets a similar
pattern (*ibid.*, p. 50, ll. 8–10), but Traianus in seventh place again omits
the clause ποιούμενος τὸν λόγον, and all after him follow, including, of course,
Leontius in ninth place. Here again, however, *every* signature includes an
ὑπέρ clause like that of Hesychius. It is perhaps of interest that Leontius
is the only member of a delegation of fifteen whose signature to the
Libellus monachorum ad Agapetum, read in the first session, does *not* include a
similar ὑπέρ clause (*ibid.*, p. 145, l. 34 f.). I burden the reader with such
detail only in order to establish once and for all that at least among the
monks of Palestine the phrases in question do not imply peculiar ecclesiastical office or dignity.
[95] For Leontius' signatures, see the description of the evidence of the
acta, supra, p. 158 f.

tius the Origenist monk by either of these titles. Then perhaps he is not the Leontius of the Council? We must ask first what the Origenist Leontius *could* have been; but, for the moment, not whether he could have been τοποτηρητής—for the title τοποτηρητής, "representative," demands here more definition than it offers—but whether he could have been ἡγούμενος, an abbot.

Could Leontius have become an abbot in or before 536? For it is above all with the Leontius of the Council of 536 that we have to do.[96] We may begin by asking: abbot when? Before 531? If so, presumably an abbot in Palestine, and in Palestine abbot of the New Laura only; or so anyhow the notices of Cyril of Scythopolis in the *Vita Sabae*. However, if Leontius had been an abbot at the time of his separation from Sabas, we would expect Cyril to say so, and he does not.[97] Besides, with his separation from Sabas he would in effect have been relieved of the post; and the more so as he remained in the capital. Then, if not before 531, perhaps between 531 and his reappearance in the New Laura about 537,[98] in Palestine, say, after the death of Sabas? Nonetheless, Cyril's sudden mention of Leontius in 537 seems to hint that he had been in Constantinople until rather recently; that is, had not been in Palestine since 531, and so could hardly have become abbot of a laura there. If here we adduce the *acta* of 536, we may ask besides: even if Leontius had returned to Palestine, become abbot, and sailed back to Constantinople for the Council of 536, why did the *acta* describe him and why did he sign as ἡγούμενος without qualification of place, that is, as ἡγούμενος καὶ μοναχὸς ἰδίου μοναστηρίου? Why not as abbot of the *New Laura*? In any case, Leontius does not seem to have been

---

[96] However, there is no evidence that Leontius became abbot of the New Laura after his return there from Constantinople about 537 or shortly later. The manuscript tradition of the theologian Leontius, as we have seen, suggests quite the contrary; for it calls Leontius ἐρημίτης, μονάξων, ἀββᾶς, μέγας ἀσκήτης, μοναχός, but never ἡγούμενος; and yet, if Leontius had become an abbot only in the last years of his life, or again only after the publication of his works, it seems highly unlikely that the manuscript tradition of his works would have failed to notice his promotion.

[97] Cyril's account of the separation describes Leontius only as Λεόντιος... εἷς ὑπάρχων τῶν μετὰ τοῦ Νόννου εἰσδεχθέντων ἐν τῇ Νέᾳ λαύρᾳ μετὰ τὴν Ἀγαπητοῦ τοῦ ἡγουμένου κοίμησιν; i.e., about 520 by Agapetus' successor Mamas (see *VSabae*, p. 176, ll. 12–14, a reference to events described in p. 125, ll. 15–22).

[98] *Ibid.*, p. 189, l. 10ff., and especially p. 190, ll. 3–7.

abbot of the New Laura *in 536*; first, because Cyril clearly implies that on their voyage to the Council of that year, Domitian and Theodore Askidas found Leontius in Constantinople;[99] but second, because in the very same passage Cyril describes Theodore himself as τῶν τῆς Νέας λαύρας ἐξάρχων; and even should ἐξάρχων here be better translated "leading spirit" than "abbot," we might expect that Cyril would clarify the relation between Theodore ἐξάρχων and his abbot, Leontius, were Leontius abbot.[100] Then, if not abbot of the New Laura, perhaps abbot of a monastery in Constantinople. But again, why does Leontius not sign in the *acta* of 536 as abbot of that monastery? Why is he numbered there among the Palestinian delegation? Why does he, as it seems, abandon "his own monastery" to return to Palestine and the New Laura so soon after the Council, and remain there for some three years?

Prima facie, then, there is no shred of evidence that the Origenist Leontius was at any time abbot of any monastery whatsoever; so that to the degree to which the notices of the *acta* of the Council of 536 are right in calling their Leontius an abbot, it is reasonable to doubt that the Leontius of the Council is one and the same with the theologian Leontius.[101]

(b) *The solution: Leontius* ἐρημίτης. The question is: could Leontius the Origenist theologian have been an abbot and, more exactly, ἡγούμενος...ἰδίου μοναστηρίου?

Not, we see, if an ἡγούμενος is what we now call an abbot and a μοναστήριον is what we now call a monastery or *coenobion*. Yet, need these words mean just what we suppose? In fact, this interpretation of them renders the phrase ἰδίου μοναστηρίου oddly vague. Is the Leontius of the Council merely stating that he is abbot of the monastery in which he himself resides? The phrase then becomes sheer tautology: in the case at hand, he could of course be

---

[99] *Ibid.*, p. 189, l. 1 ff.

[100] *Ibid.*, p. 188, l. 26 f. 'Εξάρχων certainly seems to imply abbot; and so of course Siméon Vailhé, "Les monastères de Palestine. Les monastères de saint Passarion et de l'abbé Marcion; la Nouvelle Laure," *Bessarione*, IV (1898), pp. 201, 208. Still, why does Cyril not say ἡγούμενος, and why does Theodore appear in the *acta* of 536 only as διάκονος καὶ μοναχός, etc.?

[101] To the best of my knowledge, this difficulty was first raised by L. Duchesne, *L'Eglise au VIe siècle*, p. 83, note 1, and p. 167, note 1.

abbot of only that monastery in which he lived. Why then did he
not satisfy himself with the title ἡγούμενος alone, as did the
scribe who enrolls him in the lists of observers at the first four
sessions? Or, more to the point, why did he not identify himself
as "abbot and monk"—of itself a rather unusual pair in the
acta—of a certain monastery? Why does he not specify his
monastery by name? Almost everyone else does.[102] Or does the
phrase "his own monastery" mean only that Leontius had himself
founded the monastery in which he lived? The *acta* of 536 include
the signature of such a monk: one of the delegation from Constantinople, Θεόδωρος ἐλέει Θεοῦ πρεσβύτερος καὶ ἡγούμενος μονῆς
χάριτι Θεοῦ ὑπ' ἐμοῦ συστάσης πλησίον τοῦ ἁγίου μάρτυρος

---

[102] Exceptions are surprisingly few. The most important is a group of
seven monks from Palestines I, II, and III—a group quite distinct from
what we have been calling the Palestinian delegation. As a group, it appears
only in the signatures to the two *libelli* of the last session, *Ad Justinianum*
II and *Ad Menam*; only one member of the delegation, Strategius, had signed
the *Ad Agapetum* and been present at the first four sessions. (N. B.:
Strategius is not among the happy few who sign the *Ad Justinianum* I of the
first session: *ACO*, III, p. 133, l. 31 ff.) Before the last session, Strategius
regularly stands, with insignificant variations, as Στρατήγιος διάκονος καὶ
μοναχὸς μονῆς τοῦ μακαρίου Ἰωάννου ὑπὲρ πάντων τῶν ὑπὸ Σκυθόπολιν μοναχῶν
(p. 130, l. 38 f.; p. 146, l. 16 f.; p. 159, l. 1 f.; p. 166, l. 1 f.; p. 174, l. 21 f.);
that is, he identifies his monastery. However, of the seven monks who sign
the *libelli* of the last session, only one gives his monastery, and he is not
Strategius —who now signs as Στρατήγιος ἐλέει Θεοῦ διάκονος καὶ μοναχὸς
καὶ ὑπὲρ πάντων τῶν ἐν τῇ δευτέρᾳ Παλαιστίνῃ μοναχῶν, etc. (p. 37, l. 37 f.)—
but a certain Photinus of Jamnia (p. 38, l. 5 f.). Nonetheless, each member
of the delegation claims to represent the monks of either a clear and distinct
political unit (Palestine I, II, or III), or of a certain city (Augustopolis,
Petra, or Aela, that is, Aelana or Aqaba).
The other exceptions seem at least insignificant. The monastery of
Marianus, the chief of the delegation from Constantinople, is omitted in his
signatures to the *Ad Justinianum* I and *Ad Agapetum* of the first session
(p. 133, ll. 32–34; p. 142, l. 1 f.), but included everywhere else, that is, at
the head of the lists of observers and among the signatures to the *libelli* of
the fifth session. *Item*, the monastery of one John, a presbyter of the
Pedias, is omitted on p. 130, l. 35; p. 158, l, 40; p. 165, l. 41; p. 174, l.
18; and p. 146, l. 11 f.; but finally identified on p. 37, l. 31 f., and p. 51, l.
19 f. Of John, more immediately *infra*. *Item*, the monastery of a certain
Paul, otherwise regularly specified—p. 129, l. 41; p. 158, l. 3; p. 164, l. 44;
p. 173, l. 23; and p. 46, l. 3 f., if the Paul in question is the same—is
omitted on p. 144, l. 39, probably by accident. He does not seem to have
signed the *Ad Justinianum* II. Notice that in each of the three cases just
mentioned, the omission of the name of the monastery of the man in
question is corrected elsewhere and so proved insignificant. Not so with
Leontius, as we shall see. I do not number one Σέργιος πρεσβύτερος καὶ
περιοδευτής (p. 130, l. 15; p. 158, l. 20; p. 165, l. 21; p. 173, l. 41) of the

Λαυρεντίου, etc., as he signs the *Ad Agapetum*.[103] In comparison with this, however, Leontius' words are so vague as to suggest that he meant nothing of the kind.

Suppose, however, that Leontius' μοναστήριον here is the equivalent not of κοινόβιον, that is, what we moderns call a monastery, but of κέλλιον.[104] Leontius' signature then means only that he was *abbot of his own cell*, that is, an ἐρημίτης or a member of a laura. In fact, precisely such is the hitherto unnoticed suggestion of Eduard Schwartz,[105] who thereby might reasonably have supposed that he had transformed the last serious objection to his thesis into a proof; for the Leontius of the *Vita Sabae* of Cyril of Scythopolis was indeed an ἐρημίτης and member of a laura.

What is the value of Schwartz's suggestion?

To begin with, Leontius is not the only monk to sign in the *acta* as *of his own monastery*. Among the signatures of the delegation of Constantinople to the *Ad Menam* of the fifth session we find: Ἰσίδωρος ἐλέει θεοῦ πρεσβύτερος καὶ ἡγούμενος μονῆς ἰδίας τῆς οὔσης ἐν φυτοῖς πλησίον τοῦ ἁγίου μάρτυρος Ἐπιμάχου ὑπὸ Φωτεινὸν τὸν ὁσιώτατον ἐπίσκοπον Χαλκηδονίων ὑπέγραψα.[106] What is Isidore's μονὴ ἰδία? Simply his cell in the woods near the church or

delegation from Antioch among the exceptions. As περιοδευτὴς τῶν ἁγίων ἐκκλησιῶν ἐπὶ χωρίων τῆς πρώτης Σύρων ἐπαρχίας (*Ad Agapetum*, p. 146, l. 32 f.), he is more than sufficiently identified. He does not sign the *libelli* of the last session only because a certain Paul signs for the whole delegation.

[103] *ACO*, III, p. 145, l. 20 f. This Theodore is not listed among the monks observing the first three sessions. At the fourth, however, the presence list identifies him as Θεόδωρος μονῆς τῆς ὑπ' αὐτοῦ καταστάσης πλησίον τοῦ μαρτυρίου τοῦ ἁγίου Λαυρεντίου (p. 173, l. 28 f.); and he signs the *Ad Menam* of the fifth session (p. 47, l. 5 f.) with a formula almost identical to that with which he subscribed the *Ad Agapetum*, quoted in the text *supra*. There is no reasonable doubt that this Theodore is the same Theodore who signs the *Ad Justinianum* II of the fifth session with a rather less specific formula (p. 35, l. 38 f.).

[104] For μοναστήριον as equivalent to κέλλιον, see E. A. Sophocles, *Greek Lexicon of the Roman and Byzantine Periods* (New York, 1900), article μοναστήριον, 2 b, and E Schwartz, *KyrSkyth*, pp. 289 and 295 (*s.v.* μοναστήριον [*Einsiedelei*]).

[105] E Schwartz, *KyrSkyth*, 391, on the notices of the *acta* of 536: "Gelegentlich nennt er [i.e., Leontius] sich auch ἡγούμενος eines eigenen μοναστήριον [= Einsiedelei]; die hat er sich, nachdem Sabas ihm die Gemeinschaft gekündigt und ihn mittelbar aus der Neuen Laura ausgewiesen hatte, in Konstantinopel eingerichtet."

[106] *ACO*, III, p. 49, ll. 9–11. This seems to be Isidore's only appearance in the *acta*.

monastery of the martyr Epimachus; and it is of his cell alone that he is abbot.[107]

A conclusion too farfetched, or perhaps not to be applied to Leontius' signatures? We are fortunate in possessing strong evidence to the contrary: an anecdote in nothing less than our major source for Leontius' life, the *Vita Sabae* of Cyril of Scythopolis. In the passage in question, Cyril is at great pains to emphasize the close personal bond between his hero, Sabas, then archimandrite or, in a broader sense, ἡγούμενος of all the monks living as eremites, and Theodosius, archimandrite of all the κοινόβια of the desert. "One could see them," Cyril tells us, "joking with one another, and in the love and affection of the Spirit speaking with perfect candor and freedom. In these conversations, the blessed Sabas would very often say to Theodosius (now among the saints): 'My lord, you are ἡγούμενος of mere children, while I am ἡγούμενος of ἡγούμενοι; for since each of the monks under me is autonomous, each one is ἡγούμενος of his own cell.'"[108] Better confirmation of Schwartz's interpretation we could not ask; an anecdote from Leontius' own milieu interprets his words; and so we may take it as established that the Leontius of the Council is abbot and monk only of his own cell; is, in short, an eremite. We may add: and that he is one man with the Origenist eremite Leontius is more certain than ever.

This resolution of the evidence also clears up certain other questions about Leontius' notices and signatures in the *acta*.

---

[107] Immediately after the signatures of the Palestinian delegation to the *Ad Agapetum* in the *acta* of the first session, we find an apparently similar subscription: ᾽Ιωάννης ἐλέει Θεοῦ πρεσβύτερος μονῆς ἰδίας ἐν τῇ πεδιάδι καὶ ὑπὲρ πάντων..., etc. (*ibid.*, p. 146, l. 11 f. The name of the same man—᾽Ιωάννης πρεσβύτερος τῆς πεδιάδος καὶ ὑπὲρ πάντων..., etc.—stands in the lists of observers at the first four sessions immediately after the names of the Palestinian delegation: p. 130, l. 35; p. 158, l. 40; p. 165, l. 41; p. 174, l. 18). However, that John's ἰδία μονή is not his cell but his laura seems clear from his signature to the *Ad Justinianum* II of the fifth session: ᾽Ιωάννης ἐλέει Θεοῦ πρεσβύτερος καὶ μοναχὸς λαύρας τῶν ἀμμίων τῆς πεδιάδος καὶ ὑπὲρ πάντων..., etc. (*ibid.*, p. 37, l. 31 f. A similar formula in John's signature to the *Ad Menam* of the same session: p. 51, l. 19 f.).

[108] CyrScyth, *VSabae*, p. 166, ll. 21–26. The text of Sabas' speech (ll. 24–26): κύρι ἀββᾶ, σὺ μὲν παιδίων ὑπάρχεις ἡγούμενος, ἐγὼ δὲ ἡγουμένων εἰμὶ ἡγούμενος· ἕκαστος γὰρ τῶν ὑπ' ἐμὲ αὐτεξούσιος ὢν τοῦ ἰδίου κελλίου ἡγούμενός ἐστιν.

Leontius does not name his monastery because it has no name. It is only a hermit's cell. He does not give its location—as the eremite Isidore did — because his cell, presumably in or near Constantinople, is far, far away from the lauras of the desert whose inhabitants he claims to represent. Above all, however, we now know if not the meaning, at least the implications of the title which all four lists of observers ascribe to him and which he claims for himself in his signature to the *Ad Agapetum*: τοποτηρητὴς τῆς ἐρήμου πάσης. Leontius must claim to speak for the whole desert because he cannot speak for any part of it. Of all the monks present at the Council of 536, he alone claims the title τοποτηρητής, "representative," because he alone speaks only as an exile. In that sense, he may be called *delegate at large*; and it is in some such way that we must translate τοποτηρητής.

III. CONCLUSIONS

We may now draw our conclusions. There can be no serious doubt, we see, that the Leontius of the Council of 536 is identical with Leontius the Origenist monk and theologian. However, if the Leontius of the Council is the same as the Leontius of the colloquy, then the latter must be our Leontius also; though, of course, the probability of this last conclusion clearly varies with the probability that the Leontius of the colloquy is the Origenist Leontius; that is, with the probability that the Origenist Leontius is indeed *apocrisarius patrum sancta civitate constitutorum*.

These conclusions do much to complete our picture of Leontius' life and work between the years 531 and 536. He is above all occupied with that phase of the controversy between Orthodox and Monophysite which opens with what we may call the policy of toleration of 531. In the controversy he stands on the side of the Orthodox Chalcedonians and represents their views not only in public discussions both formal and informal, but also in writing. However, within the ranks of the Chalcedonians, Leontius holds a special place: he is the theologian of that party among the Chalcedonians which we may call *Origenist Chalcedonian*, that is, the party which expounds the formulae of Chalcedon by means of the Origenist Christology of Evagrius of Pontus.

Here we must pause to consider the last serious objection to our identification of the Origenist Leontius with the Leontii of colloquy and Council. If all these Leontii are one, it follows, as we have just now been saying, that Leontius plays no small part in the controversy against the Monophysites. This of itself suggests that Leontius and his party must somehow have been a factor in the religious policies of Justinian in these years. We may go further. If Leontius did indeed attend Justinian's colloquy in 532, and if he may have been responsible for the Origenistic tint of the Palestinian delegation to the Council of 536, it is perhaps not unreasonable to suggest that he and the Origenist Chalcedonians were in fact willing agents of Justinian; or, more exactly, that it was by means of Justinian's favor that they hoped to advance their views. Now, we have already heard Marcel Richard reject such an account of the matter *in toto*. Leontius, he says, was never a member of Justinian's theological *camarilla* and never could have been; for he was a *Strict Chalcedonian* to the very end, and no way inclined to fall in with the express *Neochalcedonianism* of the imperial policy.

Our reply? Let us grant at once that we have no evidence that Leontius himself commanded the imperial ear. Neither is there evidence that he did not. Our estimate of the probability here will depend entirely on our answer to the questions: was Leontius a Strict Chalcedonian? Is it impossible that he could have cooperated in Justinian's campaign against the Monophysites? The answer to both questions: emphatically *no*. Leontius was not a Strict Chalcedonian but an Origenist Chalcedonian; and as such he had every reason to hope for the imperial favor.

The difference, then, between Strict Dyophysites and Origenist Chalcedonians? We need only resume our earlier findings. Granted one point of agreement: both Strict Dyophysites and Origenist Chalcedonians (among them, Leontius) refuse to canonize the theological formulae of Cyril of Alexandria, that is, to identify Jesus Christ's μία ὑπόστασις with the Logos himself. Rather, both locate the μία ὑπόστασις (and name) of Christ in a *tertium quid*. Nevertheless, they define that *tertium quid* very differently. The Strict Dyophysites speak of a properly indefinable event, of which all proper attributes of both divine and human natures must be predicated simultaneously. The Origenists to the contrary define Jesus Christ not only dialectially but also positively: he is the single, unfallen *nous* of a primordial κόσμος νοητός, and as such perfectly united to the Logos in that contemplation of the Logos which constitutes the very nature or activity of νοῦς. The one hypostasis of Jesus Christ, the subject of the incarnation, is not a name or an event, as the Strict Dyophysites hold, but a real being. In defining Jesus Christ positively, of course, the Origenist Chalcedonians approach Cyril, the Monophysites, and the Neo- or Cyrillian Chalcedonians; for whom, nevertheless, the one hypostasis of Jesus is not a *nous* but the Logos himself.

Just here, of course, we catch a glimpse of how it was that the Origenists hoped to attain their ends. The Monophysite criticism of the formulae of Chalcedon and above all the attacks of Severus had found the Achilles' heel of the Strict Dyophysites: their genuinely radical helplessness to lend content to the one hypostasis of Jesus Christ, indeed, to Jesus Christ himself. How now to defend the Council? How to define the unity of God and man in Christ, and yet preserve the difference? The Origenist Chalcedonians— not only the Neochalcedonians, but also the Origenists—had an answer, and in the crisis of the Monophysite schism the Emperor was willing to listen. For a few years after 536 the Origenists had every reason to hope that their Christology might become the official interpretation of the formulae of Chalcedon and they themselves the agents of the Emperor in promulgating it. They failed, we know, but we must add: it seems to have been none other than the Origenist Leontius who first introduced Justinian to the answers of the Origenists and so laid the ground for their later and greater triumphs, the promotion of Theodore Askidas and the condemnation of the Three Chapters.

Bibliography

The following bibliography is organized under two headings: *The Scholarly Literature on Leontius of Byzantium* and *Other Works Cited in This Volume*. Of the second group, nothing need be said. Of the first, please note that I list works of two kinds only: *either* works which have dealt with Leontius explicitly and at length *or* works which have advanced our knowledge of him in some specific detail. I have therefore omitted handbooks or reference works which only summarize the then current state of the question, and omitted also the innumerable theological works which merely reproduce what they please to call Leontius' doctrine of the *enhypostasia* of the human nature of Jesus Christ.

With a few exceptions, this bibliography cites only the volumes in question, not individual works which may be included in the volumes; e.g., it does not list the works of Leontius of Byzantium, but cites the volumes in which his works are included: Jacques-Paul Migne (ed.), Patrologiae cursus completus ... series graeca.

THE SCHOLARLY LITERATURE ON LEONTIUS OF BYZANTIUM

Acta conciliorum oecumenicorum, ed. Eduard Schwartz, 4 tomes in 13 volumes (Berlin, Berlin-Leipzig, Strasbourg, 1914–1940 [incomplete])

ALTANER, BERTHOLD, "Der griechische Theologe Leontius und Leontius der skythische Mönch," *Theologische Quartalschrift*, CXXVII (1947), 147–165

BALTHASAR, HANS URS VON, *Kosmische Liturgie. Das Weltbild Maximus' des Bekenners*, 2nd rev. edition (Einsiedeln, 1961)

BARDY, GUSTAVE, *Paul de Samosate. Etude historique*, Spicilegium sacrum Lovaniense, fasc. 4, new ed. (Louvain, 1929)

BIBLIOGRAPHY

BASNAGE, JACOBUS (ed.), *Thesaurus monumentorum ecclesiasticorum et historicorum sive Henrici Canisii lectiones antiquae...*, 4 tomes in 7 parts (Amsterdam, 1725), I

CANISIUS, HENRICUS (ed.), *Antiquae lectionis (sic)...*, 6 vols. (Ingolstadt, 1601–1604), IV, 1 (1603)

CARAZA, I., "Doctrina hristologica a lui Leontiu de Bizant" (in Romanian), *Studii teologice*, XIX (1967), 321–333

CASAMASSA, ANTONIO, "I tre libri di Leonzio Bizantino contro i nestoriani e i monofisiti," *Bessarione*, XXV (1921), 33–46; reprinted in *idem, Scritti patristici*, I (Rome, 1956), 88–103

DEVREESSE, ROBERT, *Essai sur Théodore de Mopsueste*, Studi e Testi, 141 (Vatican City, 1948)

— "Le florilège de Léonce de Byzance," *Revue des sciences religieuses*, X (1930), 545–576

DIEKAMP, FRANZ, *Analecta patristica: Texte und Abhandlungen zur griechischen Patristik = Orientalia Christiana Analecta*, 117 (Rome, 1938)

— *Die origenistischen Streitigkeiten im sechsten Jahrhundert und das fünfte allgemeine Concil* (Münster in Westphalia, 1899)

— (ed.), *Doctrina patrum de incarnatione verbi. Ein griechisches Florilegium aus dem Wende des siebenten und achten Jahrhunderts* (Münster in Westphalia, 1907)

DRAGUET, RENÉ, *Julien d'Halicarnasse et sa controverse avec Sévère d'Antioche sur l'incorruptibilité du corps du Christ* (Louvain, 1924)

DUCHESNE, LOUIS, *L'Eglise au VIe siècle* (Paris, 1925)

EHRHARD, ALBERT, Review of Friedrich Loofs, *Leontius von Byzanz*, etc., in *Literarischer Handweiser*, XXVII (1888), 504–508

— "Zur Catalogisirung der kleineren Bestände griechischer Handschriften in Italien," *Centralblatt für Bibliothekswesen*, X (1893), 189–218

ELERT, WERNER, *Der Ausgang der altkirchlichen Christologie. Eine Untersuchung über Theodor von Pharan und seine Zeit als Einführung in die alte Dogmengeschichte*, eds. Wilhelm Maurer and Elisabeth Bergsträsser (Berlin, 1957)

ERMONI, V., *De Leontio Byzantino et de eius doctrina christologica* (Paris, 1895)

FESTUGIÈRE, ANDRÉ-JEAN (ed. and trans.), *Les moines d'Orient*, 4 vols. (Paris, 1961–1964 [incomplete])

FUNK, FRANZ XAVER VON, Review of Friedrich Loofs, *Leontius von Byzanz*, etc., in *Theologische Quartalschrift*, LXX (1888), 316–319

GLAIZOLLE, G., *Un empereur théologien: Justinien* (Lyons, 1905)

GRABE, JOHANN ERNST, *Spicilegium sanctorum patrum ut et haereticorum seculi post Christum natum I, II et III*, 2nd ed., 2 vols. (Oxford, 1700)

GRUMEL, VENANCE, "La sotériologie de Léonce de Byzance," *Echos d'Orient*, XL (1937), 385–397

— "Léonce de Byzance," *Dictionnaire de théologie catholique*, eds. Alfred Vacant *et al.*, 15 vols. (Paris, 1903–1950), IX (1926), cols. 400–426

— "Le surnaturel dans l'humanité du Christ viateur d'après Léonce de Byzance," *Mélanges Mandonnet*, 2 vols. (Paris, 1930), II, 15–22

— "L'union hypostatique et la comparaison de l'âme et du corps chez Léonce de Byzance et saint Maxime le Confesseur," *Echos d'Orient*, XXIX (1926), 393–406

GUILLAUMONT, ANTOINE, *Les "Kephalaia gnostica" d'Evagre le Pontique et l'histoire de l'Origénisme chez les Grecs et chez les Syriens*, Patristica sorbonensia, 5 (Paris, 1962)

HAMMERSCHMIDT, ERNST, "Einige philosophisch-theologische Grundbegriffe bei Leontios von Byzanz, Johannes von Damaskus und Theodor Abu Qurra," *Ostkirchliche Studien*, IV (1955), 147–154

HELMER, SIEGFRIED, *Der Neuchalkedonismus. Geschichte, Berechtigung und Bedeutung eines dogmengeschichtlichen Begriffes*, Inaugural Dissertation, printed reprod. (Bonn, 1962)

JUGIE, MARTIN, "La béatitude et la science parfaite de l'âme de Jésus viateur d'après Léonce de Byzance et quelques autres théologiens byzantins," *Revue des sciences philosophiques et théologiques*, X (1921), 548–559

— "Quelques témoignages grecs nouveaux ou peu connus sur la doctrine catholique de la procession du Saint-Esprit," *Echos d'Orient*, XXXIX (1936), 257–273

JUNGLAS, JOHANNES PETER, *Leontius von Byzanz. Studien zu seinen Schriften, Quellen und Anschauungen*, Forschungen zur christlichen Literatur- und Dogmengeschichte, Band VII, Heft 3 (Paderborn, 1908)

[LEONTIUS OF BYZANTIUM], "Extracts from Leontius of Byzantium [in English translation]," in Edward Rochie Hardy and Cyril C. Richardson (eds.), *Christology of the Later Fathers*, The Library of Christian Classics, 3 (London, 1954), 375–377

LEUNCLAVIUS, JOANNES (ed.), *Legatio imp[eratoris] caesaris Manuelis Comneni aug[usti] ad Armenios.* ... (Basel, 1578)

LOOFS, FRIEDRICH, "Leontius von Byzanz," *Realencyklopädie für protestantische Theologie und Kirche*, 3rd ed., ed. Albert Hauck, 24 vols. (Leipzig, 1897–1914), XI (1902), 394–398

— *Leontius von Byzanz und die gleichnamigen Schriftsteller der griechischen Kirche*, Texte und Untersuchungen zur Geschichte der altchristlichen Literatur, Band III, Heft 1–2 (Leipzig, 1887)

— Review of Johannes Peter Junglas, *Leontius von Byzanz*, etc., in *Theologische Literaturzeitung*, XXXIV (1909), 205–209

— Review of V. Ermoni, *De Leontio Byzantino et de eius doctrina christologica*, in *Byzantinische Zeitschrift*, VI (1897), 417–419

— Review of Wilhelm Rügamer, *Leontius von Byzanz*, etc., in *Byzantinische Zeitschrift*, V (1896), 185–191

— ["Selbstdarstellung"], in *Die Religionswissenschaft der Gegenwart in Selbstdarstellungen*, ed. Erich Stange, 5 vols. (Leipzig, 1925–1929), II (1926), 119–160

MAI, ANGELO (ed.), *Scriptorum veterum nova collectio e vaticanis codicibus edita* ..., 10 vols. (Rome, 1825–1838), VII, 1 (1833)

— (ed.), *Spicilegium romanum*, 10 vols. (Rome, 1839–1844), X, 2 (1844)

MIGNE, JACQUES-PAUL (ed.), Patrologiae cursus completus ... series graeca, 161 vols. (Paris, 1857–1868)

MOELLER, CHARLES, "Le chalcédonisme et le néochalcédonisme en Orient de 451 à la fin du VIe siècle," in *Das Konzil von Chalkedon: Geschichte und Gegenwart*, eds. Aloys Grillmeier and Heinrich Bacht, 3 vols., revised (Würzburg, 1959), I, 637-720

MÖLLER, WILHELM, Review of Friedrich Loofs, *Leontius von Byzanz*, etc., in *Theologische Literaturzeitung*, XII (1887), 336–339

ORBE, ANTONIO, *La Epinoia. Algunos preliminares históricos de la distinción* κατ' ἐπίνοιαν. (*En torno a la Filosofia de Leoncio Bizantino.*) (Rome, 1955)

PITRA, JEAN-BAPTISTE (ed.), *Analecta sacra spicilegio Solesmensi parata*, 7 vols. (Paris *et al.*, 1876–1891)

REES, SILAS, "Leontius of Byzantium and his Defence of the Council of Chalcedon," *Harvard Theological Review*, XXIV (1931), 111–119

— "The *De Sectis*: A Treatise Attributed to Leontius of Byzantium," *The Journal of Theological Studies*, XL (1939), 346–360

— "The Life and Personality of Leontius of Byzantium," *The Journal of Theological Studies*, XLI (1940), 263–280

— "The Literary Activity of Leontius of Byzantium," *The Journal of Theological Studies*, XIX (1968), 229–242

REINDL, HERBERT, *Der Aristotelismus bei Leontios von Byzanz*, Inaugural Dissertation, unpublished (Munich, 1953)

RELTON, HERBERT M., *A Study in Christology: The Problem of the Relation of the Two Natures in the Person of Christ* (London, 1922 [first published 1917])

RICHARD, MARCEL, "Léonce de Byzance était-il origéniste?" *Revue des études byzantines*, V (1947), 31–66

— "Léonce de Jérusalem et Léonce de Byzance," *Mélanges de science religieuse*, I (1944), 35–88

— "Léonce et Pamphile," *Revue des sciences philosophiques et théologiques*, XXVII (1938), 27–52

— "Le Néo-chalcédonisme," *Mélanges de science religieuse*, III (1946), 156–161

BIBLIOGRAPHY

— "Le traité 'De Sectis' et Léonce de Byzance," *Revue d'histoire ecclésiastique*, XXXV (1939), 695–723

RÜGAMER, WILHELM, *Leontius von Byzanz. Ein Polemiker aus dem Zeitalter Justinians* (Würzburg, 1894)

SCHWARTZ, EDUARD, *Kyrillos von Skythopolis*, Texte und Untersuchungen zur Geschichte der altchristlichen Literatur, Reihe 4, Band 49, Heft 2 (Leipzig, 1939)

— *Zur Kirchenpolitik Justinians*, Sitzungsber. d. Akad. d. Wiss., Philos.-hist. Abt., 1940, Heft 2 (Munich, 1940), 32–81. Reprinted in *idem, Gesammelte Schriften*, 5 vols. (Berlin, 1938–1963), IV (1960), 276–328

SLYPII [Slypyi], JOSEF, *De principio spirationis in sanctissima Trinitate* (Lvov, 1926)

SOKOLOV, VASILII ALEKSANDROVICH, *Leontii Vizantiiskii: ego zhizn' i literaturnye trudy* (Sergiev Posad, 1916)

THEODOROS, ANDREAS, Χριστολογικὴ ὁρολογία καὶ διδασκαλία Λεοντίου τοῦ Βυζαντίου, *Theologia*, XXVI (1955), 212–222, 421–435, 584–592; XXVII (1956), 32–44

VAILHÉ, SIMÉON, "Les monastères de Palestine. Les monastères de saint Passarion et de l'abbé Marcion; la Nouvelle Laure," *Bessarione*, IV (1898), 193–210

WATT, J. H. I., "The Authenticity of the Writings Ascribed to Leontius of Byzantium," *Studia Patristica*, VII, Texte und Untersuchungen zur Geschichte der altchristlichen Literatur, Band XCII (Berlin, 1966), 320–336

ZAHN, THEODOR, Review of Friedrich Loofs, *Leontius von Byzanz*, etc., in *Theologisches Literaturblatt*, VIII (1887), 89–92

OTHER WORKS CITED IN THIS VOLUME

ABEL, FÉLIX-MARIE, *see* VINCENT, HUGUES, and ABEL, FÉLIX-MARIE

ARISTOTLE, *Generation of Animals*, Greek text, trans. A. L. Peck, Loeb Classical Library (London, 1943)

— *Parts of Animals*, Greek text, trans. A. L. Peck, Loeb Classical Library (Cambridge, Mass., 1937)

— *Categoriae et liber de interpretatione*, ed. L. Minio-Paluello, Oxford Classical Texts (Oxford, 1956)

ARNOU, RENÉ, "Unité numérique et unité de nature chez les Pères, après le Concile de Nicée," *Gregorianum*, XV (1934), 242–254

ATHANASIUS, *De incarnatione*, ed. Frank Leslie Cross, Texts for Students, 50 (London, 1939)

BASILE, SAINT, *Lettres*, ed. and trans. Yves Courtonne, Collection Budé, 3 vols. (Paris, 1957–1966)

Commentaria in Aristotelem graeca, 23 vols. (Berlin, 1882–1909)

Corpus juris civilis, ed. Simon van Leeuwen, 4 vols. (Venice, 1836–1844); eds. Paul Krüger *et al.*, 3 vols. (Berlin, 1928–1929)

DUCHESNE, LOUIS, *Eglises séparées* (Paris, 1896)

FRANKENBERG, WILHELM (ed.), *Euagrius Ponticus*, Abhandl. d. Königl. Gesellsch. d. Wiss. zu Göttingen, Philol.-hist. Klasse, Neue Folge, Band XIII, 2 (Berlin, 1912)

GEORGIUS CEDRENUS, *Historiarum compendium*, ed. Immanuel Bekker, 2 vols, Corpus scriptorum historiae byzantinae (Bonn, 1838–39)

GUILLAUMONT, ANTOINE (ed. and trans.), *Les six centuries des "Kephalaia gnostica" d'Evagre le Pontique*. Edition critique de la version syriaque commune et édition d'une nouvelle version syriaque intégrale, avec une double traduction française = *Patrologia orientalis*, tome XXVIII, fasc. I (Paris, 1958)

— and GUILLAUMONT, CLAIRE, "Evagre le Pontique," *Dictionnaire de spiritualité ascétique et mystique*, eds. M. Viller *et al.*, 6 vols. (Paris, 1937–1967 [incomplete]), IV (1961), 1734–1744

BIBLIOGRAPHY

— "Le texte véritable des 'Gnostica' d'Evagre le Pontique," *Revue de l'histoire des religions*, CXLII (1952), 156–205

HAUSHERR, IRENÉE, "Nouveaux fragments grecs d'Evagre le Pontique," *Orientalia Christiana Periodica*, V (1939), 229–233

JANIN, RAYMOND, *Constantinople byzantine. Développement urbain et répertoire topographique*, Archives de l'Orient chrétien, 4A, 2nd ed. (Paris, 1964)

MANSI, GIOVANNI DOMENICO (ed.), *Sacrorum conciliorum nova et amplissima collectio* ..., 31 vols. (Florence and Venice, 1759–1798)

MARCHAL, L., "Migne, Jacques-Paul," *Dictionnaire de théologie catholique*, eds. Alfred Vacant *et al.*, 15 vols. (Paris, 1903–1950), X (1928), cols. 1722–1740

MELCHER, ROBERT, *Der 8. Brief des hl. Basilius, ein Werk des Evagrius Pontikus*, Münsterische Beiträge zur Theologie, Heft 1 (Münster in Westphalia, 1923)

MUYLDERMANS, JOSEPH, *Evagriana* (Paris, 1931)

PROCLUS, *The Elements of Theology*, ed. and trans. E. R. Dodds, 2nd ed. (Oxford, 1963)

QUASTEN, JOHANNES, *Patrology*, 3 vols. (Westminster, Maryland, 1950–1965 [incomplete])

RIEDMATTEN, HENRI DE, *Les actes du procès de Paul de Samosate. Etude sur la christologie du IIIe au IVe siècle*, Paradosis, Etudes de littérature et de théologie ancienne, 6 (Fribourg, 1952)

SOCRATES, *Ecclesiastica historia*, ed. Robert Hussey, 3 vols. (Oxford, 1853)

SOPHOCLES, EVANGELINUS APOSTOLIDES, *Greek Lexicon of the Roman and Byzantine Periods* (New York, 1900)

STEIN, ERNEST, "Cyrille de Scythopolis: A propos de la nouvelle édition de ses oeuvres," *Analecta Bollandiana*, LXII (1944), 169–186
— *Histoire du Bas-Empire*, 2 vols. (Paris, 1949 [vol. II]–1959 [vol. I])

THEOPHANES, *Chronographia*, ed. Carolus de Boor, 2 vols. (Leipzig: Teubner, 1883–1885; reprinted Hildesheim, 1963)

VINCENT, HUGUES and ABEL, FÉLIX-MARIE, *Jérusalem*, II: *Recherches de topographie, d'archéologie et d'histoire. Jérusalem nouvelle* (Paris, 1914–1926)

Indexes

Proper Names

TECHNICAL TERMS

JUN 1 1986

APR 3 0 1980   JUN 1 1987

AUG 2 8 1970   OCT 1 6 1974

DEC 3 1 1979

OCT 2 2 1970   FEB 2 9 1980

OCT 1 1 1972   JUN 1 1981

DEC 7 1972   JUN 1 1982

                 JUN 1 1983

NOV 1 4 1973   JUN 1 1984

JUN 2 6 1970   JUN 1 1985

JUN 2 6 1970
DEC 1 3 1973